TALES FOR THE DYING

SUNY series in Hindu Studies

Wendy Doniger, editor

TALES FOR THE DYING

The Death Narrative of the Bhāgavata-Purāṇa

E. H. Rick Jarow

STATE UNIVERSITY OF NEW YORK PRESS

Published by
STATE UNIVERSITY OF NEW YORK PRESS
ALBANY

Printed in the United States of America

For information, address
State University of New York Press
90 State Street, Suite 700, Albany, NY 12207

Production by Kelli Williams
Marketing by Anne M. Valentine

Library of Congress Cataloging-in-Publication Data

Jarow, Rick.
Tales for the dying : the death narrative of the Bhagavata-Purana / E.H. Rick Jarow.
p. cm. — (SUNY series in Hindu studies)
Includes bibliographical references and index.
ISBN 0-7914-5609-9 (alk.) — ISBN 0-7914-5610-2 (alk. paper)
1. Puranas. Bhāgavatapurāña—Criticism, interpretation, etc. 2. Death—Religious aspects—Hinduism. I. Title. II. Series.

BL1140.4.B437 J37 2003
294.5'92—dc21

2002191120

10 9 8 7 6 5 4 3 2 1

This book is dedicated to the late Barbara Stoler Miller: master-scholar, educator, critic, and colleague. The grace she exhibited during her long battle with cancer was awe-inspiring. Indeed, she exemplified what it may mean to be taught by the wisdom one has read and written.

CONTENTS

ACKNOWLEDGMENTS

There are many faces and places that arise in association with gratitude for the growth and development of this volume: Harvard Square, where I had my first darshan of Krishna and of Vaishnava dharma from A. C. Bhaktivedanta Swami; Vrindaban, where Anna McDowel and Asim Krishna Das were my first guides, where Shrivatsa Goswami engaged in endless discussions with me on Jīva Gosvāmī's "oneness in difference," and where Shripad Baba offered council when I felt this work was impossible to complete; Morningside Heights, where I was nurtured by the Department of Asian and Middle East Languages and Cultures at Columbia University, where Barbara Stoler Miller proposed that I work on "the theme of separation," and where Wendy Doniger urged me to complete my work on the *Bhāgavata-Purāṇa;* Vassar College, where I have received support, encouragement, and friendship from my colleagues in the religion department, and where Deborah Dash Moore encouraged me to focus this work on "death."

Many friends and colleagues have read over this manuscript and have moved me to refine my thinking and expression. I particularly want to thank Steve Rosen and the *Journal of Vaiṣṇava Studies,* Paul Sherbow, David Crismond, Cora Zoller, Nadine Berardi, and Griff Foxley in this regard. I also want to acknowledge the work of Celine Sigmen and Griff Foxley in the preparation of this manuscript and to thank Nancy Elegate and State University of New York Press for their patience and support.

A NOTE ON TRANSLATION AND TRANSLITERATION

Translations of passages in this volume are credited either with endnote references or in parentheses immediately following the text. When no translator is indicated, these are my own, original translations. Since there is no critical edition of the *Bhāgavata-Purāṇa,* I consulted a number of editions of the Sanskrit text for translation purposes. Most of them were consistent, with the few minor differences not crucial to particular translation issues. Various texts do, however, have differences in the numbering of verses. For all citations, therefore, I have used the Gorakhpur: Gita Press, 1962 text (with Śrīdhara Commentary), edited by Pandey Ramtej Sastri. For most translations of Sanskrit, the original text in transliterated form appears either next to it in the volume or in the corresponding endnotes. Where transliterations do not appear, the specifics of the translation itself are not deemed crucial to the particular issue being discussed. All transliterated words from Sanskrit and Hindi are italicized with the exception of capitalized proper names, places, and words from these languages that are used as English adjectives (Vedic, Puranic, etc.).

ABBREVIATIONS

AIOC	All India Conference (Summary of Proceedings)
BG	Bhagavadgītā
BhP	Bhāgavata-Purāṇa
HV	Harivaṁśa
JG	Jīva Gosvāmī
JAOS	*Journal of the American Oriental Society*
JB(B)RS	*Journal of the Bombay Branch of the Royal Society*
JIP	*Journal of Indian Philosophy*
JRAS	*Journal of the Royal Asiatic Society*
MBh	Mahābhārata
MW	*Sanskrit-English Dictionary* by Sir M. Monier-Williams
NS	*Nāṭyaśāstra*
RV	Ṛg Veda
SR	Śrīdhara Svāmī
VA	*The Practical Sanskrit-English Dictionary* by Vaman Shivaram Apte
VC	Viśvanātha Cakravartī
VJ	Vijayadhvaja
VP	Viṣṇu Purāṇa
YS	*Yoga Sūtra* of Patañjali

INTRODUCTION

MANY WAYS OF DYING

In a citation from the *Satyricon* of Petronius at the opening of T. S. Eliot's *Waste Land,* the Sibyl—who has received a "gift" of immortality from Apollo and has thus been cursed to age forever, despairingly declares, "I want to die." One might read this as a variant of the futility of the ego's project of self-preservation, but there is a particular gruesomeness in the unchallengeable cruelty of the gods here. Dying would be a relief, and the world as it is seems to possess no ethical sensibility at all.

Indeed, this is often how we feel in the face of suffering and death despite the most inventive protestations of discourses on divine justice. And, as we see in the above instance, there may even be fates worse than dying. In the Hindu-Buddhist imagination, death often comes as part of a package of inevitable "fourfold miseries" which include birth, disease, and old age; which in turn are part of another package of "threefold miseries;" those caused by nature, by gods, and by other beings. And while the specter of death haunts us as a species, when the righteous king, Yudhiṣṭhira, is asked by the Lord of Death in the Mahābhārata: "*What is the most wonderful thing?*" He responds, "*Day after day countless beings are sent to the realm of Death, yet those who remain behind believe themselves to be deathless.*"[1]

Freud declared that the unconscious refuses to recognize death, and perhaps this is one reason that I want to write on dying, to work at making the unconscious conscious, to try and meet death in its multidimensionality, not just as a feared or denied end to a short, puzzling human life.[2] I also want to meet death multiculturally, to look at imaginative discourse around death and dying (and there may only be imaginative discourse here) through a tradition which is neither my own by birth or by language.

What is the draw here beyond an affinity for Indian languages and literatures, a penchant for the "exotic-other," a training in Asian Studies, and extended residence in India? At the center of this project, I imagine, is the tormenting truth of impermanence. And what I find so intriguing about Indian Epic and Purāṇic discourse is their particular way of grappling with this universal: not by directly staring it down, or meditating on it in a cremation ground, but rather through performing another kind of meditation, an imaginative one that works through the presence and power of narrative, of stories. The Bhāgavata-Purāṇa, the focus of this work, does more than just relate stories. It is, after all, a "*Purāṇa*" and hence an immense compilation of narratives, genealogies, encyclopedic accounts of epic-lore, didactic teachings, philosophical polemics, legendary chronologies, platitudes of all kinds, and a host of other subjects. Moreover, as the great Vaiṣṇava text of devotional theism, the Bhāgavata (as it is usually called) is filled with prayers, hymns of praise, and narratives aimed at inculcating a devotional sensibility in its audience. All of this has been much discussed in both scholarly and religious-devotional circles and is clearly "above board."

What is not often discussed is the fact that the Bhāgavata also contains a collection of narratives told to someone who is about to die, and for some reason or other (could Freud be helpful here?) this fact has rarely been made the center of any discussion on the Purāṇa. It is this fact and its possible implications that I address in the following volume, not only in terms of "Purāṇic Studies," but also within the discourse of mythic and narrative responses to death, dying, and loss.

Can a meditation on this text speak through space and time? Without being hopelessly essentialistic, I would like to believe so. If religious texts (and experiences) were entirely culturally determined, they would not cross cultures and languages as easily as they do. What comes down to us as Purāṇa is, after all, already an amazingly variegated amalgam of previous discourse that has been (and continues to be) fluidly transmitted through time. Moreover, if religious texts and experiences were unequivocally unique to their place and time, they would not invite the ongoing interpretive traditions which continue to surround them. This is particularly pertinent with regard to the Sanskritic tradition, since commentaries on texts (and this holds true in the Bhāgavata) often postdate a respective work by a number of centuries. The commentaries, as essential and helpful as they are, more often than not represent particular interpretive communities with their own ideological predilections and agendas. The fact that commentators like Śrīdhara, Vallabha, and Viśvanātha, representatives of specific *sampradāyas* (disciplic lineages), have come up with such dramatically different visions of the same Purāṇa, exemplifies a characteristic nature of Bhāgavata discourse: it continues to speak, in different forms, to ongoing interpretive communities, whether they be theological, local performance-oriented, scholarly text-oriented, or otherwise.[3]

Jīva Gosvāmī, the medieval *bhakti* theoretician and commentator on the Bhāgavata-Purāṇa, coined a phrase: *acintya-bhedābhedatattva* (inconceivable oneness and difference).[4] This sensibility, I would argue, is not akin to the nihilism of a misinformed Buddhist or hyper-deconstructive practice, but resembles the compassion of the *Great Vehicle* that honors the very inconceivability upon which we live and die. Death, in this regard, is not an undiscovered country to be feared or to be heroically charted with a map and compass. There are no great voyages and returns in the *Bhāgavata* as with Gilgamesh, nor are there heroic rescue attempts from the underworld, as with Orpheus.[5] Rather, dying is met through the weaving of the paradox of essence and existence, not in an explanatory mode, but through the mythic amplification of the human longing for immortality and its encounter with temporality, necessity, and limitation. Thus, while the principle text for this meditation is one from seventh-to-tenth century India, one which continues to exert influence to this day, the questions asked are the "elemental ones," as Albert Schweitzer put it.[6]

This work shall focus on how the Bhāgavata-Purāṇa responds to one such "elemental question" through a narrative that revolves around the fundamental theme of death and dying. I want to closely read and examine the Purāṇic narrative, paying attention to its language and imagery, as well as to the commentarial traditions that have grown up around it. At the same time, I want to remain mindful of the wider connotations of the Bhāgavata, for my deep sense of the matter is that it can speak to an emerging intercultural conversation around death and loss in a variety of contexts.

James Hillman, in his earlier writings on psychology, argued for a "return to Greece" as the imaginative basis of Western discourse.[7] In this volume, I want to take to task the idea of there being any geographically limited area of the imagination in this time of "post-history" (a term which I prefer to "postmodern"). A study of the East can inform the West as much as a study of the West can inform the East. Therefore I am seeking to avoid "a camera tour of the other," no matter how powerful and sophisticated the lens might be. For I not only recognize, but freely admit, that the lens always points toward, or is filtered through one's own experience, language, and history in some respect or capacity.

In a similar vein, this volume also seeks to avoid the discourse of the "comparative," be it of religion or literature, because the intent is not to compare, but rather to flesh out the very human issues that we all face: desire, love, and loss. This need not indicate a naively universalist view of culture. Different civilizations have genuinely particular imaginative realms and they are to be recognized and respected. When we look at the "other" in any form, however, we are forced to evolve different perspectives on ourselves, and this should also be acknowledged and articulated. A serious encounter with "the other" involves a certain risk, the risk of confronting ideas and practices that challenge our culturally based assumptions, and meeting a text or tradition, neither as a partisan nor as a disinterested observer, but in an existentially engaged way, will likely be disturbing and inconclusive. But if "real living is meeting" (as Martin Buber put it), such an encounter will inevitably be fruitful and need not compromise scholarly integrity. Moreover, increasing cultural pluralism and infrastructures are reducing constructs like East and West to near absurdity. Hopefully, then, this will be more than a camera tour. For the Purāṇic narrative acts on one's own inner world as well as on an Indian one.

Is there a difference between the two (or more) worlds? Is the depth psyche universal or not? This work will not lay claim to the position of one side or the other, but assumes that cross-cultural investigations are in order. And while race, class, gender, and historical conditions certainly effect the production and reception of texts (and this is clearly so in the case of the Bhāgavata), they themselves need not be envisioned as the only important factors within the work. For every work contains something else intrinsic to it, dare I say "its spirit," which speaks to different interpretive communities at different moments. If this were not so, the words attributed to Jesus would only be effective in Aramaic. This is not to discount the important insights that have come to us, and will continue to come to us, through readings of the *Purāṇa* along historical or other extrinsic lines; I am simply pointing out my working methodology of intrinsic reading and mytho-poetic focus. If it were possible, I would eschew any and all explanation, pursuing a methodology of "amplification, density, and connection," my own version of a "thick description." But this is not possible, so some explanation is in order.

The vast *itihāsa-purāṇa* tradition draws complex, multileveled, and many-sided images of death and dying. On the one hand, it does not always welcome death with open arms: one of its major narrative themes is the effort, successful or unsuccessful, to overcome death. In well-known Epic and Purāṇic narratives, King Yayāti, seeking to curb the passage of time, demands and ultimately receives his lost youth from his sons. The epic heroine, Sāvitrī, refusing to accept the finality of her husband's death, rescues him from the realm of Yama. Demon kings like Rāvaṇa and Hiraṇyakaśipu are constantly petitioning the great gods for immortality, and Rāhu's attempt to devour the Moon during an eclipse recalls the efforts of the demon *asuras* to surpass the gods by drinking *amṛta*, the elixir of immortality that rose from the churning of the ocean of milk in the hoary past.

There is another type of Epic and Purāṇic discourse, however, that seems to welcome the end of earthly life, or to see it as a unique opportunity. In the *Bhīṣma Parva* and particularly in its Bhagavadgītā section of the Mahābhārata, the potential moment of death becomes a cornerstone for the charged-rhetoric of *bhakti* polemics. I am speaking of a type of *upadeśa* (instruction) or remembrance (*hari-smaraṇa*) at the time of death that is seen as a primary and indispensable act which can require a lifetime of preparation and which—it is said—can lead one on to liberation with one's last breath.[8] Such a practice was exemplified by Mohandas Gandhi, whose utterance of the name "*Rām*" at the moment of his death qualified him, in the eyes of many, to pass immediately on to the immortal realm.

While Purāṇic literatures tend to fall on both sides of "avoidance" or "approach" attitudes towards dying, the Bhāgavata-Purāṇa is unique in that its entire narrative is framed around a discourse on how one should die.[9] As mentioned, this central fact has been more or less overlooked in studies on the *Purāṇa*, and therefore I think it is worth investigating. Moreover, I want to explore this particular discourse through a number of perspectives; not as much in a comparative as in a dialogical sense: by looking at Purāṇic lore through the lenses of literary criticism and depth psychology as well as indology, one also explores these disciplines through the lore and insights of Purāṇic literature. This can be particularly interesting since both literary criticism and depth psychology rely so heavily on Greek imagery and mythology in their understanding and mapping of literary and psychological processes. Do the same notions of structure hold up when the focus of the lens is shifted eastward?

In this work, therefore, I look closely at the text, at the issue of death and dying in the text, and at how the two are related. While acknowledging the importance of the strong extrinsic studies (there are superb studies on the linguistics, the historical development, and philosophy of the Purāṇa, and on the Bhāgavata in relation to the Purāṇic genre) and of the major commentaries on the Purāṇa, and drawing on them when necessary, I want to look at the complex of death, loss and love, as configured within the work.[10] In any case, I cannot, at the moment, think of a better way to pass the time. I have been reading it for over twenty-five years, (the Purāṇa is some eighteen thousand verses long), and I still find myself drawn to its unique confluence of poetic imagery, eclectic philosophy, religious mystery, and hyperbolic absurdity.

I have been warned, during the course of this project, to "be careful," for prolonged attention to something like "death and dying" could bring it literally upon oneself. And indeed, this project was interrupted by a period of serious illness. Eventually, however, I came to understand how my illness was part of a larger complex of events. And in the same way, I want to emphasize that the Bhāgavata-Purāṇa does not isolate dying as an issue, and this is crucial. Just like "love" as a term may be meaningless without envisioning what kind of love it might be: the pining of lovers, the love of two friends, a parent for a child, a patriot for her country, and so forth, death also comes in a cloak of many colors.[11]

The "many colors" place one in the province of myth, and Purāṇic literature is, after all, myth par excellence, with all its variance and complexity. Its tales have been passed down in numerous versions and recensions since at least the early Brāhmaṇical era (500 B.C.E.), and they continue to exist through a living tradition, embodied in regional literatures, the performing arts, and contemporary electronic media.[12]

Among the principal Purāṇas, the Bhāgavata has been conspicuous through its propagation of popular devotional religion (Bhāgavatism) and through its celebrated performance modalities such as *Bhāgavat-saptas*—seven-day ritualized recitations of the *Purāṇa*. The celebrated Sanskrit work—probably produced in South India between the seventh and tenth centuries, and canonized as an integral part of the Vaiṣṇavaite *bhakti* tradition in India—became the cornerstone of medieval devotional theism and Kṛṣṇaism in particular. It has spawned hundreds of retellings of its most poetic passages in various mediums and genres. The esteem in which the Purāṇa is held by many led the late A. K. Ramanujan to describe the Bhāgavata as a "cult book" in a sense similar to James Joyce's *Ulysses*—a book that holds its adherents together through ritualized readings and debates that continue on for generations.[13] One can only wonder if, through some collective phenomenon, the Bhāgavata-Purāṇa's popularity may also have to do with the fact that it deals with the core issue of death and dying in such a unique and provocative way. The Bhāgavata-Purāṇa, whatever else it may be, is a collection of stories told to one who is about to die for the purpose of helping him meet his death. Indeed, a good deal of the Purāṇa, one could argue, is an elaboration upon Parīkṣit's initial and crucial question: *puruṣasyeha yat kāryaṁ mriyamāṇasya sarvathā*, "What, in every respect, should be done by a person who is about to die?"[14]

Such a question, while asked within a specific cultural context, is certainly ubiquitous in its application. For, as far as we know, human beings have always been mortal. Within the realm of Parīkṣit's immediate circle, however, the preparation for dying takes on the aura of a particular ritualized and theatrical performance. The surviving heir of the Pāṇḍu clan participates in the ongoing "construction" of his death (the Purāṇic narrative) before a wide audience of sages and bards, and the narrative that is "performed" will continue to serve other audiences as a luminous guide through the perilous age of Kali, the last of the four *yugas*, characterized by (among other things) a severely shortened life span.[15]

A further note on methodology may be in order here, because when one encounters the Purāṇic literature (or lore to perhaps be more accurate), many methods that have been long used in indological studies may not be appropriate for focusing on the "literary" nature of a text, and may miss the fact that Purāṇas are as much collections of stories as they are sectarian theological tracts or encyclopedic compilations on multifarious topics ("the duties of different *varṇas*, funeral rites, and cosmologies" etc.).[16] I am even reticent to employ the word "myth" here, at least for the moment, for I fear that contemporary clinical connotations around myth often tend to take us away from the story and back into theoretical abstractions, (this, despite the fact that one meaning of the Greek word *mythos* is "plot").[17] It is as though we are unconsciously Platonic in our habitual readings that devalue the poetic at the expense of the prosaic. Even the Sanskrit commentarial traditions, which focus almost exclusively on theological concerns, appear to skirt the centrality of story: this is most important in regard to the Bhāgavata which A. S. Biswas, J. A. B. van Buitenen, and others have labeled "the literary *Purāṇa*."[18]

The Bhāgavata, like other Purāṇas, is, ultimately, a collection of stories. The stories have likely been filtered down through oral history, transposed into written form, and from very early on in Indian religious traditions—earlier than we have often been told—have been considered canonical texts.[19] The canonizing process, a major research project in itself, is viewed differently by representatives of particular interpretive communities. (For the "origin" of these stories is a charged question, so much so, that the Bhāgavata will spend a good deal of time discussing its own composition.) What is fascinating, in this regard (and what I shall discuss in detail in chapter three of this volume) is that the composition of the Bhāgavata itself is said to be shrouded in death, the death of Kṛṣṇa, and the ending of an era. Therefore, along with discussing the Purāṇic stories themselves, I will be looking at the text's own myth of composition, at exactly how the Bhāgavata sees itself in relationship to dying and its own narrative process.

Therefore, I speak of "many ways of dying," to amplify the thematic resonance of death in all of its associations. On the mimetic level, the text focuses on impermanence through the intrusive and shocking finality of death: no one is immune, and the Bhāgavata will continually assert this. Impermanence enters into everything, whether or not it is invited. A sustained reflection on impermanence challenges often dominant family and social values—be they partisan to the normative-brahminical primacy of *dharma* or contemporary preoccupations with building a humane society. It flouts desired outcomes, makes light of melodrama on any level, and forces one to take a new look at constructions of history, particularly those that fudge the problematics of mortality by transposing the finite-fated individual onto an assumed identification with a continuous cultural entity through time.

The Bhāgavata-Purāṇa, thus, weaves death into its narrative on many different levels. On one level, it focuses on preparing for the end of life. Not only is the main character cursed by a *brāhmaṇa* to die, but numerous stories are introduced in which the "death-walk" is tantamount. But this is not the only manner in which death and dying are located in the Purāṇic imagination. While awareness of impermanence and loss are built into the center of Bhāgavata's vision of dying, the movement of desire, and unsatisfied desire in particular, forms an ironic background to it: kings leave their kingdoms in disgust, unrequited lovers pine in despair, families are unable to remain together, and an entire dynasty dissolves in a drunken fray. One recalls Nietzsche's reference to "man as the sick animal," the only animal whose wants generally exceed its circumstances. And this phenomenon of wanting, of never being satisfied, is a major part of the Purāṇa's discourse on death. Indeed, the confluence of desire, sexuality, and death in the Bhāgavata is quite resonant with contemporary discussions of masculine ideology, like those of Camille Paglia, that see men as creating a defense against a complex of nature, woman, and death, seeking to transcend the "miasmic swamp whose prototype is the still pond of the womb."[20] The Bhāgavata is, after all, a text composed by an elite class of men seeking to maintain their social position and adhering to a belief system that often associates death and dying with the "lower elements" of an ever-changing natural world. The portrayal of death in the Purāṇa, is so pervasive, however, that it touches everything and everyone, cutting across barriers of family, lineage, and locality.

If this is beginning to sound a bit like Buddhist doctrine it should be noted that Buddhist and Hindu traditions share age-old perspectives. I recall my recent visit to Buddhist temples in Śri Laṅkā, finding them ringed with Hindu as well as local deities, and how a number of residents and *sādhus* in Braj—one of the Bhāgavata-Purāṇa's major institutional arenas—continually referred to the Buddha's sojourn in Mathurā, adding even further prestige to the land of Kṛṣṇa's appearance and childhood. This kind of popular pluralism is much more the rule than the exception in India (although you would never know it from reading text books on world religions that offer a neat version of Hinduism as one religion distinct from others). The lack of comfort in any form of absolutism is often thought of as the hallmark of Buddhist teaching, but both Buddhism and Bhāgavatism grow from similar soil.

The Buddha's visit to Mathurā may or may not be able to be historically documented, but the challenge of his presence is clearly felt in *Bhāgavata-dharma*. The Bhāgavata-Purāṇa continually focuses on human suffering and propounds the reality of impermanence in the face of the desire for something greater. What the Bhāgavata proposes, however, is more of a "homeopathic" resolution.[21] Impermanence and relativity are dealt with, not only by eradicating desire or by mindfully observing it, but by intensifying it into a conscious anguish which has transformative effects. Thus, the Purāṇa comes down on both sides of the "logocentric" issue: philosophically it invokes an absolute reality that is *nitya*, ever-existing; narratively it speaks extensively of inevitable frustration and loss in one form or another without any compensation. And at other times, as in the *advaitic* Uddhava's visit to the dualistically stricken cowherd lovers of Kṛṣṇa, the Bhāgavata consciously juxtaposes these two positions. In this manner, the narrative of the Purāṇa offers various ways to negotiate loss.

I am using the word "loss" as opposed to death rather frequently here, and this merits explanation. "Death" itself takes on many faces in the Purāṇa, some literal and some figurative. At times, death is spoken of as an intrusive "terror." At other times, it is not a problem at all, as when the hero, Dhruva, steps on Death's head in his ascent to the heavenly spheres, and at other times the loss of a loved one is said to be more painful than death. The variant scenarios all work to give meaning to the fact of dying, and this may be what the Purāṇa's project is ultimately about. I do not speak of "meaning" here in a purely cognitive sense, but rather in a visceral one. Death, as part of human life, must fit into some life-practice as well as world view. Humans ceremonialize their dead in different ways to accomplish this (the *Garuḍa-Purāṇa*, in this regard, has entire sections delineating the performance of the *śrāddha* rites for the dead). The Bhāgavata, on the other hand, accomplishes this by framing death with all kinds of circumstantial colorations. Here are some of the major ones I have isolated.

Clinical Death

Contemporary medicine defines death in numerous ways, most of which have to do with the cessation of physical functions (i.e., the irreversible cessation of all functions of the brain, circulation, and respiration).[22] The Bhāgavata offers its own set of clinical discussions, based on its strict body-mind dualism, about just what death is. In Kapila's discourse to his wife Devahūti in the third *skandha*, or "book," of the Purāṇa, he explains that the living being (*jīva*) attracts a suitable mind and sense organs through its activities (*karma*) and when the karmic reactions of that body come to an end, it is known as death. This is compared to the eyes losing their capacity to see objects. When this occurs, the sense of sight also gets deadened and the living being loses his power of vision. In the same way, when the physical body is incapable of perceiving, this is known as death. Likewise, the identification with the mind and the body as oneself is known as birth.[23]

Kapila's discourse has more than a clinically descriptive purpose, however. It is meant to engender dispassion and leads to the affirmation that one should neither view death with horror, nor identify the self with the body. Rather, one should be free of attachment and realize the true (deathless) nature of the living being. This refrain, which maintains the strict nature-spirit dualism of the Sāṁkhya school, shall be repeated throughout the text. Death is a natural fact, but it is not ultimate, and as we shall see, Hindu traditions develop this idea much differently from prevailing Christian religious sensibilities.

Kapila's instruction is reminiscent of the dialogue in the Gītā where Kṛṣṇa declares to Arjuna that "for one who is born, death is certain. And for one who has died, birth is certain. Therefore, in the unavoidable discharge of one's duty, one should not lament."[24] The basic understanding, shared by the Bhāgavata, is that the living being never dies, but has mistakenly identified itself with material elements and forms. In reading the text and its consideration of death, then, one will continually come up against its assumption of another life. I, myself, take a theologically neutral stance throughout and propose that one need not accept or discount this assumption to fully engage the text. Rather, like the discourse of death itself, it is there to be examined in all of its possible manifestations, both literal and metaphoric. And while the Purāṇa's unquestioned exposition of the deathlessness of the living entity certainly colors its visions of dying, the various crises that occur throughout the text around the "end of life" suggest other forces at work as well.

If who we are is deathless, then why do we die? Why does the living being misidentify itself as mind and matter? The Bhāgavata does not broach this question from a singular standpoint, although there is very little sense of a "fall" or of original sin in the text. Rather, the Bhāgavata offers a treasury of stories and theologies, and it is through a multiplicity of stories as opposed to one story that the thirst for origins is dealt with.

Separation

Along with clinical definitions of death, there are figurative types of "dying" that play a major role in the Bhāgavata-Purāṇa and in later

Vaiṣṇava theology. I am speaking of "separation" as a major thematic element in both Indian literature and religion. Technically called "*viraha*" or "*viyoga*," instances of separation highlight the intense anguish that can ensue from being apart from one's beloved or from one's own true nature. And often, this is depicted as a much more agonizing situation than "mere death."

The metaphor of "separation" can be (and has been) extended, to include the separation of human and divine as well as from loved ones. Both levels appear in the Purāṇa and are often juxtaposed. Fathers are constantly losing sons, wives lose husbands, parents lose children, and lovers lose their beloved. The entire Purāṇa may be read as a sustained meditation on loss, and this perhaps is its force. Rather than seeking to avoid loss (perhaps a correlate to the Buddhist truth of *duḥkha),* the Bhāgavata, as ironic as this may seem, celebrates it and makes it a fulcrum of personal transformation. This is most clearly visible in the climactic story of Kṛṣṇa and the cowherd women (*gopī*s) where love and loss, human and divine, intermingle dramatically.

Extending the discourse on dying to separation and loss moves us away from literalism to areas of our imaginings. Even if we remain with clinical death for a moment, a number of questions arise. What kind of death is it? How, when, and where does one die? Is dying a purely personal event or a social one as well (as in the death of Bhīṣma, the grandfather of the great Kuru dynasty, which is played out in front of a vast audience). How is it understood by others? How do the living memorialize the dead and what are their said motivations for this? What particular images, colors, and scenarios surround a death? At one point in the text, for example, a *brāhmaṇa* holds a king responsible for the untimely death of his son. In this case, an individual's death becomes a social and political issue. And, whatever the exact relationship between nature and culture may be, the Bhāgavata's death-narratives clearly participate in its social polemics.

As we extend our idea of what it may mean to "be dead," we see that some of the strongest characters in the text are "dead to the world." The *avadhūta,* who has wholly renounced worldly ties, and the mad lover, who gives up all self-striving in the fires of longing, are primary in this regard. Tragedy abounds in the text as well, through circumstances where romantic union leads to ultimate separation, very much in opposition to Sanskrit dramatic sensibility. And there are other dimensions in which this gets played out: ironic unions demonstrating their own impossibility and paradoxical unions and separations together. And if there is any "rule" here, it would be "variance," as "Many Ways of Dying" indicates. By not binding oneself to a particular method or view, let us look at some of the other principal ways in which the Purāṇa configures death.

Murder, Suicide, and Sacrifice

The Bhāgavata is filled with all types of violence and murder, war, fits of rage, and personal jealousies. Patricide, matricide, infanticide abound as the Purāṇa often paints a ghastly portrait of human existence. Perhaps the most celebrated of these is the mass murder, rewritten from the epic, of the Yadu dynasty. One cannot really call this a mass suicide as in the case of Rāma's subjects walking voluntarily into the Śarayū river after their hero-God has left. Here, the dynasty ends in a drunken brawl (providential, of course) in which the members of the great Yadu clan kill one another with blades of *kuśa* grass that have been unknowingly treated with iron.

Outright war, on the other hand, is more often than not spoken of in terms of ritual sacrifice, particularly the Bhārata war (as Hiltebeitel has elegantly described in his work on the epic). The epic warriors Arjuna and Bhīṣma both stand on the verge of dying, much like Parīkṣit in the Purāṇa. Arjuna's theophony in the Gītā, in fact, results from encountering Kṛṣṇa's awesome aspect of death. The elder Bhīṣma, who has the power to choose the time of his death, waits to impart instruction to Yudhiṣṭhira on how to rule the kingdom. So the moment of death during the heat of battle is seen as an excellent time for both giving and receiving instruction.

At other times in the Purāṇa, war and killing take on a playful aspect as in descriptions of wars between Śiva and Viṣṇu. When Kṛṣṇa destroys his various rivals in battle, the descriptions of rolling heads and running rivers of blood are given in a ludic, hyperbolic mode as a celebration of another *līlā* or amusing pastime of Kṛṣṇa. And one may wonder, in these instances, what or whose agenda may actually underlie such descriptions. Rarely is death "done as melodrama" in the Purāṇa. Major figures do not stab themselves or each other in tragic solemnity, probably because dying is understood as a passage as opposed to a finality. This is also the case in the Bhāgavata's "resurrection scenes," in which various characters matter-of-factly return from (or are brought back from) the dead, usually to offer discourses on the futility of material attachment.

The most ritualized and solemn deaths in the Purāṇa are the suicides. They are mostly sacrificial ones, as in the *satī* of Gāndhārī when she willingly enters her husband's blazing funeral pyre. The Dakṣa myth, retold in the Purāṇa, has Satī burning herself to ashes in a self-created yogic fire due to her outrage over her husband, Śiva, being slighted by Dakṣa, her father. There are also detailed descriptions of *yogīs* leaving their body and leaving mortal life consciously. The Yudhiṣṭhira of the Bhāgavata (as opposed to the epic) gives up his life in this manner of a master *yogī*.[25]

Death as Consequence of Ignorance

One repeated pejorative "death-image" in the Purāṇa is that of the "serpent and the rat:"

> Alert as the serpent that grabs a rat, licking the ends of its lips through hunger, You as Death suddenly overtake the *jīva* who is utterly careless, engrossed as he is in the thought of his projects and totally given up to the pleasures of the senses, and is seized with inordinate greed.[26]

Here, as in many other places, death is envisioned as a fitting reward for ignorance of one's true nature. Death, in fact, is often spoken as a symptom of dualistic ignorance. The divine sage Kapila declares, "Figuring as death, I cause great fear to him who makes the least discrimination between himself and another because of his differential outlook."[27]

Death is not merely retribution for ignorance, however, it is emblematic of ignorance itself and is often conflated in the Purāṇa with women, sensual attachment, the family, and the external world. The Bhāgavata declares woman to be the personification of *māyā* that slowly entraps man, advising one to regard her as "death to oneself like a well whose mouth is covered with grass."[28] Man, however, is also seen as death for woman, as sexual attraction in general is condemned as *hṛd-rogam* or a "disease of the heart."[29]

Other Types of Dying

As discussed, I want to look through physical death to the many associations that come with it: the "death" of projections and identifications, the "death" of a life-stage or social designation, the "death" of a lineage or dynasty. The Bhāgavata deals with all of these in one place or another and more often than not counsels renunciation, which is enacted as a symbolic social death: kings leave their kingdom, sages leave society, and children even leave their parents right after birth.

The death of one's identification with a place may be brought about by exile, and the Bhāgavata plays upon this theme heavily. We remember that both great Indian epics revolve around temporary exiles, but the restoration of the kingdom is always fraught with contradiction. In the Mahābhārata, the lineage continues, but only after a holocaust that claims almost all the heroes and villains of the world. The *Rāmāyaṇa* tradition never makes up its mind about a final "return." In some texts, Rāma and Sītā return triumphantly to their home, Ayodhyā, while in others, there is a final exile and mass suicide. In the *kṛṣṇa-carita* (story of Kṛṣṇa) of the Bhāgavata, the infant Kṛṣṇa is separated from his parents at birth and brought up by foster parents. Later on, when he returns to claim his kingdom, Kṛṣṇa must leave behind the loves of his youth from the cowherd village of Vṛndāvana. This becomes a focal point of the Purāṇa, as we shall see, (for in the Bhāgavata, as in the Hindu religious imagination, Kṛṣṇa's place of exile, Vṛndāvana, is his "real home").

Exile, in the Bhāgavata does not correlate with a "fall into history." There is no original paradisial place, no singular search for an ultimate abode. In one narrative, the creator god Brahmā is born from a lotus and tries to find his origin. He descends down the stem as far as he can and finds nothing so he returns to his place of birth where he hears the word "*tapas,*" or "penance." He then enters into meditation, and Viṣṇu, his progenitor, appears. But this Viṣṇu is one of many Viṣṇus who appear and reappear like bubbles in the causal sea. Here again, we witness the "*advaitic* theism," the uni- and multicentered sensibility of the Purāṇa.[30] Death is seen as a form of ignorance which one can conceivably cross over, and yet there is no one time or place when the descent into death happened. There is no search for a first cause, only *līlā*, the ongoing play of the divine.

Time and Destiny

More often than not, both natural and unnatural dying in the Purāṇa are accompanied by discussions on the inevitability of fate and time. Though fate and time are not necessarily synonymous with death in the Purāṇa, they do seem to accompany it in many guises. At one point, after the violent death of King Dhruva's brother, Manu, the progenitor of the human race, tells Dhruva that it was not his enemies who slew his brother, but *daivam* (destiny) which alone was the true cause of his death.[31]

In an extended allegory about a king whose city of nine gates (the body) is on fire, the daughter of time is said to range over the three worlds seeking a husband. When refused by the sage Nārada, she curses him to be unable to stay in one place for a long time. She then marries Fear, the Lord of the Yavanas, and together they bring about the death of living beings.[32]

In another narrative, Kāla ("time") is referred to as "the ruler of rulers," who, being the support of all, enters the heart of all living beings and devours them through other beings. This Kāla is said to be none other than Viṣṇu, the presiding deity over sacrifices.[33]

Not only is time equated with God here, but also with death and procreation, with fear, and with foreign low-caste peoples (Yavanas).

The high-born sage, Nārada, will have nothing to do with time's daughter, and he thus becomes a fleeting traveler rather than a fixture in the world. The complex of birth, death, fear, eating, and being eaten, all are set squarely under the province of time. We get a sense here of time not only as an immutable and all-powerful devourer, but also as a lower aspect of the divine power, one to which low-caste peoples (Yavanas) are subject.

Death as Creative Renewal

The paradox of Death as creator as well as destroyer is often envisioned through sexuality where the loss of precious male seed, though often equated with death, also contains the power of creation. Death, as in sexuality and sacrifice, engenders life. And as the ashes of the dead are thrown into the Gaṇgā to "feed the river" with the "crystallized semen" of burnt bone, the story of Parīkṣit's death, woven through the eighteen thousand verses of the Purāṇa, will be seen as a sacrificial rite meant to "seed" the future.[34]

Perhaps, then, the central axis around which all this turns is still "sacrifice," in which the principles of exchange and conservation of energy predominate over beginnings and endings. The text describes its own reading as a "sacrifice," a literal one where sages have gathered in the forest to hear the Bhāgavata for the good of the world. The sacrificial metaphor, like the literary one, is gustatory. Sacrifice is offered to be devoured and, through being eaten, is transformed.[35]

Overcoming Death

The Bhāgavata often envisions freedom from death as true knowledge and the reward of devotion, as the god Śiva affirms in the text.

> Though destroying the universe even with his brows contracted as a token of his majesty and energy, Death does not seize the soul who has taken shelter under those feet [of Viṣṇu] as subject to his authority.[36]

The entire story of the Purāṇa, as I shall describe, is spoken to a man who is about to die, and it enables him to come to terms with his own dying. Moreover, there are a number of characters in the text who die consciously and painlessly, usually while meditating on some form of the supreme. And this is significant, since the "problematic" of death and dying is played out, in the Bhāgavata, against a backdrop of "non-problematic" dying. Thus, the possibility of mastery over the incongruities of the physical world is a given in the text, at least as far as certain types of people are concerned.

Death and dying, as a particular occurrence then, exists within wider, more numinous connotations: separation, as an archetypal dynamic underlying the very structure of occurrences; the narrative process itself as a corrective of sorts to inevitable loss; and the ongoing, emblematic presence of those who have visibly triumphed over death. It is through the interplay of a strong sense of absence and loss with an equally strong sense of unity that the Bhāgavata develops its enduring power.

1

EXAMINATIONS OF THE PAST

Purāṇas participate in a similar mythological universe to epic and *kāvya* (poetic) works. However, they are structured as exhaustive compendiums of the Epic lore seen through particular (one may say "sectarian") perspectives. The word *purāṇa* means "ancient," and a good deal of its oral lore may have been coexistent with the Veda itself, sharing the nebulous ground of a most extensive oral tradition.[1] Regardless of extrinsic chronological possibilities, Purāṇas see themselves as narrating events that have taken place in the "distant past." Such narratives, of course, have little to do with measurable, historical continuity. Rather, "the past" becomes the paradigm for the present through the mythic shadows cast by its great characters—gods, kings, saints, and sages.

The Purāṇic past is highly structured. But the tradition's classification of the Purāṇas by *pañca-lakṣaṇa*—the five qualities that define a Purāṇa—functions primarily as a "myth of composition" as E. W. Hopkins and others have noted. The *pañca-lakṣaṇa*s, or "five characteristics," have in fact never been strictly followed.[2] Furthermore, the Bhāgavata speaks of possessing "ten characteristics," *daśa-lakṣaṇa* as opposed to *pañca-lakṣaṇa*, prompting much commentarial speculation on the arrangement and purpose of the *lakṣaṇa*s themselves.[3] What may be significant here is that the Purāṇic narrative constructs itself through categories, perhaps indicating a "past" that lends itself more easily to lateral, associative classification then to successive chronology.

The question of Purāṇa as being history or myth is not really an issue here, for—as Eliade has noted in his early work on ritual and as Sudhir Kakar has shown in particular case studies—history in India has tended to bleed into myth in a matter of two or three generations.[4] The Purāṇas do not claim to be history, in a contemporary sense, as much as they envision themselves as a collective memory, a memory that turns around particular persons in particular situations. They do not offer a master narrative that states "what happened." Rather, they are as situational as the ethics of Manu, and therefore welcome the coloration of subjectivity that contemporary readers would attribute to myth as they reconstruct the past. Thus, the Bhāgavata relates stories found in the Epics and in other Purāṇas, but it does so from its own unique perspective, and while its perspective is clearly a Vaiṣṇava one, and a Kṛṣṇaite one at that, the fact that its narrative turns around a conversation between a dying man and a sage, who has come to help him die, is unique in Indian literature.

What is really crucial to understanding the Bhāgavata's "death narrative" is the Purāṇic sense of the past. For the mythical revisioning of the past is what Purāṇas essentially do, and this is what Parīkṣit is given to do in preparation for dying. Unlike the *Bar do thos grol* (the *Tibetan Book of the Dead*), the dying person is not given instruction on what she/he will encounter upon leaving the physical body. (The Bhāgavata does, however, have an "after-death section" in the third book, and like other Purāṇas does catalogue an impressive series of heavens and hells in the fifth *skandha*.) But more pointedly, Parīkṣit is led through a series of rich, diverse stories that combine variant theologies, narrative forms, and philosophies in a pastiche of Vedic, Āgamic, Epic, and other modes of discourse (a pastiche which led Friedhelm Hardy to marvel at the author, if indeed there is one, not becoming schizoid).[5] Rather than a weakness, however, this borrowing effect may be a strength of the Bhāgavata-Purāṇa. As in the case of the Bhagavadgītā, encompassing diversity has led to monumentality.

Moreover, this "collage-like" structure should be considered one of the principal psychologizing devices of the Purāṇa. It takes leave of literal history and authorship, as well as linear narrative, and enters into a liminal world of figures who represent the cultural *mythos* of the past, the world of Parīkṣit's ancestors. The name "Parīkṣit" literally means "the examiner." In the Mahābhārata he is the grandson of Arjuna, and is the last surviving heir of the Pāṇḍava line. In both the Epic and Bhāgavata versions of his story, Parīkṣit is saved by Viṣṇu, who incarnates in the womb of his mother and protects him from Aśvatthāmā's irreversible *brahmāstra* weapon.[6] Having seen the form of Viṣṇu while still in the womb, Parīkṣit goes on searching for that likeness throughout his life.

Parīkṣit, cursed to die within seven days, then, is still examining. He will be asked to hear a recapitulation of the imaginative history of his lineage, he must return to the past, he must "psychologize" in order to make peace with his past. As an interesting aside here, Parīkṣit's own son, Janamejaya, will not at all be at peace with his father's death; instead, he will seek to exterminate the entire race of serpents in a ghastly sacrifice (since a serpent-bird, Takṣaka, is the actual instrument of Parīkṣit's death).

It is important to note that the recounted Purāṇic past—unlike a contemporary analytic session—is not composed of Parīkṣit's personal history, but rather of the history of his lineage which is significant. This position is in marked contrast to normative depth psychology's notion of a personal mytho-history, or a "myth of individuation," to use C. G. Jung's terminology (which was arguably coined in conscious contradistinction to non-Western metaphors of "absorption" into an undifferentiated Absolute). As Alan Roland, and more recently Stanley N. Kurtz, have pointed out, Indian psychology in general offers a model of health focused somewhat differently from that of post-Enlightenment humanistic psychology: the healthy ego is not the "individuated" one, but is one which has successfully integrated into its significant group—the "we-self"- versus the "I-self." Thus, personal history defers to collective history, and personal values to collective values. One's very existence is conceived of as part of the collective matrix, not apart from it.[7]

In its reconsideration of the past, then, the Bhāgavata does not focus on personal events but evokes as best it can the sense of a monumental collective identity. Through archaic language and sanskritization of regional themes, and through its narrative constructed from a mosaic of common lore, the Bhāgavata seeks the universal, hoping to appeal to as broad a base as possible. Thus, commentators from varieties of different schools claim the work as their own.

Moreover, Purāṇic stories do not exist within the covers of a book, nor even within the genre labeled "Purāṇa." They are chronicles of the collective imagination, confluences of ongoing discourse, and will be continually revisioned and retold through varieties of dramatic and performance traditions. The intertextual echo of the Purāṇas always resonates strongly, for the Purāṇas are dialoging with the Epics by retelling their stories and with the *Veda*s by trying to emulate them (as in the case of the Bhāgavata's *gāyatrī*-like verse), refer to them, or align with them.[8] In the Bhāgavata's own words, it, itself, is the *nigama-kalpa-taror galitaṁphalam,* "the delicately ripened fruit from the *kalpa* (wish-fulfilling) tree of the Vedic tradition."[9]

Another important aspect of the Purāṇic narrative is its sacral nature. These are not just collections of stories as in the *Kathāsaritsāgara*, or *Daśakumāracarita.* The original narrative is attributed to the Supreme Being, Nārāyaṇa, and the immediate author, Vyāsa, is also said to be an aspect of the Supreme.[10] Jīva Gosvāmī, in this regard, cites a verse from the *Bṛhadāraṇyaka Upaniṣad* stating that the Vedas, Itihāsas, and Purāṇas have all emanated from the breath of the "Great Being." And the Bhāgavata, itself, refers to the *itihāsa-purāṇa* as the fifth Veda.[11] By wrapping itself in the mantle of the Veda, the Purāṇa supports its claim to divine status and attempts to elevate its narrative to the level of Vedic orthodoxy.[12] In this sense, the Bhāgavata-Purāṇa corresponds to scholarly definitions of myth as "a story that is sacred."[13] And this sense of its own sacredness characterizes the Bhāgavata's narrative along with its aesthetic and narrative sensibility.

The Purāṇa thus aims at more than an extrinsic synthesis of variant subjects and perspectives, for it resists presenting itself as an unicentered text promoting a singular theological position.[14] For the Bhāgavata is mytho-poetic narrative in its most anagogical sense. It sees itself as the very incarnation of the Godhead, the "ripened fruit" from the tree of the Vedic tradition whose *arka*, a Vedic word for "ray," will bring light to the dark Kali age.[15] Beyond both its efforts to present itself as a Vedic evolute and its philosophical predilections and historical reconstructions, however, the narrative/aesthetic focus of the Bhāgavata stands as predominant. Taking its lead from a phrase of the *Taittirīya Upaniṣad*, "*raso vai saḥ*"—"He is *rasa*"—the Purāṇa continually refers to its own narrative as "ambrosial," as it seeks to embody both the Vedic idea of *rasa* as blissful liquid essence and the Ālaṁkārika tradition's notion of *rasa* as aesthetic mood.[16] In this regard, the text frequently employs classical (*kāvya*) instead of Epic śloka meters and moves its narrative toward the figurative dimension whenever possible.

The Bhāgavata, of course, will assert that its own "devotional mood," or *bhakti-rasa*, is the apotheosis of these traditions. Just how far and in what way it lays claim to the Vedic and classical aesthetic traditions will be discussed in the third chapter of this volume. What I want to investigate here is the Bhāgavata's sense of "narrative as aesthetics" as opposed to "narrative as representation." "Narrative as representation" places one in the realm of *itihāsa*—the recounting of said events. But the series of interwoven stories that make up the Purāṇa exist in such a seemingly oblique (versus literal) relationship to one another that one can hardly account for them as necessary components of the Purāṇic genre. Moreover, the idea of the Purāṇa as *kathā*—in the Epic sense of a descriptive or historical narrative—cannot account for its multiplicity, visions of the future, and sustained heights of poetic rapture.

The Purāṇic form can be understood, perhaps, through the conventional theories of Sanskrit poetics as they are interpreted by the Vaiṣṇava commentaries of Jīva Gosvāmī, Vallabha, Viśvanātha Cakravartī, and others.[17] In such commentaries the narrative itself is envisioned as the chief aesthetic element, and the various *skandhas* (or chapters of the Purāṇa) are seen as containing "complementary" *līlās,* or "divine plays," each exhibiting their own particular flavor or *rasa*s. The appropriate mixing of aesthetic flavors sets the stage for the climactic tenth *skandha* in which *mādhurya-bhāva* (the mood of conjugal love) eclipses all the others. While *mādhurya* is often referred to by commentators as "*ādi-rasa,*" or the "original mood," the text itself moves on and winds back down to a harmonious, more worldly conclusion, much like an Indian *rāga* recapitulates its original themes after a climactic movement.[18] This "narrative as aesthetic" becomes the Purāṇa's primary and ongoing response to Parīkṣit's existential situation.

The question is why, and the answer is offered here in hypothetical form. Could it be that the Bhāgavata-Purāṇa recognizes an inherently "aesthetic" nature of the world? Could it be that the Purāṇa understands interior processes to be akin to narrative itself—not Epic, or dramatic, narrative as a description of psychic processes, but a pluralistic narrative that bends, dips, and doubles back on itself? What Hardy speculates to be schizophrenia, and what others may deplore as relativism, may be a deeper, more accurate, and even more therapeutic image of the cultural, mythic terrain than the non-aesthetic models commenting upon it could have imagined. The multivalent story lines, flashbacks and flash-forwards, and repetitions of similar themes in innumerable forms may be a more accurate map of the imagination than can be captured in any singular design.

James Hillman, for the last three decades, has boldly asserted the human psyche to be decentered and polytheistic, taking the Greek mythological imagination as his model.[19] The Bhāgavata's vision, on the other hand, is neither that of a fragmented multiplicity (as the rhetoric of deconstruction would see it), nor even that of an uneasy, extended family (as in Hillman's vision of the Greek Gods), but rather is a multiplicity of unity held together by "narrative as aesthetics." In fact, the aesthetics of classical Indian dance, while drawing on both *kāvya* and *nāṭya* establishes a technique that disrupts the linear narrative by injecting diverse elements from a wide range of cultural forms in an improvisational manner. And, while I would not go so far as to say that the Purāṇic narrative is modeled after *nṛtya* (dance), it seems to share a good deal of its sensibility. Is it any wonder, then, that the ultimate figure of reality that the Purāṇa has to offer is that of a dance? The dance, or *rāsa-līlā*, appears in the tenth *skandha* and is simultaneously a narrative event, a performance (with the denizens of the upper worlds as the audience), and an emblem of the sublime to be contemplated upon by devotees. This "emblem" is discussed in terms of "unity and difference being inconceivably and simultaneously united" (*acintya-bhedābheda-tattva*—Jīva) as well as it being "a resting place of contradictory characteristics" (*viruddhadharmāśrayatā*—Vallabha). I will explore the *rāsa-līlā* in detail in the sixth chapter of this volume. For the moment, I want to examine the power and centrality of the Bhāgavata's narrative patterning.

What is woven through this Purāṇic form, then, is a sustained focus on a narrative which will, according to its connotations and audience, produce an emotional response of deep feeling (*bhāva*), maturing into *bhakti-rasa*.[20] This is crucial to the project of preparation for dying because it supports the idea of listening as an end in itself, an end which is discussed in the first *skandha* as being superior to liberation from birth and death!

> *ātmārāmāś ca munayo nirgranthā apy urukrame*
> *kurvanty ahaitukīṁ bhaktim ittham-bhūta-guṇo hariḥ*
>
> Even sages and those who delight in the *self,* who are freed from all ties, perform unalloyed devotion unto the Supreme Lord, Urukrama, being attracted by his wonderful qualities.
>
> (BhP. I.7.10)

In the above verse, *bhakti* (loving devotion) is spoken of as desirable even for those who are liberated (literally "delighted in themselves"—*ātmārāma*), and even for those who have "gone beyond texts"(since the word *nirgrantha* can literally mean "without books" as well as "without ties"). The implication of this word *nirgrantha* is crucial to the narrative's sense of itself because even those who are beyond language, as *jīvanmuktas* are said to be, willingly participate in the language of devotion. The Bhāgavata repeatedly associates *bhakti* with the act of *śravaṇa-kīrtana*—the hearing and singing narrative process—as its own reward. Thus, the Purāṇa promotes neither an absolutist cognition that frees one from the phenomenon of dying and its consequences, nor a relative conclusion that will abandon the "dying enterprise" as hopelessly unresolvable.

While the *bhakti-rasa* is the undeniable thread that strings the various Purāṇic narratives together, the Purāṇic narrative itself is inseparable from this thread. The polemical conclusions, innuendos, and didactic assertions of the Purāṇa are all delivered through the medium of story, not in the sense of an easily graspable tale, or even necessarily an allegory for the fallen minds of the Kali age, but in the sense of a rambling, episodic collage that incarnates patterns of meaning and cultural value while incorporating religious, moral, historical, and aesthetic dimensions of experience.

A Note on the Mytho-Poetic Tradition

Let me return to what I have been refering to as either the "mythopoetic" or "depth psychological tradition." By these terms, I do not mean the one school of Jung and his followers, but also the work of James Hillman, Northrop Frye, Wendy Doniger, and others who point to story as a most authentic model of the mythological process; not myth seen as reflecting a semidynamic structured psyche of *ego, id,* and *superego* (Freud), or even *persona*, *anima*, and *self* (Jung), but an open-ended mythic field of variance, filled with assorted characters, plot lines, and few clear-cut resolutions.

If *mythos,* seen as plot, is in some way analogous to the structure or patterning of the psyche, then the narrative process is itself the significant event; the telling of the story, which is what a Purāṇa does, has its own logic. Focusing on such "narrative logic" would be described by Frye as an "intrinsic" or "literary" method: one which does not subordinate narrative and its nonconclusive, anthropomorphizing, and even sometimes pathological tendencies to either historical grids or philosophical considerations.[21] I would further add that what Frye labels as "literary," and what Hillman labels as "psychological" or "psychologizing" are one and the same thing: the focusing on the imaginative, either interiorized or projected outward, as the primary movement of narrative.[22] In this sense, as Frye has noted, literature, Purāṇic or otherwise, may serve in the same way as the structured visualizations of *maṇḍala*s, *ḍākiṇī*s, and *yi dam*s do in Tibetan Buddhist traditions—as psychic constructs (often personified) that are evolved and dissolved through the imagination. In this sense, literature does not try to represent the external world but rather to transform the relationship between the imaginary and the real (as Lacan might put it), or between the inner and outer worlds.

Another important aspect of the mytho-poetic narrative process is variance. And, as one explores the narratives of the Bhāgavata, one cannot help but be impressed by their multivalence. The Purāṇa, for example, does not privilege a young male hero struggling for independence from a mother (although heroines are few and far between), nor does it focus on an old king, nor on a young maiden, nor even on a great paradigmatic war as the Epics do. Instead, demons such as Bali and Prahlāda become exalted; virtuous heroes such as Mucukunda succumb to the ravages of time; children die at birth; Viṣṇu, the "main character" of the Purāṇa (if there is one), appears in a multitude of forms—human, animal, male, female, young, and old; and the same stories, such as the *Varāha-līlā*, of Viṣṇu, rescuing the earth in the form of a boar, are told differently in separate sections of the Purāṇa.[23]

What kind of story, then, does the Purāṇa tell? Not an original story, not even a uni-authored one, for the narrative is depicted as a collaborative effort. The ripened fruit of the Purāṇa is said to be passed down literally from reciter to reciter as ambrosial liquid from the mouth of

Śuka, the parrot-narrator whose touching of the narrative, the commentators tell us, makes it even sweeter.[24] The commentarial tradition here affirms the psychology of the collective rather than that of the individual. As it is passed down, the story is embellished. Unlike the Veda, it is not expected to be passed down verbatim. At one point, Śuka speaks of the Purāṇa as originally having been spoken by Nārāyaṇa in the form of four *ślokas*. And Sūta, the bard who has heard the narrative of Śuka and who is said to be "bathed" in the discourse of the tradition (*viṣaye vācāṁ snātam*),[25] is asked to narrate to others what he has heard. And so the narrative technique of "someone always talking to someone else about something" (J. L. Mehta), a technique which Tzvetan Todorov called "embedding" in *A Thousand and One Nights* and which David Shulman has referred to as "emboxing," goes on.[26] If one looked at this narrative through the eyes of a psychoanalyst, one would see it as a practice of collective free association. And this, I think, would be quite acceptable from the Purāṇic viewpoint. The Purāṇa is, after all, an admittedly collaborative re-telling, a re-visioning of the Epic-past with new additions, differing perspectives, and variant conclusions.

There are some fascinating family dynamics present in the text. The principal narrator, Śuka, is the son of the principal narrator of the Mahābhārata, Vyāsa, and so the Bhāgavata, as J. L. Mehta notes, represents itself as the offspring of the Epic for a new age.[27] In this regard, we may remember that the death of the Pāṇḍava brothers is one of the thorniest Epic conundrums, which, like the Epic itself, is never clearly resolved.[28] Therefore the children, Śuka and Parīkṣit, must take up the task, by trying "a different way of dying," so to speak.

Let us return again to "The Examiner" and his preparation for death. Is this the Bhāgavata's principal point of focus? Not really. The Bhāgavata does not have a singular focus or not a literal one anyway. One could thematically say that *bhakti* is its focus, yes, but I would argue that *bhakti* is more of its polemic or its underlying mood, than its focus. Beneath the various family and dynastic dramas, prescriptive behavioral guides, and geographical descriptions of the world, there is the ongoing narrative practice of telling the tale of "what happened in days of old" *(purāṇa)*. So the "death-drama" of Parīkṣit does not remain on center stage, and this too is central to the mytho-poetic stance of the Purāṇa. If the narrative kept returning to the existential situation of Parīkṣit in Sartre-like fashion, we would have a psychology of singular focus, a dualistic tension between *eros* and *thanatos*. We do not. Rather, the Bhāgavata frames the Śuka/Parīkṣit narrative by scores of other narratives. Are there thematic relationships? Yes, but the focus never becomes fixed or static. The Purāṇa eschews the psychology of an "integrated personality." Even the Absolute Truth, when discussed philosophically, is said to reveal itself in three different aspects, *brahma, paramātmā*, and *bhagavān*,[29] while *Bhagavān*, the Absolute personified, plays—and this is a literal translation—through twenty-one different forms or *avatāras*.[30] What this begins to resemble is Hillman's description of the Greek polytheistic terrain, and that might be attractive. But the Bhāgavata, as I mentioned, does not uphold a universe of loosely related familial powers. Rather, there is inconceivable oneness in difference, and this is what I would call the "multivalent psychological stance" of the Purāṇa.

Part of this position is reflected in the Bhāgavata's uncompromising attitude toward death and dying. It rewrites, for example, the Mahābhārata version of the Parīkṣit story, expunging any effort on the monarch's part to escape from death. In the Epic narrative (followed by the *Skandha Purāṇa* and the *Devī Bhāgavata*), Parīkṣit tries to circumvent his fate with the aid of his ministers and *brāhmaṇa*s by having an impregnable palace constructed on a huge pillar and surrounding the structure with physicians, healing herbs, and ritual adepts. Takṣaka, the snake bird, however, takes the form of a small worm and hides inside a fruit that his Nāga allies (disguised as ascetics) offer to the unsuspecting king. When Parīkṣit sees the small copper colored worm, he imagines that he has found a way out: if this worm would bite him, the curse of death would be figuratively enacted, and his real death would be averted. As the king places the worm to his mouth, however, it transforms into Takṣaka, who leaps out hissing, coils around the monarch, bites him, and sends him on his way.[31]

In the Bhāgavata version, on the other hand, Parīkṣit immediately accepts his fate, abandons his kingdom and possessions, and makes his way to the Ganges to fast until death. When Parīkṣit pointedly asks what one should do to prepare to die, however, he is met with a discourse of multiplicity, a panoramic story of what happened in days of yore, all the way back to primary and secondary creations of the universe. What does it mean to rehash the old here? Might this be a larger and earlier version of the therapeutic method, the "talking cure?" Not exactly, because the Bhāgavata would better be described as a "listening cure": chanting (*kirtana*) follows hearing (*śravaṇa*)in the Bhāgavata's "therapeutic" process. Both of these processes, however, privilege the imaginative, or more precisely, privilege narrative. The Bhāgavata does not see itself as "imaginary" or as "fantasy," but as "history." Freud, and those who followed him, it could be argued, believed that fantasy could have a greater impact and interior accuracy than history, or to take it a step further, that there may only be Purāṇa, the recorded cultural fantasy analogous to the fantasy of the individual. Whatever the case, in this regard, one cannot help but be struck by Purāṇic images, such as the one of *Mahā-Viṣṇu* dreaming the world and then reabsorbing it back into his body. This is a micro-macrocosmic image of the world as *māyā*, as the dream-like emanation of the divine, in which the past and future are woven together, rising and falling on the billowy breaths of the inconceivable and the unknowable. Such an image literally identifies myth with history because the reality of the world emerges from a dream.

As unknowable as the world may be, however, the all-too-human phenomenon, the "cognitive imperative" tends to assert itself: the drive to organize unexplained stimuli into some coherent cognitive matrix.[32] The imaginative-explanatory need is envisioned by a number of scholars as a primary human need. In this vein, one might better understand the repeated reminders from the Epic oral tradition that story is at the heart of life. Without stories the collective body cannot maintain its *mythos* which is its cognitive matrix, especially when the social order shatters, as in a war—be it the Bhārata war or Viet Nam. Indeed, this is what happens to Parīkṣit: when his world shatters, he hears the stories of his predecessors and ancestors, leading up to sublime stories in the tenth *skandha* for the initiated alone. He hears the knowledge of the collective which allows him to take his place in mytho-history.

The Story of Parīkṣit

Why tell a story, or more pointedly, hear a story at the end of your life, the moment that presumably represents the height of ultimate concern? Unlike Scheherazade's *Thousand and One Nights*, this story is not told to procrastinate, to put off one's inevitable demise, nor to change fate in any way. And unlike some literature found in the pseudepigraphic *Testaments of the Twelve Patriarchs*, there is no balancing of accounts in terms of an individual's life, no sustained emphasis on ethical or eschatological instruction.[33] Hillman, in *Revisioning Psychology,* discusses Plato's death narrative as a type of "soul-making," Keats' poetic phrase signifying the development of depth-psychological awareness.[34] The story of one's death, or the story told at one's death, is seen as an important activity, one that can lead toward a deeper, more reconciled modality of being, a "healing fiction," to use Hillman's own words.

One might expect death dialogues, therefore, to melt things down to their so-called essentials, but this is not necessarily the case. Socrates, in the *Phaedo*, accepts his fate and discusses the pleasure of freeing the soul from the body. He also, in Bhāgavata-Purāṇa fashion one could argue, discourses on a wide variety of subjects including the geography of the universe, absolute beauty, and the good life, before insuring the settling of his final debts (the cock to Aesculapius) and accepting the administered poison.[35] Don Quixote, on perceiving the warning signs of death, recants his past illusions, receives confession, and pragmatically prepares his will.[36] According to Philip Aries, there were specific formulae for dying in preindustrial Europe, "the same words passed on from age to age," specific ritual confessions, testaments, and customs that good Christians would follow before dying; such as lying quietly upon the ground or sickbed, spreading one's arms out to form a cross, and turning one's head east toward Jerusalem.[37] One knew exactly what to do in these public ceremonies. But, unlike Aries' examples of Christian European death narratives, the Bhāgavata's goes on for eighteen thousand verses! Unlike Plato's or Cervantes' narrative, the focus of the final moment—as I have mentioned—is not on the individual and his fate, not on his or her immediate surroundings and loved ones, and not even about dying itself. The Bhāgavata's "death-narrative" is an amplification, an expansion of the collective past as opposed to a personal confession or statement of belief. Nevertheless, the stories told do help Parīkṣit complete his life and approach death with dignity, even with exaltation, although this happens almost as an afterthought to the ongoing, all-encompassing story itself.

Umberto Eco has remarked that ". . . death, once it has occurred, and only then, constitutes the one and only referent, or event which cannot be semioticized."[38] Eco reasons that a dead semiotician no longer communicates semiotic theories. This is understandable because, from the materialist viewpoint, death is ultimate: it cannot be represented. The vision of death as an unequivocal finality charges it with eschatological power. However, when the scenario is framed by rebirth, as is the case in most Indian religious traditions, death ceases to be as ultimate. In the discourse of endless transmigration, the heroic quest for elevation, adventure, *cleos*, or even for salvation itself, loses some of its grip. From this perspective, which is the perspective of the Bhāgavata, death can become a call to a greater awakening while remaining part of the natural order of things.[39]

In the first *skandha* narrative of Nārada, which we shall discuss in detail later on, the fated death of the protagonists's own mother is seen as an opportunity for liberation, and he leaves home, without mourning, to follow his destiny. When Nārada, himself, gives up his body, he is immediately transferred to another divine one.[40] Such a vision of dying, whether it be a wish-fulfillment fantasy or not, is seen as an important event that can open one to the greater truth, that one, in fact, has never died. What dies or who dies in normative Indian traditions is not the essential person, the *ātman*, or *self*, but the ever-changing forms of the *guṇas*, or elements of nature. There indeed are, as we shall see, fates worse than death in the Bhāgavata, and they have to do with *viraha*, being separated from one's beloved. The narrative will build up to this vision, which ironically sees death and dying as a subset of *saṁsāra*, and *saṁsāra* itself—or the illusory condition of duality in the mind—as the real issue which one opens to in dying. It is important, therefore, to keep in mind the Bhāgavata's perspective on this: its focus on the collective biography as opposed to the biography of a lifetime, the hope-and-fear-based narrative of a mortal individual. Even this idea of an Indian collective-social ego is subsumed under the power of *kāla* (endless time) in its saṁsāric aspect. The great solar and lunar dynasties, for example, reveal themselves to be players in the *līlā*s that appear and reappear through the cycling ages. The Bhāgavata, then, integrates human psychology into cosmology. The individual and social narrative expands into cosmic dimensions, not as some peculiar altered state but as the way things actually are.

It is fitting, then, that the hero of the Purāṇa, if one would dare use such a word, is spoken of neither as a great warrior nor as the founder of a dynasty. The hero is the inheritor of a holocaust, the one surviving grandson of the Pāṇḍu clan who has seen Viṣṇu in the womb of his own mother. He exemplifies the new generation, the possibility to build upon what was; and his great act will be to die. Likewise, the narrator, Śuka, the son of Vyāsa, is also of a new generation. He is a peerless, pure sage who retells the vision of the past by offering a very different narrative. What, then, should one do who is about to die? The Bhāgavata declares that one should immerse oneself in the treasury of stories whose perspectives on living and dying are healing in a way different from what we may be accustomed to. Parīkṣit's is not a night-sea journey, not a descent into the underworld. He does not return to the world of the living in order to better accomplish his tasks and lead his people. This is all the more ironic since Parīkṣit has survived, indeed has been saved, in order to die. And there is no sense whatsoever, of the king's death serving an historical purpose, offering hope for the future, or redeeming the world. Perhaps his task is simply to die more consciously than his predecessors. And, in living and dying with Parīkṣit, one may learn to negotiate loss through the ritual of hearing and singing, envisioning the individual, not as an isolated entity, nor even as part of a sociohistorical collective, but as something greater which cannot be grasped but which can be shared through deepened participation in narrative form.

2

THE SEMIOTICS OF SEPARATION

The Bhāgavata-Purāṇa combines its own version of Epic narrative with the aesthetic sensibility of poetry (*kāvya)* and dance (*nṛtya*). Its theology is thus imbued with an aesthetic as well as narrative "logic" that operates around the centrality of absence. In discussing "many ways of dying" and the pastiche-like nature of the Purāṇic narrative, I have emphasized the *complex* of dying, the multifaceted imaginings around death as opposed to literal death. This, as mentioned, places one in the imaginative province of myth. There are, however, several specific modes of narrative in the Bhāgavata, strands of discourse appropriated from different traditions in a seemingly less than unified fashion. In this chapter, the principle strands of *Veda* (theological iconic), *alaṁkāra* (poetic), *itihāsa* (Epic), *bhakti* (devotional), and *darśana* (philosophic), will be untangled to see how they influence the representation of death and loss in the Purāṇa.

The centrality of loss also blends into a series of self-reflective issues around representation itself which underlie much of the Bhāgavata's project. By focusing on the "semiotics" of the text, or "how it produces meaning," one may see different ways in which the Bhāgavata grapples with a "tension between fusion and separation" which Sudhir Kakar claims continues to characterize much Hindu subjective experience.[1]

Perhaps as fundamental to the death-narrative as the various tales of the dying, is the semiotic issue of the basic incompleteness in linguistic representations of reality. This "incompleteness," interestingly enough, is often equated with mortality, and with language as well, for they are both part of the dualistic world which normative Vedāntic ideology relegates to the realm of illusion. One philosophical term often used to describe such dualism or "difference" is "*bheda*," which is used in the Epic to mean "wound" (among many other things). This may point to a connection between philosophical discourse and subjective experience, an anathema to traditions that maintain strong subject-object distinctions, but quite accurate in regard to normative Indian thinking. For the "woundedness" which difference often implies (i.e., the woundedness in the sense of suffering from birth, disease, old age, and death, as well the "difference" implied in their phenomenologies of transition) all too often proceeds from the arrows of Kāma, the movement of desire personified.[2] In Bhāgavata discourse, language and love intertwine, being bound up in the movement of desire, ever wanting but never arriving at finality. The problem, known in the post-structuralist world as that of the "floating signifier," (the absence of any ultimate stability to the linguistic sign and hence to any narrative), haunts this work, much as the "problem of desire" does. Again and again one meets situations in which finalities collapse as the flimsy moorings of apparently stable situations are graphically and searchingly portrayed.

In the case of this Purāṇa, however, there is the philosophical assertion of an *āśraya*, or "ultimate resting place." Language and love do have an end. Thus, one may initially be tempted to label the Bhāgavata-Purāṇa as "logocentric" in the Jacques Derridean sense of its having an ultimate finality. Indeed the Bhāgavata states, "All these are parts and portions of the Supreme Being, but Kṛṣṇa is the Supreme himself."[3] This "logos," however, is quite an unusual one in terms of Western experience. "It" plays a flute and operates *along with others*, for example within the confines of a small cowherd village. The common and unfortunate interpretive reaction to this scenario is to reduce it to one's own terms through one's own language (i.e., "Kṛṣṇa is God,"), although there is no one word in the Purāṇa that could actually translate as such). The actual epithet "*Bhagavān*" (possessor of *bhaga*—prosperity, fame, glory) implies greatness and wealth, while the devotional mood, in which Bhagavān is realized, already implies a community, a "holding company" if you will, in which numerous participants have shares (since *bhakti* has the meaning of a "portion" or "share"). In the Bhāgavata, moreover, the "problem" of the floating signifier can be likened to the problem of *saṁsāra* itself. Language keeps revolving through endless association, while Absolute Beingness (like death and dying) challenges efforts of representation.

Indian philosophical traditions, beginning with the *Upaniṣads*, have often discussed the dilemma of repeated birth and death in semiotic terms, with debates over the stability of meaning as experienced through thought or language. The *Chāndogya Upaniṣad* VI.1.4, for example, describes the entire manifest creation as nothing but a modification of language based on names (*vācārambhaṇaṁ vikāro nāmadheyam*). This model creates an endless "cause and effect" relationship between the signifier and signified, the repetition of the birth and death of "meanings" with no finality, no original word. The only relief from this endless semiotic chain (*saṁsāra*) is to perceive "the one real substance which pervades all modification" (*mṛttikety eva satyam*).[4] But as the *Taittirīya Upaniṣad* makes clear, in this absolute perception "words turn back," since they are incapable of signifying ultimates.[5]

If this be the case, conventional methods of signification such as perception, inference, and analogy, must be false or at best relative, and many commentators point this out. *Śabda*, the fourth traditional *pramāṇa* or "means of obtaining knowledge" is considered to be the strongest by many Bhāgavata commentators.[6] However, the serious question arises as to how such sound vibration or testimony, a seemingly material product, can be authoritative or absolute. To put this issue in Bhāgavata, as opposed to *Mīmāṁsā* terms, how can the stories about Kṛṣṇa or his entourage transport the reader/hearer beyond "saṁsāric" difference when the stories themselves are composed of material words and letters? After all, do they not also participate in the relativity of linguistic signification?

King Parīkṣit, in fact, asks this exact question to his preceptor Śuka in the tenth *skandha* of the work.[7] The Purāṇa's answer to this is once again, a story. Instead of offering direct advice or even philosophical dictums, Śuka, after declaring that the Almighty evolved the material faculties of living beings for attaining the four aims of human life (*puruṣārtha*s), narrates an "ancient legend" which turns out to be a dialogue between sages containing a report about another discussion on the nature of ultimate reality (*para brahman*) that took place in another realm in another age.[8] The "story" is a long, convoluted discussion on the nature of the Absolute in relation to the manifest creation narrated by Sananda Kumāra, one of the four mind-born sons of Brahmā, the creator deity. Sananda speaks of the personified scriptures (*śruti*s) awakening the sleeping Supreme Person, who is lying, with all his entourage in yogic trance, as if asleep at the juncture between dissolution and a new creation. The Śrutis, like bards to a king in early morning, sing hymns describing the glories of the Lord. More often than not, these hymns repeat Upaniṣadic dictums about the world being a transformation (*vikāra*) of *Brahman* (i.e., clay remaining constant through its variant modifications such as pots and pitchers). The argument is made that, since all is in actuality *Brahman/Bhagavān,* all language is ultimately signifying the "Transcendental One." On the other hand, sages are said to concentrate their mind and speech on the Absolute (spoken to in the second person honorific, "You"), as opposed to the world of "modifications." It is declared that the "spiritually wise" immerse themselves in the "ambrosial ocean of story" to wash off the dirt of the world and rid themselves of sins.[9] Such people, it is stated, free themselves from the effects of time and "do not fall again into the jaws of death."[10] In this way, the Purāṇa seeks to chart a course between non-duality and apparent duality, what D. P. Sheridan has called the "Advaitic Theism" of the Bhāgavata-Purāṇa.[11] Bhagavān, the Supreme Person, is said to exist within the entire creation, to be in fact the entire creation, and to yet be untouched by it.

In a trope that the Purāṇa repeats continuously, those who are immersed in the "ocean of ambrosial stories" have renounced home and family and even the desire for liberation. The enjoyment of household life is said to rob one of virtue, for the core of the "problem" is spoken of as the illusory identification with "the physical body that wanders in *saṁsāra*." The Bhāgavata, however, concedes another possibility. Those whose minds become attached to the supreme reality, by one method or another, see the entire universe as Truth, a projection of the Supreme Being, just as a person seeking gold would not discard gold ornaments, the knowers of the *self* see the universe as their very self and are then able to "plant their foot on the head of death."[12]

True knowledge, in this regard then, is envisioned as immortality.[13] What appears to be death-ridden is but an appearance, although such "appearances" may indeed be daunting. And therefore, those who try to overcome the world by their own means are compared to merchants embarking on a voyage without securing the services of a helmsman. The "helmsman," more often than not, will be construed as the text itself. Thus, the Bhāgavata sees itself as an entity existing over and above the "difference" of the conventionally signified world, the "place of exile" in which names and forms (*nāma-rūpa*) do not directly correspond to any ultimate ground of meaning. Such a world of illusion, or *māyā*, however, is also said in the Purāṇa to be nothing but a transformation of *Bhagavān* who, it turns out, is the ultimate signified of every signifier.

> *sa vācyavācakatayā bhagavān brahmarūpadhṛk*
> *nāmarūpakriyā dhatte sakarmākarmakaḥ paraḥ*
>
> Bhagavān assumes the form of Brahmā and takes
> on names, forms, and activities, himself being
> both the things designated and the words denoting
> them. He is both the doer of activities and the non-doer.
> He is beyond both
>
> (BhP. II.10.36)

To revisit to the aesthetics of the text for a moment, the Bhāgavata often discusses the inconceivable interfacing of duality and non-duality in the dramatic terms of a theater production, with Bhagavān as the actor on the stage of the world.

> Just as an ignorant person does not understand the performance of an actor, dull-witted beings cannot comprehend by mind or words the play of the Creator, who emanates his name and forms.[14] (BhP I.3.37)

In this way of "hide and seek" (a way that may be seen as a philosophical sleight of hand or as an extension of its own "reconstructive" project) the text seeks to circumvent its own body-mind, signifier-signified, life-death, dualism. It seeks to reintegrate itself into life, even everlasting life, and therefore relegates the isolated, dualistic notion of death and dying to the realm of ignorance.

For the Bhāgavata, the illusory vision of difference is the ground condition of the mundane world, and its chief characteristic is death, symptomized by the false identification with the temporal body. This initial place, often spoken of as *ahaṁkāra,* expands into other forms of identification: family, country, friends, and loved-ones, as the text tirelessly points out. The correlative of this condition is desire, which creates attachment, and initiates the chain of *saṁsāra*, or perhaps more accurately keeps the wheel spinning. Now, according to the "normative ideology" as discussed by Friedhelm Hardy, desire contains no inherent resolution and must be willfully, even violently, eradicated. Śiva, as the destroyer, burns Kāma-deva to ashes, but Kāma simply becomes *anaṅga*, bodiless and thus even more elusive. For desire cannot be willfully annihilated (since willfulness is already a form of desire). The Bhāgavata offers an alternative to this problematic through its *bhakti* polemic: aligning one's desire with loving service to the Supreme. This is generally considered to be a less restrictive and more humanly attainable path. After all, no matter how ingenious and comprehensive Vedāntic philosophy may have been, it could never capture the image and emotion-laden Indian cultural imagination, on its own. For desire creates gods, myths, realms, and narratives, and even renunciation. Thus, hymns to various gods had to be attributed to Śaṅkara.[15]

Narrative is a product of desire as well. Instead of seeking to eradicate narrative, however, even the narrative of the ego (in the forms of biography or history), the Bhāgavata offers its own *hari kathā* narratives as "antidotes" to the conditions of loss and death. By doing so, it follows in the poetic tradition of the *Rāmāyaṇa* and certain *kāvya*s (such as the *Meghadūta)*, positing narrative as the healing response to irrevocable loss. Here, we return to Parīkṣit sitting by the Ganges listening to the narrative of Śuka. Death is already the assured outcome: it has been related to the condition of the saṁsāric-world and to its language as well, but hearing and speaking will be the cure, and language, far from being negated, will be redirected through the project of specific Purāṇic narratives.[16]

Since this is a Purāṇa, the traditional Purāṇic categories and narrative forms must be observed. The Bhāgavata-Purāṇa, however, depicts itself as a culmination of all (as opposed to merely Epic) previous discourse (*nigama-kalpa-taror galitaṁ phalam* [I.1.3]), and its response to the issue of language, signification, and the absolute has to reckon with the entire spectrum of the tradition. Therefore it is intertextually drawing from Vedic, Epic, poetic, dramatic, and other materials, as it seeks to weave its own polemic out of the tradition.

The Vedic Tradition

It has been said that the Bhāgavata mimics the Veda, deliberately employing archaic forms to gain prestige and authority.[17] Indeed, the Bhāgavata's very first verse employs the verb *dhīmahi*, found most accessibly in the *gāyatrī mantra*, to place it in Vedic resonance. "*Dhīmahi*" (we meditate) is held to be the essence of Vedic knowledge and is pointed to by Śrīdhara (BhP. I.1.1) and other commentators as evidence of the same knowledge.[18] Over and above this, however, is the text's declaration of itself as the "ripened fruit" of the Veda, and it repeatedly makes the point that it supersedes both Vedic and Epic traditions. While this can easily be read as "the partisan tradition making a power play," the fact that the story is spoken of as the "fruit of a tree," suggests an organic development.[19] A narrative evolves through successive narrations, and in this sense is historical (*itihāsa-purāṇa*). The Bhāgavata narrative has indeed evolved organically, like the rings of a tree, representing the layerings of mythic variants. It does not declare itself to be the Veda, but the fruit of the Veda, the extremely palatable distillation of the past, bearing traces of its long developmental process while it matures into its own form.

The Bhāgavata is certainly not unique in its search for Vedic roots. Purāṇas, in general, build themselves upon Vedic foundations, and some (like the *Matsya* and *Vāyu*) declare themselves to be older than the Veda.[20] And there is, in fact, a good deal of scholarly speculation that the Purāṇic literatures may have been, at their oldest level, coeval with the Veda.[21] Whatever the extrinsic case may be, the Purāṇas prefer to see themselves as "Vedic" in many respects, and the Bhāgavata-Purāṇa extends this effort: linguistically, it employs Vedic verbal forms and meters; semantically, it establishes itself through the lineage of Vyāsa, the "compiler" of the Vedas; and polemically it invokes the ever-sermonizing character of Nārada, who is associated with the Vedic Goddess of Speech (Vāc) as Vyāsa's preceptor. While it is not unusual for a Purāṇa to exalt itself as such, what is especially noteworthy here is the confluence of traditions that emerges through the Purāṇa. Along with the self-conscious Vedic echoes and the ever-present theme of *bhakti* is a third major element, an aesthetic one.

The *Ālaṁkārika* Tradition

While the Bhāgavata is often characterized as a "literary Purāṇa,"[22] it may be more accurate to speak of it as that Purāṇa which proposes to incorporate an "aesthetic solution" into its repertoire of truth claims, actually raising (or lowering, depending upon one's perspective) aesthetics to a *yoga* or a spiritual discipline. It does this by combining the absolute principle, Viṣṇu-Bhagavān-Kṛṣṇa, with an aesthetic vision that is based on, but ultimately diverts from, the classical *rasa*-aesthetic of the *Nāṭyaśāstra*. Viṣṇu is realized, not through arduous yoga exercises, through the practice of philosophical inquiry, or as the final destination of a long line of questing signifiers, but through the constant process of narration. The problematic of irrevocable loss, which has provoked Indian thinking from Vedic sacrificial dismemberments to succinct Buddhist formulations, is not resolved into any source. Instead, it is further intensified through the narrative process of *hari kathā*, which the Bhāgavata claims supersedes all previous modes of discourse.

Just what is this aesthetic vision? When we look at Sanskrit aesthetics we find a deeply developed and categorized map of the human emotional terrain which is said to be stimulated by the work of art, literary or otherwise. The purpose of art is not expressive (to give vent to emotions) as much as it is contemplative, to experience the refined "universal" of emotion known as *rasa*. Bharata's celebrated dictum, *vibhāvānubhāva-vyabhicāri-saṁyogād-rasaniṣpattiḥ,* is a culinary one of mixing and blending: *rasa* emerges from the combining of environmental ambience (*vibhāva*), mental impressions (*anubhāva*) and accessory emotions (*vyabhicārin*).[23] *Rasa*, the stated goal of the work of art, is more than sentiment; it is the distillation of sentiment and a deepening of the level at which it is experienced or "tasted."[24] This was expressed by the word *alaukika* or "non-worldly," often used in the critical literature to describe the aesthetic experience. Abhinavagupta, the celebrated tenth-century Kashmiri aesthetician, emphasized the difference between *rasa* and quotidian emotions. *Rasa* is aroused in artistic environments as opposed to daily situations, and it approaches the yogic ideal of "pure contemplation."[25]

The Aesthetic classifications of the Sanskrit critical tradition are deeply psychological. They are said to describe dispositions of the psyche or *(bhāva*s) which are inherent in the mind as deep memories (*vāsanās*, also called "*saṁskāras*") and are developed into specific aesthetic moods.[26] *Vāsanās* are said to be impressions of anything remaining unconsciously in the mind, but the verbal root *vas* denotes "be fragrant" as well as "abide." The idea that art or literature can revive a latent impression in the mind sounds quite Platonic, indeed in Kālidāsa's famed verse on the subject in the drama, *Śakuntā,* the work of art ignites deeper memories.

> Seeing rare beauty, hearing lovely sounds,
> even a happy man becomes strangely uneasy . . .
> Perhaps he remembers, without knowing why,
> loves from another life buried deep in his being.[27]

Indian aesthetic speculations, however, can move into other dimensions of recollection. They may insist that certain experiential realities, existing above and beyond the purview of the individual personality, can be tasted and smelled as well as recalled. Impressions can be strongly olfactory. One Buddhist text, in fact, describes a realm where the holy teachings (*dharma*) are transmitted through fragrance alone.[28] When I speak of an "aesthetic vision" therefore, I am not simply referring to the Bhāgavata's appropriation of complex lyrical meters and *ālaṁkārika* ideals in order to ground itself in brahmanical legitimacy and satisfy the Sanskrit *literati* as Hardy has suggested.[29] I am envisioning the aesthetic as the primacy of the imaginative; and as psychological, in the sense that the psyche itself may be aesthetic, given to inherently expressing itself in dramatic and poetic form.[30] In other words, rather than the measured appropriation of form employed for a particular emotional effect, form itself becomes content, and style becomes paramount. Quality, timbre, and emotional resonance reveal layers of meaning that lie below the level of denotative content. *Stotra* (the genre of praise) is employed, but the text is not *stotra*, philosophy is employed, but the text cannot be placed in the philosophical camp. Epic narrative is followed, but the text does not offer a linear storyline of successive events. In the Sanskrit Aesthetic tradition this sensibility was called "*dhvani,*" usually translated as "suggestion" but having connotations of resonance and undertone as well (since the verbal root *dhvan* is literally to roar or reverberate). This sensibility mirrors the imaginative associative functions of thought. Rather than proceeding in direct, literal fashion, the suggestive, metaphorical sense moves into depth, amplified feeling, and emotive cognition.

The Bhāgavata-Purāṇa's Aesthetic dimension is revealed in its focus on emotive versus cognitive discourse. It employs cognitive discourse, but subordinates it to its immense narrative project. In displaying an acute awareness of its own use of language, employing diverse poetic meters and figurative forms (*alaṁkāras*), and making use of the conventions of classical Sanskrit poetics, it incarnates feeling through its effects. Moreover, without adhering to the strict poetic conventions, it appropriates *rasa-śāstra*, building upon the idea that the erotic sentiment (*śṛṅgāra-rasa*) is the ultimate *rasa* and that love overcomes death.

The Bhāgavata conspicuously uses the words *rasa*, *rasika*, and other classical poetic terms. As in *nāṭya*, its *rasa* is not evoked solely through the suggestive powers of language but emerges through a larger process that, in the Bhāgavata's case, involves a narrative based around immanent death, a central scenario of love, loss, and longing, and a constant focus on the source of all *rasa*, Śrī Kṛṣṇa, the personification of absolute love, in one form or another.

In this final respect the Bhāgavata-Purāṇa, and its commentarial tradition, seek to fully insert aesthetic experience into the realm of *brahmāsvāda* (the taste of the Absolute) and to jump off from the point where Abhinavagupta would be obliged to halt. Abhinavagupta, Bhoja, and other Sanskrit poeticians declared that *rasa* was akin to *brahmāsvāda*, that is, that aesthetic experience is close to the taste of Absolute Being, *Brahman*. Abhinavagupta declares the experiences to be "akin" but not "identical," but the Bhāgavata tradition takes this a step further.[31] Commentators on the Purāṇa note the constant use of *rasa* and *rasika* in the context of Absolute Love, *bhakti*, and declare that *rasa* finds its fulfillment in the Absolute as the source of all feeling. The commentaries frequently cite a verse from the *Taittirīya Upaniṣad*, "He is *rasa*" (*raso vai saḥ*) to accentuate this point and place it under a Vedic umbrella.[32] All *rasa* is envisioned in this sense as an aspect of *bhakti-rasa* and all levels of sentiment can be accepted in this regard.[33]

The transformation of an aesthetic doctrine into a religious one is central to the Bhāgavata's theological "solution." The Purāṇa does not simply offer an unusual ontological principle, but actually presents an aesthetic parade or "*līlā*," the centered-decentered inconceivable play of the Absolute, that is realized through *tasting* the narrative. It is this ever-continuous *līlā* which rises through the traditional Purāṇic categories of unfolding creations and royal genealogies, through the lives of "paradigmatic devotees," and through "death-narratives" and poetic figuration.[34]

On one hand then, the Bhāgavata can be seen as a hybrid collage, tailored for popular religious consumption, as opposed to *kāvya* whose virtuosity resonates with court culture, or "purer" forms of devotional poetry.[35] If we develop the depth-psychological or mytho-poetic metaphor, however, which privileges imaginative over didactic, informative, or even formal-poetic discourse, we may see how central this mosaic-like sensibility is. The fact that the Bhāgavata assimilates philosophy and aesthetic principles into its narrative may reflect a psychological process of integration as much as it may reflect a conscious ecumenical effort to combine variant elements. The need to assimilate previous forms before venturing into new territory may be much like the projects of Pablo Picasso or James Joyce in the Western modernist traditions of art and literature. While one can "deconstruct" the Purāṇa through layers of its historicity (as Hardy has done) or discourse, the Bhāgavata constructs meaning by interweaving style, content, and traditions, and its effort to align aesthetic and religious sensibility will later resonate throughout the *bhakti* tradition.

By combining material of probable folk origin with classical lyric figures and meters, and then infusing them both with religious ideology, the Bhāgavata seeks to invest its own narratives with super-referential ability, declaring that having its audience will free one from the vices of the age of Kali.[36] The contention is that, as with Vedic *mantras*, hearing these tales alone can lead one beyond the realms of duality and death.[37] This is because *hari kathā* is thought of as different from conventional language and literature, since *hari/bhagavān* is "in the heart of all." When one hears the narrative in a devotional mood, akin to aesthetic mood of the *sahṛdaya* or "sensitive-hearted" receptor, the deep *self* or *ātman* is said to be pleased.[38] Thus, narratives about Kṛṣṇa are believed to participate in absolute as opposed to relative signification.

This participation is achieved through the aesthetic process of "tasting" the ecstatic nature of the absolute narrative. As in classical aesthetics, the revelatory importance of indirect language (*vakrokti* or *vyañjanā*) is noted, as is the elevation of figurative language and intertextual resonance over any teleological plot outcome. This whole complex is clearly visible in the third verse of the Purāṇa where the text makes its most direct claim to being a uniquely powerful *rasa-śāstra* wrapped in a Vedic mantle.

> *nigama-kalpa-taror galitaṁ phalaṁ*
> *śuka-mukhād amṛta-drava-saṁyutam*
> *pibata bhāgavataṁ rasam ālayaṁ*
> *muhur aho rasikā bhuvi bhāvukāḥ*
>
> Oh you of refined poetic understanding
> keep drinking this *Bhāgavata*, this *rasa*
> here on earth and hereafter. It is the fully
> ripened fruit from the heavenly wish-yielding
> tree of Vedic wisdom passed from the mouth of
> Śuka filled with pure, liquid nectar.
>
> (BhP. I.1.3)

Here, the Bhāgavata speaks of itself as the fully ripened fruit from the *nigama*: literally "root," in Purāṇic usage, that which all enters into, a synonym for the Vedas or their auxiliary works.[39] Aside from claiming its own supremacy, however, this verse initiates the reader/hearer into the aesthetic vocabulary and sensibility of the text. It is not concerned with specific aesthetic categories, for the distinctions between *rasa* and *bhāva* are blurred (*rasika*s are equated with *bhāvuka*s). The particulars do not matter as much as the taste itself in this verse where meaning is equated with drinking (*pibat*).

One is commanded to drink the Bhāgavata's *rasa*, flowing from the ripe fruit of the Veda, on this earth (*bhuvi*) and beyond (*ālayam* as "final abode" or "liberation," following Śrīdhara—*ālayaṁ layaṁ mokṣaḥ*), for the Bhāgavata as a text is a *rasa*-filled abode. The concept of *rasa* is expanded beyond its technical term to become the feeling of ecstatic bliss on the platform of eternity. The fluidity of the *rasa* is emphasized here, along with its immortality (*amṛta-drava*).

Amṛta and *drava* are both, in their own ways, synonyms for *rasa*: *amṛta* as immortal nectar and ambrosia, and *drava*, as liquid with connotations of distilled liquid and essence. The word *drava* has also been used in instances of deep loss and separation to refer to the melting of the heart, and is said by Abhinavagupta to be a principal quality of the erotic (*śṛṅgāra)*, compassionate (*karuṇa)*, and anguished (*vipralambha)* moods.[40] So, with allusions to Veda and classical poetics, the Bhāgavata emphasizes its "aesthetic liquidity" declaring itself to be the *galitam-phalam*, the ripened or fallen fruit of the Veda. One is struck by the use of *galita* here because it is not the usual word for ripe. It has meanings of falling, liquidity, and the extreme sensitivity of full ripeness. Śrīdhara and other commentators, therefore, see in *galitam* indications of the *paramparā,* the carefully handed down ripe fruit from the source through traditional transmission.[41] Through its *galitam* or descent in this way, the fruit literally matures. This maturation is corroborated by the pun on the word *Śuka*, which means both "parrot" and is the name of the son of Vyāsa who narrates the Purāṇa to Parīkṣit. The parrot, it is said, is only attracted to the best fruits, and makes them sweeter through his pecking at them.

The fruit is not just ripe, commentators claim that it is at its apex of ripeness, almost on the verge of decay and therefore in need of the expert handling of the *rasika. Rasika* is the Aesthetic tradition's term for the "sensitive hearted" connoisseur of *rasa*, and is here transformed into an epithet for the ecstatic devotee.[42] Thus, we are dealing with a "well-ripened text," which speaks through the language of poetics. The extended gustatory metaphor suggests that one does "understand" such narrative through "tasting." Moreover, the reception of the text is related to drinking which is even beyond tasting. One can drink this *rasa* because it is liquid. Commentators interpret this as indicating its distilled essence, fruit without pit or rind, and therefore supremely pleasurable.[43] While apparently simple, this idea of pleasure should be emphasized. Understanding involves ecstatic pleasure and deepened feeling. It is this level of narrative which Parīkṣit participates in. He is not merely "hearing" stories at the time of death, he is tasting them, drinking them, and they have a marked visceral effect.

The "aesthetics of tasting" will continue throughout the Purāṇa. The sages at Naimiṣāraṇya, the mythical forest where the Epic recitation also takes place, implore Sūta to recite the *līlā*s of the Supreme, claiming never to be satiated while hearing the glories of *uttama-śloka*, the Lord as one who is the "Supreme Verse" or "Who is praised by the best of verses," which, according to the knowers of *rasa*, increase in sweetness with every word.[44] In this early verse, the Purāṇa sets its own categories of meaning, categories that combine the religious and the aesthetic. While the weight of tradition is more than acknowledged, and other sources are thoroughly suppressed (South Indian folk tales, for example, as Hardy convincingly demonstrates), the Purāṇa will not hesitate to forge its own form. "*Bhakti*," for example, cannot be reduced here to an insular "path" (*mārga*). It is, instead, produced by a complex of phenomena including the presence of the hallowed Veda, elaborations on the power of poetic language, the centrality of loss—whether through literal dying or some form of separation—and the devotional sensibility as the thread which ties the others together. The end product mirrors the mytho-poetic process itself. It is a conglomerate of times, places, ideas, and styles, a *maṇḍala* that weaves disparate elements into a particular formal cohesion, a meditation on living and dying that moves through the imagery of a cultural cosmology. Like a ripened fruit from the tree of origins, it asks to be tasted as well as cognitively understood.

3

NARRATIVES OF ABSENCE

The Bhāgavata-Purāṇa, like the Mahābhārata, features narratives followed by their own metanarratives, forming successive layers constellated around a major theme. Within these laminated-like structures one finds the unifying motif of *bhakti* appearing through various characters in modes of both union and separation. This particular devotional element distinguishes the Purāṇa from its precursor, the great Epic, in which *dharma*, the "over-arching" sacred law, predominates thematically, (although Bhāgavata themes are present and are more than hinted at in the Epic).[1] Both texts, interestingly enough, bring one face-to-face with a holocaust situation. The Mahābhārata actually chronicles the decimation of a race while the Bhāgavata extends the chronicle as it narrows the focus to the annihilation of an individual representative of that race (Parīkṣit).

The Bhāgavata-Purāṇa preserves much of the Epic's narrative form. Like the Mahābhārata, it is said to be the creation of Kṛṣṇa Dvaipāyana Vyāsa, although it does not share the Epic's narrators. The principal narrators and interlocutors in the Bhāgavata are Vyāsa's son, Śuka, and Arjuna's grandson, Parīkṣit. In this way, as J. L. Mehta noted, the Purāṇa literally presents itself as an offspring of the Epic and as a culmination of the creative process of Vyāsa.[2] Moreover, by casting its narrative in the mode of genealogical succession, the Bhāgavata awards itself legitimacy. However, in seeing itself as an improvement on "the ripened fruit of the Vedic tree," the Purāṇa is not merely echoing the past in order to derive its authority. On the contrary, it reveals its own polemical purpose explicitly: that if *dharma* does not lead to *rati* (pleasure) in *hari kathā* (discourse on God), it is mere toil.[3]

Along with its concentration on Kṛṣṇa and on the profound pleasure of *bhakti*, the Bhāgavata, more than the Epic, looks toward the future.

With its strong awareness of the rupture caused by the Bhārata war, of the disappearance of the *avatāra* and his dynasty, and of the end of the age that these events portend, the Bhāgavata offers itself as a means to negotiate a new and more difficult era. In this way, too, the narrative grapples with death, not only an individual's death, but the death of an epoch

After the opening "*gāyatrī*" verse followed by two other *stotra* verses, the text begins, in conventional Epic/Purāṇic fashion, by speaking of (just who actually narrates is not exactly clear) a gathering of *ṛṣi*s at Naimiṣa forest who question Sūta, their preceptor, through the voice of Śaunaka, the leader of the assembled sages.[4] The position of the *sūta* in the Bhāgavata is a bit ambiguous. He is certainly not an ordinary bard, being *anagha*, "faultless" or "sinless." While he does not recite directly from the Veda, (as a *sūta* should not) he has learned all that Bādarāyaṇa (Vyāsa) knows, Vyāsa being *veda-vidāṁ śreṣṭhaḥ*, "the best among those who know the Veda."[5] Therefore, he can expound upon the *kathā* of Śūka's. This is yet another way in which the Purāṇic narration continues to associate itself with the Veda.

I mention the *sūta* here not only because of his pivotal position in the text's narrative scheme, but also because his position is an acknowledgement by the text of the importance of its oral transmission. As Mehta points out in reference to the Epic, the narratives are always "told to someone by someone face-to-face, somewhere, at some point of time,"[6] and to this day, *sūta*s (now either *bhaṭṭas* or *brāhmaṇas*) continue to recount "Purāṇa" in formal as well as improvisational settings throughout India.[7]

The *ṛṣi*s gathered in the forest then ask Sūta to speak on the ultimate good of humankind.[8] Instead of a direct reply from the bard, however, Vyāsa, the reputed "author" of the Purāṇa, narrates Sūta's reply, embedding Sūta's narrative within his own.

Sūta discourses on ultimate good (*śreyas*), on devotion to Bhagavān, and on the benefits of hearing about Bhagavān. The very first verse he speaks, however, highlights the concurrent themes of glorification and absence. In this verse, which has been the object of much commentarial attention, he praises the *muni* (Śuka) and mentions the loss that Śuka's father, Vyāsa, feels after his son leaves home:

yaṁ pravrajantam anupetam apeta-kṛtyaṁ
dvaipāyano viraha-kātara ājuhāva
putreti tan-mayatayā taravo 'bhinedus
taṁ sarva-bhūta-hṛdayaṁ munim ānato 'smi

I offer respects to that silent sage whose
heart is that of all beings. He was not yet
endowed with a sacred thread when he set out
as a recluse. Dvaipāyana [his father], grieving

> in separation, cried out, "O son," to which
> only the trees, with which he had merged,
> responded.
>
> (BhP. I.2.2)

Sūta begins his narrative by acknowledging a genealogical lineage of transmission, and then indicates the rupturing factor of loss which is inherent in this process. In this instance, it is Śuka, the detached son of Vyāsa, who renounces the world of his father (*pravrajantam*) and who is glorified for his action.[9] Still, the trees seem to echo a sentiment that will pervade the rest of the text. Vyāsa, the father, cries after his son who merges into the trees. The son does not respond, but the trees do. Their actual response, however, is not indicated. Is it their rustling upon absorbing Śuka, their echoing back of the father's voice, or their vast silence? What response, finally, can be given in face of inevitable loss? Answering this question is one task that the Bhāgavata-Purāṇa takes upon itself, a task that has quite a different focus from a text like the Garuḍa Purāṇa, which largely concentrates on rites to avoid hellish after death conditions and to assume improved rebirths. The Bhāgavata may occasionally pay lip service to the social concerns that occupy a number of Hindu ritual works and practices having to do with death and dying, but its overwhelming polemic is one of renunciation. It is as if this is the only card in the deck that can match the absoluteness of death itself. The text's response to loss is thus illustrated through this portrait of the disappearance of Śuka into the forest, and its argument for a deeper unity outside the realm of mortal social relations is given through Śuka's being characterized as "the *muni* who is one with the heart of all beings."[10]

On the one hand, there is *viraha*, separation from (and renunciation of) the family and in particular, the father and all that the figure of the father symbolizes. On the other hand, there is a suggestion of total union/identification (*tanmayatā*) with everything and everyone. This oxymoronic juxtaposition, part of a long-standing classical tradition in which mystical union breaks personal ties, will be repeated in different ways throughout the Purāṇa, offering a paradox of detachment and union. Such a paradox demands investigation, and the Bhāgavata will push this investigation to its limits when the closest associates of Kṛṣṇa leave their mortal frames in a swoon of separation and unite with him on another level. Since the Purāṇa presents its "investigations" as narratives (as opposed to philosophical, ethical, or logical forms of discourse), the very multiplicity of narrators and narratives serves the purpose of amplifying this central paradox by highlighting, contrasting, and weaving thematic resonances through variant versions of similar and dissimilar stories.[11]

Sūta explains that he was present on the bank of the Ganges when the Bhāgavata was narrated to Parīkṣit, and will try to elucidate it accordingly. Vyāsa again interjects his voice to introduce the chief disciple of Sūta. The narrative then becomes a dialogue between the teacher, Sūta, and the student, Śaunaka. The *guru-śiṣya* dialogue will be the principal model for all following narratives. Such narratives are rarely linear, but instead they work concurrently with other narratives and ongoing dialogues. When discussing the authorship of the Purāṇa, for instance, Sūta will relate an interlocution between another teacher-student pair, Nārada and Vyāsa.

The narratives in the first book, however, serve more as a frame, setting the stage for the principal teacher-student narrative-dialogue between Śuka and Parīkṣit. The bulk of the Purāṇic material consists of Parīkṣit's questions to Śūka, whose responses are interspersed with didactic tales, genealogical legends, and other assorted material. In continually shifting back to the forest dialogue of Sūta and Śaunaka, the narrative at times serves as a frame for another set of *guru-śiṣya* narrative dialogues, including those in the third book between Vidura and Maitreya. As the text progresses, like an ancient version of a serialized variety show, different illustrious (guest-star) narrators are brought in. These narrators include sages like Nārada and Dakṣa, gods like Yama, Brahmā, and Śiva, great demons who reveal their former divine embodiments, like Vṛtra and Hiraṇyakaśipu, and ultimately Viṣṇu himself, who sits at the top of this Purāṇic hierarchy.

Now there may be many good reasons for these various narrators in terms of historical layerings of the text and the Purāṇic oral tradition, but the narrative structure also says much about the text's view of its own creation and of authorship in general. Let me reiterate here that this has nothing to do with issues of extrinsic authorship. Rather, as one sees varying and seemingly paradoxical myths of the work's own origin, one is led to wonder about an entirely different conception of authorship, of origin, and of creativity.

The first statement on "authorship" appears in the second verse of the text, where it is stated, *śrīmadbhāgavate mahāmunikṛte*, "(in) this beautiful Bhāgavata created by the *mahāmuni*, the great sage." Just who is this sage? Neither Vyāsa nor any other name is explicitly mentioned, and even the commentators are divided on the subject. Vīrarāghava and many others assume that Vyāsa is the "great sage." Śrīdhara and Jīva Gosvāmī, however, state that the *mahā-muni* is none other than Nārāyaṇa, Viṣṇu himself. Both views can be supported by the text whose second "myth of authorship" appears in the third *skandha*. There, the Bhāgavata is said to have descended from Saṇkarṣaṇa to Sanat-Kumāra:

> Wanting to know the truth about the
> Highest, the *muni*s, with (Sanat) Kumāra
> as their chief, questioned the eternal god Saṅkarṣaṇa,
> the original Lord seated at
> the base of the world.[12]
>
> (BhP. III.8.2)

The complete lineage given in this section of the text is Saṅkarṣaṇa to Sanatkumāra to Sānkhyāyana to Pulastya to Parāśara to Maitreya to Vidura.

In another place in the text, following the *Catuḥ-ślokī* Bhāgavata—four verses uttered by Viṣṇu to Brahmā in the second *skandha* (II.9.32–35) which are considered to be the germ of the entire work—Viṣṇu is said to be the author and origin of the Bhāgavata's lineage:

> *tasmā idaṁ bhāgavataṁ purāṇaṁ daśa-lakṣanam*
> *proktaṁ bhagavatā prāha prītaḥ putrāya bhūta-kṛt*
>
> Thus, this Bhāgavata-Purāṇa of ten characteristics
> spoken by the Lord, was joyfully told by the creator
> of beings, Brahmā, to his son.
>
> (BhP. II.9.44)

Notice the numerous puns on "*bhagavat/bhagavān*" in this verse. The name of the text itself is a secondary derivative of *bhagavat*, and let us not forget that Vyāsa himself is Kṛṣṇa-Dvaipāyana. Clearly, the Bhāgavata's conception of authorship is not one of personal invention but one of retelling what has been received.[13] If we extend the exploration of narrative as *mythos* (rather than narrative as representation), we see a narrative world that recollects and organizes itself thematically as well as linearly. On the one hand, a story can be told about something that happened ten years ago or over ten thousand years ago, and there will be no appreciable difference in tone. On the other hand, there is a very particular type of "linear logic" to the narrative, the logic of transmission which must be adhered to.

The variant versions of textual lineage in the Bhāgavata underscore the importance of the myths of transmission. No matter what the particulars, a story is sanctioned through its lineage, which must therefore be included in the narrative. It would thus seem that lineage functions as myth, as opposed to history. But it is a myth that is binding, or binding up to a point. One only has to think of the many conundrums surrounding Epic genealogies to wonder to what degree transmission itself becomes the all-important issue of narrative. The transmission of lineage, in its deepest sense, brings together issues of sexuality, power, and continuity, for all are necessary to create a lineage. Moreover, textual transmission mirrors diachronic, linguistic development as the evolution of a discourse through time. In this sense, transmission may even be viewed as "a myth of historicity."

Although a requisite order of continuity is followed in the Bhāgavata—father to son, teacher to pupil, *avatāra* to *avatāra*, and so on—there is more than one such order. The "hoary past" revealed in the Purāṇic lore becomes multiplied through various legitimate versions, none of which need be seen as incongruous, since there is no "authorial" problem in the numerous switchings from one set of dialogues to another. Tradition itself, in a sense, becomes the narrator, and the tradition, as the *Catuḥ-ślokī* Bhāgavata makes clear, proceeds from Viṣṇu, as does everything else (I.12.47). Now, a critical reader could make the argument that Viṣṇu, in fact, proceeds from the tradition (so much for a *myth* of origin). If one does not want to take that step, however, one can at least ask, "Which Viṣṇu? Which Bhagavān?" After all, the three different tales of authorship mentioned previously discuss three separate forms of Viṣṇu—Saṅkarṣaṇa, Viṣṇu, and the *mahāmuni* (this last one being Viṣṇu by insinuation since Vyāsa is an *avatāra* of Viṣṇu). The Bhāgavata thus speaks of divine authorship as well as human authorship in multiple terms.

The text, then, is not seen as revealing the mind or message of a particular individual, human or divine. There is no singular divinity who dictates the Purāṇa, as the Archangel Gabriel dictated the Qur'an to Mohammed. There is no master narrative about a particular people at a given time in history, and there are no universal laws that apply to everyone at every time. One can even go so far as to say that, according to the epistemological tradition of the Bhāgavata, the human authorship of anything is an impossibility. Vyāsa (literally, the compiler) creates under the command of his preceptor, and ultimately on the power of his being another manifestation of Viṣṇu (literally, the all-pervading one).[14] This is very much in line with the idea of human psychology interfacing with cosmology, as human authorship cannot be separated from tradition, which sees itself as emanating from a divine origin. It is just this issue, of course, which the post-Enlightenment (Buddhist as well as post-structuralist) era brings into question. The "phallacy" of an authorial-authoritative tradition is challenged; its claims are deconstructed and shown to be a power play of various priestly classes. The Bhāgavata certainly belongs to the "old school," but it offers its own curious wrinkle on transcendental authorship and origins. Instead of the text growing out of a premeditated, authorial presence, it emerges out of absence. Here one finds a very particular situation, as the "sensibility of loss" is alluded to by Sūta when he explains the generation of the text itself:

kṛṣṇe svadhāmopagate dharma-jñānādibhiḥ saha
kalau naṣṭa-dṛśām eṣa purāṇārko'dhunoditaḥ

Now that Kṛṣṇa has left for his own abode
along with *dharma*, *jñāna*, etc., this *Purāṇa-Sun*
has risen for those who have been blinded by
this age of *Kali*.

(BhP. I.3.43)

The fallen age of Kali is said to begin with the disappearance (death) of Kṛṣṇa from the Earth, bringing on all misfortune. The text, then, appears in the wake of this loss. In a sense, the passing of an era and the absence that ensues create the text, since the Purāṇa looks forward to the troubled age to come. Vyāsa himself is led to write the Bhāgavata out of a sense of despondency that he feels after compiling the Vedic and Epic literatures (I.4.25–28). This sense of loss manifests itself subtly, as a feeling of incompleteness. Vyāsa is described as *nātiprasīdad-dhṛdayaḥ*, "not satisfied at heart" (BhP. I.4.27), and it is this yearning intuition that leads to resultant action. Vyāsa's situation is not caused by the loss of a son or lover, but rather by the absence of "the Beloved," Bhagavān himself, as Nārada, his preceptor, will make clear to him.

Nārada appears as "if smiling" (BhP. I.5.1), a smile that occurs in a somewhat similar situation in the Bhagavadgītā.[15] Vyāsa asks Nārada to illumine the cause of his despondency, and Nārada explains that, although he has delineated spiritual knowledge for the welfare of living beings, he has not sufficiently glorified Bhagavān Vāsudeva. Philosophical works *(darśanas)*, which do not satisfy Him, Nārada says, are inferior. Nārada's catechism, while seemingly a standard *bhakti* polemic, carries the kernel of the Bhāgavata's aesthetic philosophy that will be repeated throughout the text. Nārada declares:

na yad vacaś citra-padaṁ harer yaśo
jagat-pavitraṁ pragṛṇīta karhicit
tad vāyasaṁ tīrtham uśanti mānasā
na yatra haṁsā niramanty uśik-kṣayāḥ

That speech, no matter how charming,
that never describes the glory of Hari,
which can purify the world, is thought
by the wise to be a pilgrimage site
for crows. The swan-like beings who
abide in absolute beauty take no pleasure
there.

(BhP. I.5.10)

Nārada goes on to say that, even if imperfectly composed, that creation of speech (*vāg-visarga*) which is marked by the glory of the unlimited Lord wipes out people's sins and is heard, sung, and repeated by the pious. The resonance of these verses ripples through philosophy and aesthetics as well as theology. *Citra-padaṁ* is a rhetorical term, *citra* being one of the three main divisions of *kāvya,* indicating charm. "*Citra-kāvya*" was decried by many critics as being preoccupied with its own form and rhetorical wit, as opposed to serving *rasa*, the sole purpose of the poetic vehicle.[16] Here, then, we may see an indication that, in the Bhāgavata, Hari will replace *citra* with *rasa* as the central principle of poetic utterance—since *citra,* or charming speech, without Bhagavān/Hari is likened to speech without *rasa*.

The *vāyasa-haṁsa* crow-swan analogy is also significant. It puts forward an opposition between the vulgar and the purified, between the volant and the grounded, one that points to the superior nature of the Bhāgavata's *rasa*. The idea of a transcendental abode, in which "the wise ones" (*mānasāḥ*) live just as the swans in lake *mānasa*, is incorporated within the verse to emphasize this. Here, levels of enjoyment through eating and abiding are suggested by the comparison of the crow, who eats refuse, with the discriminating *haṁsa,* or swan, who can separate milk from water. Once again, the tasting metaphor is central, as the Bhāgavata likens itself to ultimate, refined essence, the fullest possible evolution of *rasa*.

Can the beautiful and the alluringly sensual be rejected by this text in the name of the source of all that is? The tension between *kāma* (pleasure) and *dharma* (duty) thus reappears. In its characteristic way, however, the Bhāgavata rejects neither the ascetic, nor indulgent polarity. It seeks to incorporate them in the same way that it seeks to incorporate conventional language, as well as so-called regional sensibilities, for that matter. One must remember its semiotic: Bhagavān is the transcendental signifier and the true signified of any and every signifier. Bhagavān, Nārada will point out, is himself the entire universe (*idaṁ hi viśvaṁ bhagavān*), but is apparently different (*ivetaraḥ*). "From Him only," Nārada goes on, "has this world emanated; in Him it rests, and is annihilated" (BhP. I.5.20). The same declaration will be made by Nārāyaṇa in the *Catuḥ-ślokī*. Therefore, Nārada can confidently tell Vyāsa that he should always remember, with an entranced mind, the various acts of Urukrama ("Viṣṇu, who strides-widely") for freedom from bondage, and that not to do so would lead to a mind agitated by names and forms like a boat swept away by the wind that will never achieve stability.[17]

Nārada's admonition to Vyāsa sounds a bit like Vālmīki's curse of the hunter at the opening of the *Rāmāyaṇa* (later said to be the first poetic verse in the tradition). In Vālmīki's verse, the hunter, having unwittingly killed one of a pair of cranes while they were mating, is cursed never to find a place to rest (*mā niṣāda pratiṣṭham*). In the Bhāgavata, however, the cardinal sin is not murder (actively provoking loss), but rather the act of perceiving the world in a dualistic manner.[18] In a manner similar to the *Rāmāyaṇa* verse there is no rest. It is this restlessness and its subsequent yearning that is the hallmark of *viraha* (separation), which may be seen also as the ever-present discontinuity between the signifier and signified. Only in Bhagavān is completion ever realized, and therefore, speech must be repossessed by the *śaktimān*, Bhagavān himself.

Vyāsa is not the only one whose narrative arises from absence. Vidura, the mixed-caste brother of Dhṛtarāṣṭra and ally of the Pāṇḍavas, sadly leaves his household after being insulted by Duryodhana, now the leader of the Kurus (BhP. III.1.15,16). While on pilgrimage he learns of the death of all his relatives in the Epic battle at Kurukṣetra. In this state of loss, he meets Uddhava on the bank of the Yamunā river and questions him. Uddhava, however, is also in a deep mood of separation, since Kṛṣṇa has just left the world, and proceeds to narrate from this perspective. Narratives given by Bharata, Yama, Yayāti, Hiraṇyakaśipu, and many others either turn around issues of loss and separation or refer directly to them, and we shall look at them in the next chapter.

After urging Vyāsa to glorify the Lord, Nārada himself narrates his own story, in which his calling to be a renunciate emerges when the sudden death of his mother causes him to go into the forest and seek the Lord. The Lord appears before Nārada, but then disappears leaving Nārada to spend the rest of his life in the grip of longing.[19]

To recapitulate, the entire Purāṇa appears with the departure (death) of Kṛṣṇa. The narrative of Śuka responds to the coming death of Parīkṣit, and the resolution of the Purāṇa is the reconciliation of Parīkṣit with his own death. The narrative strategy of the Bhāgavata attempts to incorporate death and other modes of loss into its vision, with death being doubly problematic in this regard. On the one hand, it is the clearly visible end of embodied existence, and the Purāṇa never ceases harping on its irrevocable nature. On the other hand, the tradition that the Bhāgavata represents refuses to recognize death as a finality, since it sees the living being as transmigrating from body to body. Therefore, death and dying must participate in a larger cosmos, one that is beyond cognition, speech, and separation, while yet incorporating these elements. What, then, is the type of speech, the metaphor that can contain such a vision?

One such metaphor has to do with the drinking of *rasa* in the form of the Bhāgavata narratives, whose speech is akin to nectar. The Bhāgavata describes itself as *uttama-śloka-caritam* (I.3.40). *Uttama-śloka*, aside from its literal meaning of "illustrious verse," becomes an epithet for Bhagavān himself. The only language that can adequately describe him, after all, must be nondifferent from his absolute nature.[20] Uddhava is unable to speak because of separation from Kṛṣṇa (III.2.1–2), and Dhruva, upon meeting the Lord, is also unable to speak. Thus, both separation and meeting reflect the indescribable and unutterable. It is only when Viṣṇu touches Dhruva with his conch shell (IV.9.3–4) that the latter is blessed with divine speech, "*giraṁ daivīm*," and can communicate.

If he who is being described is, in fact, indescribable, one can understand why separation/loss/absence may function as one of the major modes of description: proximity to Bhagavān silences the faculty of speech! As Jīva Gosvāmī argues in his *Bhagavat-sandarbha*, however, separation necessarily includes the polarity of union. The two must exist in the same vision. Meeting and separation play off one another in a dialectic that attempts to resolve itself through a special sense of *rasa*. Thus, one finds two basic modes of discourse relating to the *uttama-śloka*: speech born of separation, and speech of glorification. This mirrors the ontological nature of Kṛṣṇa, who is, at once, everything and is yet invisible. This paradox, discussed by Nārada early in the work, and repeatedly explored by the text, generates meaning as a noncognitive, experiential phenomenon open to the *rasika-bhakta* who shares in both the experience of beatific presence and the pang of absence.

The Bhāgavata's resolution, then, places *śravaṇa*, "hearing," and *kīrtana*, "glorification," above both death and liberation. According to Nārada's remonstration to Vyāsa, such speech is, in fact, the only speech that has any real significance.[21] From the resonant octaves of Vāc, the Vedic goddess of Sacred Speech, the Bhāgavata moves through later Sanskrit aesthetics into *kṛṣṇa-kathā,* as absolute activity, developing further dimensions of the Upaniṣadic statement, *raso vai saḥ* (He is Rasa). This process will culminate in profound *viraha* songs of the cowherd women in the tenth *skandha* of the Purāṇa. As one reads through the entire text, however, one would do well to keep this deep, aesthetic sensibility in mind: a uniquely structured narrative meant to be heard and sung illumines both the essential incongruity of separation/union which haunts the Purāṇa, and the seemingly impossible task of seeing coherence in its many diversities.

4

THE DOMINION OF DEATH

The aesthetic aspects of the Bhāgavata-Purāṇa strongly resonate with Ānandavardhana's discussion of Vālmīki's "first poetic verse" in the *Rāmāyaṇa.* In both instances sorrow (*śoka*) is transformed into verse (*śloka*), and poetic utterance is motivated by loss. More often than not in the Purāṇa, such loss is irrevocable, even when literal death is not involved. Accounts where apparent loss leads to literal reunion, as in death and revival scenarios (the Lazarus phenomenon), are quite common in Epic and Purāṇic traditions and do occur a number of times in the Bhāgavata. At other times, situations of loss will precipitate the "higher vision," characterized as *alaukika* (other-worldly, i.e., deathless). The Bhāgavata is more intriguing than the Epic in the unconventionality of its hero and his loves and losses, but in this area too, even the childhood pranks of Kṛṣṇa will be framed and invariably touched by death. The Purāṇa begins and ends with death, constantly casting a shadow of separation and loss over its narrative form.

As mentioned, death, in the Purāṇa, does not walk alone, but operates in conjunction with its principal allies: time (*kāla*), destiny (*daiva*), and sexuality (*kāma*).[1] The important connection between images of death and sexuality reveal a perspective which is less a pitting of *eros* against *thanatos* than a progression of *eros* leading to *thanatos*, as well as to rebirth and bondage in the realms of desire. Indeed, there are principles opposed to desire (*kāma)* that operate in the text, manifesting themselves as the adherence to social standards of behavior (*dharma)*, as asceticism leading to liberation (*mukti*), and ultimately as *preman*, other-worldly love. Before we can take up these matters, however, the many aspects of death in this work need to be considered.

As we do so, let us keep in mind that Epic and Purāṇic narratives continue to inhabit the Hindu imagination in a deep and powerful way.

In his psychoanalytic exploration of contemporary Hindu social life, Sudhir Kakar emphasizes the psychological importance of the theme of fusion and separation, seeing its power in the "intimate relation to the human fear of death."[2] Thus, in going through the Bhāgavata-Purāṇa and its many-layered images of loss and dying, we may be unearthing a part of the foundation upon which contemporary Hindu feelings, perceptions, and behaviors are still based. Moreover, as stated before, I would not underestimate the power of the Purāṇa to speak beyond its borders of origin. One characteristic of Bhāgavatism, in general, has been its ability to change form and locale; it has shifted between south and north India, between *advaita* and *dvaita,* and between India, Europe, and America. Perhaps this is one of the major distinguishing features of the Purāṇa whose approach to loss, death, and dissolution from many angles, highlights the encounter of the individual person (embodied by Parīkṣit) with her/his apparent destiny of annihilation.

The awareness of imminent death, its shocking and powerful quality, and the denial of death as a sort of madness, are all very powerfully present in the Mahābhārata, as in the passage, discussed earlier, describing Yudhiṣṭhira's interview with Dharma. The Bhāgavata picks up this Epic thread through Śuka's opening monologue, in which he declares that Parīkṣit's question about death is glorious, and that householders who listen to thousands of subjects and somehow forget this most important one are "mad."[3] Śuka goes on to say the following:

> Madly enamored by one's body, wife,
> children, and others, though they are unreal
> soldiers of the self—even though one has seen their
> destruction—one still does not see.[4]
>
> (BhP. II.1.4)

As in the Epic, the denial or refusal of death becomes impossible, for it constantly intrudes into the lives of the Purāṇa's major characters. Such intrusions often carry an element of fear along with the disruption of quotidian life, contributing to the text's polemic of renunciation. The Bhāgavata's concerns, however, may be more far-reaching than simply to establish an argument for renouncing the world. The king (Parīkṣit) is about to die. As an archetypal embodiment of the center of the cosmos-kingdom (to follow Perry's work on sacral kingship), the king's situation is a deeply collective and mythologized one. And as a representative of the social body, his question becomes everyone's question. If, as John Weir Perry claims (and I obviously concur), the traditional royal office served to constellate a culture's identity, the imminent death of the king reflects the fantasy of either individual or collective dissolution as well.

And it is fantasy, the imaginative response to situations, that is primary here. Whether death and dying are unknown, undiscovered, or actually mapped out, the fantasy narrative that the prospect of dying generates seems nevertheless to preoccupy much religious, artistic, and personal-psychic activity. There may be quite a bit more at stake in the recitation and hearing of these stories than is assumed at a first reading. And indeed, the Bhāgavata is not as much "read" within its tradition as it is ritually heard and enacted over and over again.[5]

Unlike the Epics, in which the issue of "home" (Greek: *nostos*) and the founding of a kingdom are at issue, the Bhāgavata-Purāṇa opens to a situation in which the "kingdom has already been abandoned."[6] Kṛṣṇa, the acknowledged *avatāra* of the text, and his dynasty have left the Earth. From the beginning, then, the Bhāgavata looks beyond the social body and abandons any humanistic hope for completion in the physical world. By standing on the very ground of dissolution, the text shifts its focus from the worldly (*laukika*) to the "other-worldly" (*alaukika*) and seems more than willing to pay whatever price such a shift may entail.

Parīkṣit does not address Śuka in a subjective, personal manner, but instead employs the official and dignified terminology of *dharma*. He asks not, "What should I do?" but, "What should a dying man do?" The issue thus becomes one of collective import. The king does not stop here, however. He immediately asks a second question, "What should people hear, chant, remember, do or not do in general?"[7] This echoing repetition is significant. It is an implicit acknowledgement that the moment of death may be every moment for every being, and that this Bhāgavata-dharma ostensively meant for the moment of death, is perhaps meant for all time. This coincides with the semiotic of the Purāṇa, in which *hari kathā,* as absolute discourse, is not envisioned as being subject to the disintegrating effects of *saṁsāra*.

In the Bhāgavata, no one escapes the finality of Parīkṣit's question. Even the birth of Kṛṣṇa is surrounded by death, and Kṛṣṇa himself is fatally wounded by a hunter's arrow, ending the play of his appearance.[8] In the sixth book, reminiscent of the Gītā, the god Śiva speaks of death as one of life's unavoidable dualities.[9] There are, in fact, frequent echoes of the Mahābhārata in the philosophical musings of the Purāṇa, and, as with the case of Arjuna, philosophical discourse serves to calm terror.[10]

Death is often viewed with horror and abjection in the Purāṇa as well. In the third *skandha*'s discourse on *Sāṁkhya* cosmology, for example (narrated by Kapila to his mother Devahūti), creation issues forth through the modification of the elements of *prakṛti*, material nature. Semen, it is said, evolved out of the water element, followed by the anus from which death appeared "causing terror throughout the worlds."[11]

The association of semen with the appearance of death will be discussed in the next chapter. Here, the association of death with the anus and with defecation places it squarely in the realm of polluted substances, adding baseness to its sense of horror. One wonders if this is one reason why death—as in the deaths of Kṛṣṇa, Bhīṣma, and Droṇa—gets associated with people of low caste, women, and *adharma* respectively. Not only, then, is death envisioned as inevitable and terrible, but it is associated with the unavoidable entropy-like process of pollution from which the brahmanical tradition seeks to escape.

In keeping with the "horror motif," Kapila, and later Śuka in the fifth book of the Purāṇa, graphically describe the various tortures of hell, often brought about through frightening messengers of death:

> Then he sees two terrible looking messengers of death with eyes full of anger. At the sight of them, with terrified heart, he passes urine and excrement. They shut him up into a body designed for torture. Fastening a noose around his neck, they drag him along the road as the king's men do to convicts. Now and then he faints in exhaustion. He tries to rise again as he is led by the hellish road to the abode of Yama.
>
> (BhP. III.30.19–23)

While horror may be a strong motif, it is not the only one. Fear of death as a manifestation of the ultimate horror of being left alone is a modern phenomenon, one in which tragic vision has lost its balancing, redemptive possibility. However, in the Indian Purāṇic tradition, where rebirth is possible, death is often not depicted as irrevocable. Kāma is reborn after being burned to ashes by Śiva, and Jaḍa Bharata is reborn after his fatal mistake of becoming attached to a deer while in solitary meditation. Perhaps death as "disappearance" is the more fitting description. After all, it is not only Parīkṣit's disappearance, but also that of Kṛṣṇa and his entire dynasty that frames the work.

Due to the unquestioned assumption of the transmigration of the *self* (*ātman*) through various bodies, birth itself becomes an integral part of the Purāṇic "death issue." As is stated in the Gītā, "For one who has died, birth is certain."[12] This is expressed in a rather ironic manner in the Bhāgavata's version of the story of the philosopher-king, Nimi. After beginning a major sacrifice, Nimi, the son of Ikṣvāku, invites the exalted sage Vasiṣṭha to officiate as the sacrificial priest (and thus accepts him as his preceptor). Vasiṣṭha begs off, however, claiming that he has already been requested to officiate at Indra's sacrifice and offers to conduct Nimi's ritual after he is done. Nimi, described as "wise," however, reflects upon the fleeting, transitory nature of life and decides to proceed with the sacrifice without Vasiṣṭha, calling on the help of other priests. When Vasiṣṭha returns and assesses the situation, he angrily curses the impudent king to die, "May the body of Nimi, who considers himself learned, fall down."[13]

Nimi counter-curses his guru to die in return, claiming that Vasiṣṭha has perverted the *dharma* with greed. Both men give up their bodies, but the text tells us that Vasiṣṭha is reborn through the semen discharged by Mitra and Varuṇa upon seeing the heavenly nymph Urvaśī. In the meantime, the sages at the sacrifice preserve Nimi's body and propitiate the gods to restore Nimi to his corporeal form at the end of the rite. The gods agree to do this, but Nimi, speaking from "beyond the grave," refuses to reenter his body. He despises birth as much as he does death, linking them together in the following verse:

> I do not desire a body which carries fear, distress,
> and sorrow everywhere, since death follows it
> as a fish in water.[14]
>
> (BhP. IX.13.10)

The gods respond to Nimi's request by offering him the boon of living without a body, and Nimi takes up residence in the bodies of all beings through the opening and closing of their eyelids.

On one level, then, the Bhāgavata states its preference for disembodied existence. But the story does not end here. The sages, fearful of the consequences of a land without a king, "churn" the body of Nimi until a son is born. This son, Janaka, is known as Vaideha (from the body), because he is born from the churning of the dead body of his father. The Purāṇa sees both birth and death as abominable, vile, and illusory, but procreation—the obverse side of dying—is necessary (by one means or another) to preserve the order of the world. Of course, procreation, without the physical act of procreation is considered superior. Thus, throughout the Purāṇa, great sages like the Kumāras are "mind-born," and gods and heroes emerge from sacrificial churnings, whether they be of Nimi's body or the milky ocean. What is fascinating in the story of Nimi is the simultaneous occurrence of death and generation, by one means or another, a notion that resonates with the sense of *saṁsāra* as an endless stream. In any case, death is not a finality in the pageant of the Purāṇic imagination.

I would like to pause here and return to methodologies of reading around the portrayal of rebirth in the Purāṇa. In terms of intrinsic reading, the literal reality of *saṁsāra* is not an issue, in the same way that the historical accuracy of dynastic lineages given in the text is not an issue.

This is not a judgment on the value of these issues, but is rather a recognition that, from the perspective of the literary text, imagination overcomes literal representation, and images of rebirth are integral to the Purāṇic portrait of death and dying.

Contemporary readers of Indian texts tend to balk at the uncritical and unsubstantiated assumptions of rebirth that are often found in religious and literary works. And like major textual conundrums tend to do, images and assertions of rebirth have provoked ingenious and creative readings of the material from scholars and practitioners, both "engaged" and "objective." Chogyam Trungpa, in his introduction to the *Bar do thos grol*, for example, emphasizes the quotidian reality of the six *gati*s, or realms of incarnation, claiming that they mirror various psychological states that one may experience here and now.[15]

Psychoanalytic readings—like Robert Goldman's interpretation of Daśaratha's memory of accidently killing a *brāhmaṇa* in the *Rāmāyaṇa* of Vālmīki—often focus on the wish-fulfillment qualities of such recalls, be they of past-lives or of earlier moments in this one.[16] Such readings look at "past-life fantasies" as disguised (or "censored" to use Freud's term) rationalizations for current attitudes and behaviors, and the way in which Epic and Purāṇic literatures use such incidents to justify almost anything (as well as to keep plots moving) certainly provides much ammunition for this kind of reading. More recently in a related vein, Stephen Batchelor has argued that the entire construct of repeated birth and death is an accretion to the basic doctrine of the Buddha, and need not be accepted or even considered within the context of the "Noble Truths."[17] Whatever the case may be, the value of an intrinsic reading that focuses on the text itself is that one can work with its imagery without having to ascertain its literal referents (if indeed there are any). Therefore, no matter what the literal truth may or may not be around rebirth, the image of being reborn is one of the fundamental ways in which the Purāṇa amplifies its discussion of life and death. It should be kept in mind, however, that the Bhāgavata's "rebirth imagery" is not very appeasing; birth, as we see, is also a type of "death," and it just serves to deepen the problem of attachment and suffering. What might be worth further exploration, in this regard, is how different cultures favor particular images of dying. Death, in the Indian literary imagination, is rarely, if ever, depicted as an "endless night" or a nihilistic void, primary emblems of lonely contemporary fantasies. Images of repeated birth and death are more correlative with repeated instances of attachment and loss, and perhaps with a need to balance the account books of *karma* (as in the ongoing saga of Ambā and Bhīṣma in the Epic).

In the third book, Kapila teaches Devahūti that before birth, the living being exists in misery, as it remembers past, present, and future, and prays to the Lord for release. Upon birth, however, forgetfulness again ensues. Thus, birth is a form of ignorance similar to death.[18] The idea that a living being can ever be born or die is continually attributed to ignorance and relegated to the illusory realm of *māyā*. Towards the end of the Bhāgavata, as Parīkṣit is preparing for his final moment, Śuka exhorts him to give up the idea that he is mortal, an idea which he describes as *paśu-buddhi,* worthy of "animal intelligence."

Throughout the Purāṇa, humanistic consolations that "one has lived a good life and contributed to society" are decried. There are no eulogies commemorating the lives and deeds of the recently departed. There are no tombs or mausoleums. Death is generally callous and untimely, and so are the dead. There are a number of instances in the Bhāgavata where the dead are brought back to life, as when Kṛṣṇa restores the life of his preceptor's son as a *guru-dakṣiṇā*, or when he restores the life of his brothers who had been murdered by Kaṁsa. Instead of being thankful, these figures depart almost as quickly as they have reappeared.[19]

One particular subset of "death and restoration" motif, in the Purāṇa, involves the severing of someone's head and its restoration. The social and psychological implications of traditional narratives in this regard, such as the sacrifice of Dakṣa and the beheading and "re-heading" of Gaṇeśa, have been amply discussed by scholars (particularly Wendy Doniger) in terms of symbolic castration and power dynamics (both social and familial), and the Bhāgavata carries on these issues.[20] I will speak of the Purāṇa's version of the Dakṣa tale in the next chapter. In terms of the "beheading type" of death narratives that appear in the Bhāgavata, I would just note that the situation gets worked out in two different ways: either a substitute head is put in place of the original to restore a ruptured social order and reconfigurate power relations (as in the Dakṣa story), or the social situation is irrevocably broken by death, but the dying person receives the posthumous consolation of an after death merging into the effulgence of Kṛṣṇa (as in the Śiśupāla and Vṛtra stories). In this last instance, the "consolation" is seen as superior to the previous embodied state, as a head (or social position) is no longer necessary in the liberated condition. In both cases, a violent, confrontational death is smoothed over through reconciliation on another level. In the second instance, tensions are placated (if not resolved) by an appeal to an other-worldly state and the insinuation that, in some cases, dying may be preferable to living.

Death as God: Time and Destiny

Death will appear as God, as Viṣṇu in the Bhāgavata, and also in the form of time, *kāla*, which is also a synonym for death. The three-way equation including the absolute, time, and death has already been introduced, and the Bhāgavata refers to it continually, often employing imagery reminiscent of the Epic theophany in the Gītā where Kṛṣṇa reveals his "universal form," declaring himself to be "time set in motion to annihilate the worlds."[21] In the fifth *skandha*, for example, the *cakra*, which is the personal disc-weapon of Viṣṇu, is said to literally be the wheel of time, ever-revolving and taking the lives of all living beings from the Creator-god, Brahmā down to a blade of grass, and in the tenth book, Viṣṇu is referred to as *puruṣakāla*, "time in the form of the supreme person," who distributes death and immortality.[22]

Generally, however, the gods are not known for their powers of discrimination. Kapila, an *avatāra* of Viṣṇu, explains that, as death himself, he creates great fear in those who even slightly discriminate between themselves and another. He then declares that *kāla*, time itself, is the "*divyam*" of the *bhagavato rūpam*, the divine form of the Lord which is the cause of different forms. Kapila ends his discourse by declaring time to be eternal and immutable, creating living beings through other living beings and destroying even the god of death:[23]

> Time, without end, is the destroyer.
> Time, without beginning, is the creator.
> Immutable, creating beings through other
> beings, He destroys through death,
> even the Lord of death.
>
> (BhP. III.29.45)

The Bhāgavata professes that not only is Viṣṇu the Personification of death, but he is the doorway beyond death as well. Maitreya declares that discourse about Hari (*hari kathā*) will liberate those who are otherwise destined to die. He gives the example of Dhruva, who stepped on the head of death as he ascended to the realm of Hari. The text declares, "by hearing the story sung by the sage (Nārada), the male child of Uttānapāda (Dhruva, literally, lifted-foot) placed his foot on the head of death and rose to the realm of Hari."[24] There is a suggestive usage of the word "*padam*" here, which actually has "foot" as its primary meaning, but can also indicate a "dwelling place," a "rank," or "station," as well as a "verse" or quarter line of a stanza. The placing of the foot on the head is an act both of defiance and of claiming possession.[25] In the ninth book, Viṣṇu, in his form of Vāmana, the dwarf, takes three steps: the first two traverse the entire universe, and with the third, he places his foot on the head of Bali, the upstart demon-king who had conquered the heavenly realm. Bali loses his heavenly station, but gains immortality through association with the feet of the Lord, which are equated with the supreme (deathless) abode.

Here, the foot placed on death's head leads one to the realm/feet of Viṣṇu, which can also be read here as the "verse" of Viṣṇu, suggesting that the *kathā,* or narrative, about Viṣṇu is not different from his realm.[26]

Daiva, or fate, also walks along with death and time. The following lines reappear in various forms throughout the Bhāgavata:

> Just as assembling and removing articles of a game
> are done according to the sweet will of the player,
> so are the union and separation of all beings
> brought about by the will of the almighty.[27]

Allied with this attitude toward destiny is the idea that death must occur at a precisely ordained moment. Fate, like death, is immutable and works above the level of the individual, as Manu makes plain to Dhruva when he tells him that *daiva*, not the Yakṣas, slew his brother.[28]

In a similar vein, the Bhāgavata continually stresses the powerful effects of time. *Kāla* is declared to be "the ruler of all rulers who devours living beings through other living beings" and is described as "the razor-sharp destroyer of all creation."[29] Time is more than a cosmic principle in the Purāṇa. It figures in many of the Purāṇa's narratives, perhaps meant to instill a sense of detachment, illustrating the reality and ramifications of impermanence.[30] Such is the case in the legend of Mucukunda, the Rip Van Winkle of the Bhāgavata, who awakens from thousands of years of slumber in a cave to find the social order he was familiar with has vanished. He notices that plants, animals, and even men have all greatly diminished in size, since the cycle of the ages has turned downward. He quickly assesses the situation, observes the uselessness of attachment to dynasty, locality, and lineage, and heads north for the mountains to renounce the world.[31] None of these images, we see, place any great emphasis or value on human agency. Time and Fate impinge upon human agendas, disregarding social contracts and individual achievements. At times, the Bhāgavata's narrative appears to function in marine boot camp fashion, systematically crushing the obstinate individual. Instead of making one into a marine, however, one is made into a fit sacrifice for death. Unlike a Gilgamesh, who finally abandons his quest for immortality to take his place in the city, the heroes of the Bhāgavata-Purāṇa are continually undermined in their attempts at any normative reconciliation with the living.

Separation, Death, and the Loss of Sons

We may now investigate the various kinds of separation which occur under this great and all-encompassing umbrella of time and death. The first one we can look at is that of the loss of sons. As one would expect, the Bhāgavata is much more concerned with the loss of sons than with the loss of daughters because the patrilinear *vaṁśa* (lineage) figures strongly in every Purāṇa (It is the male issue who must carry on the dynasty). The prospect of not having a son is nothing short of a calamity. Not only will the dynasty be finished, but offerings made by the son to the deceased father to insure his deliverance from hell will also cease.[32] Nevertheless, even such seemingly tragic events often take on ironic twists that mirror, to some degree, the ironies around lineage in the Mahābhārata, although they are less prone to the latter's heroic earnestness.

One such situation occurs in the Bhāgavata's version of the tale of Aśvatthāman, who slays the five Pāṇḍava sons, and of Viṣṇu who saves Parīkṣit in the womb of his mother. Aśvatthāman breaks the rules of war by beheading the sons of Draupadī while they are sleeping and delivers them to his preceptor who then disapproves of the act. Draupadī's deep sorrow is described through physical sensations: "heavily burning in lamentation, she cried with tears in her eyes."[33] Her warrior-husband Arjuna seeks to pacify her by swearing revenge on the killer and proceeds to capture Aśvatthāman.[34] Martial revenge, however, is not the issue here, as Draupadī asks that the captured Aśvatthāman be spared. He is driven out of the camp, just as in the Epic version, but in the Bhāgavata, there is a ritual sacrifice (perhaps a symbolic castration) of Aśvatthāman. Arjuna severs his hair and the jewel he wears on his head, following Kṛṣṇa's silent suggestion. When the rites for the dead children are performed, the sages pacify Draupadī and her brothers with exhortations on the futility of opposing the ways of time and death. One feels throughout the text, for that matter, that "sacrifices" are constantly being performed on different levels to soften the inevitable reality of separation and dying.[35]

Just as this is happening, the mother of Parīkṣit, Uttarā, runs towards Kṛṣṇa, begging him to protect her unborn child from another "burning weapon" discharged by Aśvatthāman. The "saving" of Parīkṣit is described as follows:

> Hari, the Lord of Yoga, residing within all
> living beings as their own *self*, covered the womb
> of Uttarā with his own magic potency for
> the sake of the Kuru progeny.[36]
>
> (BhP. I.8.14)

Noteworthy here is the use of the words *yogeśvara* and *māyā*. Kṛṣṇa, it is stated, controls the powerful illusory-magical potency (*māyā*), which is, in fact, "the world," through his yogic mastery (*yogeśvara*, Lord of

Yoga). From this position, he can overcome impending death; for death and dying, no matter how fierce or untimely, belong to the realm of *māyā*. In this instance, the sons of Draupadī can die (just as King Nimi can die), because the lineage will be saved or continued through Parīkṣit. Is lineage, then, the immortal connection between the worlds of the gods and men? The all-important status of lineage and the reasons for its preservation are crucial issues. Traditional Hindu death rites, for example, may serve to lesson individual anxiety through the many ongoing household-based rituals that keep one "connected" to a sense of familial continuity. Lineage, and all that lineage entails, mitigate the ultimate sense of individual death and seem to endorse the endurance of social-historical reality as a supreme value. The loss of one's collective identity, then, may be more fearsome than individual annihilation. Even figurative castration may take on a new sense here (to follow Kurtz for a moment): to be "cut off" is to be separated from the cultural *mythos*. Dakṣa would rather have the head of a goat than lose his share of the sacrifice. The laws and customs surrounding *karma* and rebirth, therefore, serve to keep the dying person within the system of the living, and this is crucial. One wonders if the Bhāgavata's strong polemic of renunciation could exist without this. Even Nārada, when he leaves his mother, graduates into another collective, another order of life, and after death takes on his *ṛṣi* form, again as a group member. When a lineage dies, as one almost does in the Bhāgavata, it therefore occurs as a catastrophic mass dissolution or *pralaya*, the ending of an epoch.

Both the Epic and the Bhāgavata are works dealing with the disruption and decimation of dynasties. Only fragments of the lineage remain, a slender thread that technically, though only barely, preserves a formal sense of continuity amidst destruction and slaughter. One wonders if the story itself, as in the *Rāmāyaṇa*, is the last thread, and whether all the dynastic contortions and trickery employed to salvage a lineage are not also psychological lifelines to a myth of continuity. Remembering that the unconscious, according to Freud, denies death, if a monumental narrative somehow reflects a collective, psychologizing process, then that narrative instinctively seeks a sense of continuity, a legitimizing energy. Have we, perhaps, returned to narrative as an "escape from death" after all?

To this I would say "yes" and "no" because while the text's continuity exists beyond lineage through *hari kathā*, it could be argued that *hari kathā* could be transmitted through its own channels which may not be genealogical. Thus, Nārada can describe his past life in a lowly family in which the ending of his family line, the death of his mother and then himself, becomes his initiation into a higher world and into a lineage which transcends death.

In the first book of the Purāṇa, Nārada discusses his previous life as the only son of a maidservant attending to a group of sages. Although a child at the time, he is attracted to their narratives of Kṛṣṇa, and receives esoteric instruction from them. When the sages finally take their leave, Nārada describes his mother's ties of affection to him as resulting from her being but a maidservant and a "stupid woman." Since she needs her only son and has "no other recourse," she "binds him with her affection," perhaps reflecting the challenging mother-son bond that Kakar and others discuss in relation to the Indian family.[37] She will not get her way, however, for people of the world are under the control of the almighty like "a doll made of wood." One night the mother goes out to milk the cow and steps on a serpent who fatally wounds her. The actual verse reads:

> Once, when my helpless mother went out
> from the house on the path at night
> to milk the cow, a serpent who was grazed by her
> foot bit her, impelled by supreme time.[38]

The Sanskrit word *kṛpaṇa*, meaning "helpless" in the verse, emphasizes the mother's innocence. She accidentally touches the serpent, moved by the force of time, *kāla-coditah*. This same word, however, can also refer to the "messenger of death."[39]

This visitation from "the angel of death" begins to set Nārada free. He does not lament, but looks upon his mother's death as "the grace of the Lord" and starts wandering about the world. Thus, like so many other characters in the Bhāgavata, Nārada is led to his spiritual vocation through an experience of personal loss. This is not, of course, unique to the Purāṇa or to Indian religious traditions. David Aberbach suggests a similar situation in the life of Teresa of Avila, whose calling to the church began at age twelve with the death of her mother.[40] Sudhir Kakar discusses his own recent interviews of members of a "mystical cult" in India and finds that "loss was the single most important factor in their decision to seek membership."[41] What is interesting in the story of Nārada, however, is how "matter-of-factly" unemotional the narrative is. The mother is described as being "helpless," and there is no mention of any lamentation over the deceased parent. I wonder to what degree this and other rhetorical strategies of the Purāṇa participate in what Alan Roland and more recently Stanley N. Kurtz discuss as the "we-versus-I" self in the Indian social milieu. For the loss of, or separation from, a son is significant in that it challenges the sense of lineage, which relates to the collective, as opposed to the individual identity. The loss of a mother, on the other hand, is taken in stride here. Indeed, it comes to be seen as a blessing. The real agent of separation, loss, and death is the "Absolute" in the form of time and destiny, and that is given a positive value in the narrative.

Eventually Nārada has a vision of the Absolute in the form of "Hari" manifesting within his heart, a vision that is described in the most ambiguous of terms:

> Then, seated under the foot of a pipal tree
> in that lonely forest, meditating on the *self*
> of all selves situated within, as I had learned,
> while focused on the lotus feet (of Hari), my
> mind was overwhelmed with feeling and my eyes
> overflowed with tears of longing. Hari, in due
> course, came into being in my heart. O Sage,
> with my hair standing on end in loving ecstasy
> absorbed in a flood of bliss, I could see neither
> one of us.
>
> (BhP. I.6.16–18)

The last line reads, *nāpaśyam ubhayaṁ mune*, "O muni, I could not see either." *Ubhayam* can refer to any number of things: himself and the Lord, Hari, himself and another self (as Śrīdhara takes it), or body and soul (as Vīrarāghava takes it). Any of these readings would see such a vision as one that obliterates the duality of the seer and the seen. To one overwhelmed with love, there seems to be no other. In fact, one can argue here that *preman* itself overcomes both Nārada and the object of his search, Hari. The very next lines, however, speak of the disappearance of that supreme form from his vision:

> When not seeing that form of the Lord which is
> so dear to the mind and removes sorrow, I
> suddenly stood up from agitation, as if
> deeply discouraged.[42]
>
> (BhP. I.6.19)

The ecstasy of union leads here to separation, it would seem. Interestingly enough, variant texts are in disagreement about this verse. A number of manuscripts omit the disappearance (even though the major commentators discuss it).[43] Nārada tries to see this form again and fails. He then hears Viṣṇu explain to him that he, Nārada, will not see the Lord again in this life. Nārada thus wanders over the earth with a "purified mind." In fact, as he explicitly states, he is just waiting for his own death, and this is how the chapter culminates, with a death that is glorious and painless, a transfer from a gross body to a pure body with a sleep of a thousand ages in between.[44] Nārada's death is glorious, not in a tragic-heroic sense but in a redemptive-heroic one. The death of his mother becomes the impetus to seek his other-worldly nature. This theme is constantly reiterated in the Bhāgavata: worldly loss leads to spiritual illumination.

The contradistinctive theme that is much more difficult to fathom, however, is that even spiritual illumination can culminate in loss. This ultimate loss, or final *viraha*, will be taken up in the tenth *skandha* of the Bhāgavata (and will be discussed later in this volume). Nevertheless, here we see an episode that culminates in a death which is not a *thanatos* of dissolution, but a simultaneous awakening to another reality, death as the *āśraya*, the final abode that perhaps is being sought after all along.

The separation from the mother, although seemingly casual in the Nārada narrative, may be so as a defensive posture of sorts. The Bhāgavata's ongoing misogynist rhetoric (here seen in the epithet, "stupid women") after all is pronounced and sustained. Whereas the feminine in all of its manifestations is somewhat censored and treated with ambivalence in the Epics, appearing negatively through shadow figures like Śūrpaṇakhā and Mantharā, these feminine manifestations become openly identified as the main obstacle to fulfillment in the Bhāgavata.[45] I would suggest a further undertone here. The vision of Hari, in any of his innumerable forms, is almost always male. Perhaps then, Nārada is unable to maintain the "purified vision" of Hari in his mortal body, since it is a body that is born of woman. The one instance when Viṣṇu appears in female form is as Mohinī (The Delusive One) in the Bhāgavata's version of "the churning of the milky ocean." Here, her expressed purpose is to delude the *asura*s (demonic beings) into forfeiting their share of the nectar of immortality that has arisen from the ocean. Otherwise, the Purāṇa consistently sets up the search for an idealized divine male form that is not "tainted" by the feminine, either in the form of nature or woman. I do not want to speculate on all the homoerotic possibilities that underlie the "spiritual quest" of masculine heroic ascent, but I do want to emphasize that male/female dynamics will become even more problematic in the Bhāgavata's tenth book. Interpreters of this book have envisioned the ultimate goal of the spiritual quest as the ability to become a woman, but more on this later.

No matter how strongly the Purāṇa strives to leave the feminine world behind, however, worldly ties do remain and are often exalted when "the battle is done." When Dhruva is ready to ascend to the heavenly abode, "stepping on the head of death," he refuses to leave until his own mother is delivered with him. Here, in contrast to the Nārada story, the strength of the maternal bond is recognized, another example of the Bhāgavata's multivalence. In the case of Dhruva, however, his mother was the less-favored cowife of his father, King Uttānapada. Dhruva, after being chastised by his step-mother for trying to sit on his father's lap, and told in no uncertain terms that he could never accede to his father's throne, leaves home and worships Viṣṇu by the bank of the Yamunā. Viṣṇu appears and offers Dhruva his kingship, but Dhruva—through the purification of his mind through penance—has realized the vanity of seeking kingship, which can only keep one in the realm of *saṁsāra*. Nevertheless, he becomes a king and is reunited with his father and mother. Once again, the Bhāgavata seems to offer contrasting alternatives.

In contrast to Dhruva's familial loyalty, the Purāṇa offers ironic twists on the family dynamic in the narrative of King Citraketu in the sixth book. Citraketu was a king who ruled the Earth with his ten million wives, all of whom were infertile.[46] When the sage Aṅgiras visits the kingdom, Citraketu laments, and asks the sage to save him from falling into the hell of one who has no progeny. The sage complies, telling the king that a son will be born to him, and that he will be a source of both joy and sorrow. A child is born to the senior queen, but the cowives, out of envy, murder the child by poisoning him. The king is devastated and, manifesting signs of intense separation and grief, falls to the floor. Amidst tears and lamentations, the mother begins to speak to the dead child, protesting the cruelty and injustice of the situation, asking the child to rise and return to the living. The end of the chapter shows the king and queen surrounded by their subjects in grief.

At this time, the sage Aṅgiras returns along with Nārada, who is now in his incarnation as a traveling celestial. The two sages attempt to console the king through a philosophical discourse on the eternal nature of the soul and its fundamental difference from any particular body it takes. Aṅgiras tells the king, who has thanked the sages for their enlightening discourse, that he would have imparted such "supreme knowledge" upon his first visit, but the king longed for something else, namely, a son.[47] "Now," he says, "you have experienced the agony of those who have sons." The "agony" here is familiar—*tapas*, the burning heat of *viraha*—and it should be enough to incite the king to leave this ephemeral world. But to really drive the point home, Nārada brings the deceased son into the vision of all the lamenting relatives, and asks him to reenter his body and enjoy the world. The departed son, however, explains that he has been revolving in various species of life according to his *karma* and asks "in which birth were these my mother and father?" The son proceeds to continue the sermon of the sages. The pure *ātman* is dispassionate, unaffected by meetings or separations, which are merely circumstantial:[48]

> All beings eventually become related to all others as kinsmen, near-relatives, those who are neutral, enemies, friends, those who are indifferent, and bitter adversaries.[49]
>
> (BhP. VI.16.5)

The child then departs and the king, now awakened in knowledge, extricates himself from the "dark well of household life like an elephant from the mire of a lake."[50]

Here, we have the Bhāgavata at its polemical best, disparaging the dualistic world-vision that puts such a premium on sons, lineages, and dynasties. But the parent-child bond continues to haunt the text. Kṛṣṇa himself is born to parents who have seen their previous children killed at birth, and Kṛṣṇa's own preceptor, after completing his pupil's instruction, asks for the unusual *dakṣiṇā* (customary parting gift) of the return of his deceased son. Kṛṣṇa searches out the son through various realms of the underworld and eventually restores him to his teacher.[51] Kṛṣṇa's own mother Devakī mentions this incident and asks that her own dead sons be restored, and Kṛṣṇa retrieves them as well. The mother hugs and suckles them, "deluded by Viṣṇu's *māyā*," and then the children immediately disappear, returning to their celestial region, freed from a curse that had caused them to incarnate in the lower human regions. Instead of the heartfelt reunion of a romance, the Bhāgavata condescends to pay lip service to mother and child, while framing it within an overwhelmingly greater vision of an a-relational reality.

A similar incident occurs later on in the tenth book, when the newly born son of a *brāhmaṇa* dies just after birth. The father blames the inappropriate loss of the child on the sins of the *kṣatriya* ruler. After the loss of nine such children, the *kṣatriya*, Arjuna, takes a vow to either protect the next born child or enter into an obliterating fire. The child is born, and immediately vanishes. Arjuna seeks him out in vain, journeying all the way to the abode of death. When he is about to enter the fire, however, Kṛṣṇa comes to his aid. They travel throughout distant worlds, passing through the darkness of matter and into a shining region of "infinite, dazzling luster." Thereafter they enter an ocean in which they find a jewel-lit mansion, the abode of Anantaśeṣa, the thousand-headed serpent manifestation of Viṣṇu. His *darśana* is awesome, for he is surrounded by *puṣṭi* (grace), *śrī* (beauty), *kīrti* (fame), *māyā* (magic), and by the eight *siddhis,* or perfections. Lord Ananta admits to having taken the children just to lure Kṛṣṇa and Arjuna to his realm to be able to have their audience. Order is restored, as are the sons, but the human situation of birth and death seems insignificant before the dazzling display of this supreme ordainer.

In the same spirit, human relationship itself, the cornerstone of so many traditions of social order, is continually disparaged in the Purāṇa as arbitrary. Though loss and lamentation are major issues in these and other stories, they are often colored by an irony that reveals such separations to be illusory or irrelevant. In its effort to juxtapose the worldly and other-worldly, then, the Bhāgavata extends and expands upon themes of union and separation. As the *kavis* of old stretched their cord between being and nonbeing, the Bhāgavata moves beyond expected codes of loss and bonding.[52] The most consistent message of these narratives, nevertheless, is renunciation, arising from the awareness of the inevitable nature of loss.

The Unexpected

There are other narrative constructions around death in the Bhāgavata that do not fit into any particular social form, but resonate with issues of fate in unusual ways. I call them "the unexpected." Such episodes often involve animals of some sort and are akin to didactic fables.

One paradigmatic episode is that of King Bharata, who renounces his kingdom to perform austerities in the forest, but becomes emotionally attached to a deer. Ironically, and certainly not just coincidentally, Bharata encounters the deer at its birth: a pregnant mother deer, being chased by a lion, has leaped over a stream and dies, giving birth at that moment. Bharata sees the incident from his hermitage and takes the baby deer under his care. His attachment for the fawn grows. He forgets his meditations and austerities, wondering why the deer is late, and so on. Bharata's affectionate doting over the fawn is seen as a symptom of delusion. Nevertheless, the descriptions of Bharata's lamentation over the prospective loss of the deer are rather strong:

> At other times his mind was filled with grief
> and anxiety like a miser who has lost his wealth.
> His heart was tormented by deep agony and anxiety
> in delirious separation from the tender deer.[53]

As Bharata's laments continue, Śuka interjects to explain that these "heart-troubling and low desires" appeared in the form of a fawn due to the "force of the king's own destiny" (*svārabdha-karmaṇā*) [BhP. V.8.26], as he wandered away from the yogic ideal. "How else," Śuka rhetorically asks, "could he develop attachment to an animal of another species, after abandoning attachment to his own sons?"

"Finally," Śuka continues, "the inevitable time of (Bharata's) death arrived with wild speed, like a serpent approaching a rat." Death is described as "very difficult to surmount," and as "*karālarambhasa.*" *Karāla*, often translated as terrible or dreadful, actually means "open wide"; thus, it suggests the mouth of the serpent. *Rambhasa* has connotations of vehemence as well as speed. Thus, Bharata himself becomes the trapped animal, prey to death, as were the mating cranes of Vālmīki.

Bharata dies thinking about his fawn; and since one's last thoughts are said to determine the next birth, he is reborn as a deer.[54] Due to his previous austerities, however, he retains his human consciousness, and laments his folly. He immediately leaves his own mother and returns to a holy place, where he eats dry leaves and awaits for his next death.[55]

In his next birth, Bharata will not bother with such trifles as human sentiment, and death will no longer move him. He becomes a seeming madman, a *jaḍa*, wandering around apparently dull-witted and refusing to speak. Internally, however, he remains fixed on the consciousness of absolute non-duality. He has suffered through emotional attachment and has transformed into a silent, asocial sage. Refusing to reveal his attainment, he even disdains the Vedic knowledge of his *brāhmaṇa* family and is thus sent out into the fields to watch the animals. This is an interesting depiction in that it portrays social convention and religious life as differing manifestations of degrees of ignorance, and asocial madness as a manifestation of true knowledge.

At one point, Bharata is captured by bandits who prepare him to be offered as a human sacrifice to the goddess Kālī. Bharata, now known as Jaḍa-Bharata, "Mad Bharata," remains unmoved. He never protests and docilely allows the "outlaws" to prepare him for ritual decapitation. The goddess, however, knows who he really is and bursts from her altar in a furious rage and, along with her attendants, decapitates the thieves and drinks their blood in an orgiastic frenzy.

Here, we witness one of the Bhāgavata's two great archetypical images of attainment in the face of worldly impermanence. The *avadhūta* is one who has "shaken off" all designations and has lost all interest in the world of time. Standing apart from physical needs, oblivious to the social world of reciprocity and obligation, unconcerned even with the gods and their appeasement, the *avadhūta* is the image (albeit a somewhat shocking one) of freedom. Life and death no longer concern him, although he may still manifest concern for others.[56]

At one point on his journey, the king's retinue passes by and, needing another body to carry the royal palanquin, they engage Bharata in the king's service. Once again, Bharata does not object, and docilely allows himself to be conscripted. He is not a very effective carrier, however, because he keeps veering off the path to avoid stepping on ants. After a number of warnings, the king stops his entourage and upbraids Bharata, asking if he realizes with whom he is dealing. For the first time in his life, Bharata speaks, telling the king that a couple of lifetimes ago, he too was a foolish king. Bharata offers a teaching on the vanity of social position in the light of eternity, and the king, realizing Bharata's attainment, begs for forgiveness.

The polemic of this story is obvious. What I want to draw attention to is the exaltation of the anti-normative, antisocial being in a culture characterized by social stratification. A. K. Ramanujan's Freudian reading of Indian saints as wish-fulfillment figures in a culture strongly constrained by class and extended family bounds is certainly relevant here.[57] And while the *avadhūta* is not an oft-seen phenomenon in India, he looms large in the cultural imagination, exalted as fearless and undisturbed in life or death.

In another of the Purāṇa's "animal fables," a great king of the elephants enters a pool to frolic with his female consorts and is attacked by an alligator from underneath the water.[58] The alligator appears as "the unexpected," the low and slimy serpent issuing perhaps from a watery unconscious as the destroyer of lofty and immortal illusions. He is stronger than the elephant, being in his own element. Moreover, the elephant is vulnerable from consorting with females. A great struggle ensues. And slowly, over a period of a thousand years, the alligator pulls the elephant into the water where death awaits.[59] The attack may be unexpected, but the "unexpected," the alligator, who attacks him in the foot, interestingly enough, is again described by the term *daiva-coditaḥ*, "inspired by fate."[60] After much struggle, the elephant, who was previously deluded by *māyā* as he bathed royally with his trunk splashing in the water, seeks refuge in the Lord "through fear of whom even death flies away."[61] Death is appropriately described in the verse as a "fearsomely powerful serpent."

Viṣṇu comes, like the cavalry, as he did with Parīkṣit. Not only does he rescue the elephant from death, but his intervention transforms the alligator as well, who resumes his original form as a celestial Gandharva. The reconciliation of opposites (slimy alligator underwater with auspicious elephant above ground) is thus accomplished through the intervention of a transcendent other-worldly principle, Viṣṇu, who descends riding on his bird vehicle, Garuḍa (who is the eternal enemy of serpents). Only Viṣṇu can save the afflicted from the dangerous serpent of death.

The animal intermediary may be significant here. Garuḍa, like Hanumān in the *Rāmāyaṇa*, is able to move easily between realms, be it underground or above ground. Perhaps the animal helper, as a positive, instinctual energy, is a vehicle through which the hidden can be brought to light. This is certainly true of Hanumān's voyage to Laṅkā in the Epic. While the Bhāgavata does not feature such "super-star" animal helpers as Hanumān, animals are often present as mediating factors: they are the cows being tended by Kṛṣṇa, the animal mounts ridden by various gods, the *avatāra*s of Viṣṇu who appear in animal form—Matsya, the fish; Varāha, the boar; Hayagrīva, the horse; or the *avatāra* who is half human and half animal, and Narasiṁha; the man-lion incarnation who rips open, with his nails, the entrails of the demon Hiraṇyakaśipu. There has been much interesting speculation on the development and meaning of the *daśāvatāra* (ten avatars) phenomenon. In terms of the death narrative of the Purāṇa, I would just note them as another example of the narrative's fluidity. Strict boundaries between divine and human—as in the Nara-Nārāyaṇa, "man-god," incarnation of Viṣṇu—and between human and animal, melt away in the Purāṇa, as do strict divisions between living and dying.

The elephant, the text explains, had recalled a *mantra* from his past life, and this brings him the *darśana* of Viṣṇu. Impending death, then, as the encounter with the unexpected in the pool, does not breed forgetfulness. Rather, its unexpected shock revives memory, and from the viewpoint of the Bhāgavata, it restores sanity.

Heroic and Ritualistic Death

The heroic and ritualistic deaths ending in liberation, so common in Epic literatures, are also found in the Bhāgavata-Purāṇa. The deaths of Bhīṣma, Yudhiṣṭhira, and enemies of Kṛṣṇa, such as Śiśupāla, are retold from their Epic versions, and all are said to attain liberation upon their death. There seems to be a repeated formula for conscious or "yogic" dying in this regard, depicted as an involutive process in which the material elements are merged back into their sources. The deaths of Bhīṣma, Yudhiṣṭhira, and Pṛthu, all follow this formula in which earth is merged into water, water into fire, fire into air, and so on.[62] Nārada's narrative to Prahlāda in the seventh book is most complete in this regard.

> When, because of disease or advanced age, one is neither able to perform one's duties, study philosophy, or pursue spiritual knowledge, one should begin to fast. Properly placing the fires (on the body) within oneself and relinquishing the notion of "I" and "mine," one should then completely merge the aggregate elements into their causes.[63] (BhP VII.12.23–5)

The end of this process is the absorption of all materiality into matter itself as "recognizing the undying self remaining in the form of absolute consciousness without a second, one should cease functioning like a fire that has consumed its own origins (BhP. *VII, 12,31)*. In terms of the source *(yoniḥ)* being consumed, here. It is interesting to note that, with the exception of Satī, all the yogic deaths in the Purāṇa are enacted by males. The female correlative to this seems to be *sati* itself as when Arci, the wife of Pṛthu, seeing her husband's yogic release complete, builds a pyre, places his body on it, performs the appropriate funerary rites, bathes, offers oblations to the gods, and then enters the flames while thinking of the feet of her husband.[64] Both types of death are considered to be exemplary by the Bhāgavata.

The Bhāgavata's version of the Indra-Vṛtra conflict also merits further discussion. Unlike the Vedic version which exalts Indra as a savior and conqueror, the Purāṇa depicts the dying Vṛtra as the more elevated character. Vṛtra allows himself to be killed because his absolute knowledge transcends his individual destiny. He knows that his death is part of the "play of the situation" and that his essential nature will exist beyond the death of his form. In this sense, he is somewhat reminiscent of Karṇa, the most profound hero of the Mahābhārata, who elects to die in the *Bhārata* war rather than assume kingship.

Vṛtra is also aware of the peculiar nature of God's grace, explaining to Indra, before their battle, that Hari frustrates the efforts of his servants to attain the non-liberative aims of humanity (*dharma*, *artha*, and *kāma*). He then asks for the release of his attachments to the "*māyā*" of body, children, wife, and household.[65] The text makes it clear that Vṛtra prefers death to victory, as when he chides Indra to pick up the thunderbolt weapon that has fallen from his hands and strike, explaining that the Lord alone (in the form of time) is responsible for victory and defeat. As Bhīṣma instructs Yudhiṣṭhira from his bed of arrows, Vṛtra instructs Indra from the battlefield. With his arm lopped off, and facing imminent death, Vṛtra calmly discourses on the nature of the *self*, the illusion of independent existence, the need for equanimity in all circumstances, and the absolute nature of fate. He maintains an equanimity and presence of mind that even impresses Indra. Indra slays Vṛtra, in the Bhāgavata, and is triumphant in the visible (*laukika*) world. Nevertheless, he remains in a fearful and anxiety-ridden state, while the light from the body of the slain demon enters into the supreme (*alaukika*) abode.[66]

The "heroism" of the ascetic, who wanders the earth completely unconcerned with whether he is alive or dead, resonates with the discussed martial-heroic sensibility. In the eleventh book, an *avadhūta* praises the boa constrictor (sometimes translated as python), who just lies on the earth, making no effort to obtain food or sustenance. The *ajagara-vṛtti,* or "living condition of a python," is discussed as an actual stage of renunciation.[67] In the seventh book, Prahlāda meets such a person lying on the road, a person whose heroism lies in his renunciation of everything, even of renunciation itself. The "python sage" just does not care, and with good reason.

> Those who hold to wealth or to life are ever fearful of royal governments, thieves, enemies, relatives, animals and birds, beggars and seekers of wealth, time, and their own selves.[68]
>
> (BhP. VII.13.33)

The sage goes on to say that the source of sorrow is clinging to wealth (*artha*) as well as to life (*prāṇa*) itself. Again, on the mundane level, clinging, as in Buddhist teaching, is declared to be the source of suffering. Beings such as the *avadhūta*, the "python-sage," Ṛṣabha, and Jaḍa-Bharata, typify those who have separated themselves from convention, from society, even from the desire to live. Their valor is their freedom from fear, and thus from any concern over dying, for figuratively speaking, they are already dead.

The stoic hero-renunciate and the mad lover both refuse to cringe in front of dying. Bilhaṇa, the "mad lover" of the twelfth century, reminisces on his love, implying that it was worth it. He'd do it again, despite his impending execution. The same holds true for the "love-crazed" devotee of God typified by Caitanya, an avid propounder of the Bhāgavata-Purāṇa who did not seek freedom from death but asked for *bhakti* in birth after birth.[69] Parīkṣit, too, while awaiting his death, learns not to grieve. Śuka tells him that he cannot in fact die, because he was never born. He is told to listen to the narratives of Hari, and above all, to the narratives of love and longing in the tenth book. Parīkṣit's death is thus a kind of ritualized celebration. Numerous sages have assembled on the banks of the Ganges to witness it. The text records it. Death and celebration become intertwined, as do death and liberation.

In the tenth book, the high point of the work, death frames the charming, playful pastimes of Bhagavān. The entire *līlā* of Kṛṣṇa is, in fact, motivated by the prophecy heard by the reigning king, Kaṁsa, as he is driving the chariot of his newly wedded sister. It is customary for the brother to drive his sister and brother-in-law back to his village in order to ease the pain of familial separation that the bride may feel. While driving, a voice from the sky scoffs at the king, telling him that the eighth son of the very sister whom he is driving in the chariot will kill him.[70] At the mention of his impending death, Kaṁsa, who reacts even more swiftly than Laius, raises his sword to kill his own sister. He tries to destroy death at its source, which is birth in the womb of a woman. Here, as elsewhere, the Bhāgavata links death to birth, to generativity, and thus to sexuality. However, the "great-souled" Vasudeva, Devakī's husband, delivers a sermon on the inevitability of death and on the fundamental difference between the body and the self. Vasudeva repeats a favorite image of the Bhāgavata's, one which should be kept in mind when thinking of the text's attitude toward dying:

> Just as the luminaries, when reflected in earthen
> vessels filled with water, appear to move
> or change with the movement of the wind,
> so is a man deluded being attached to the qualities
> created by his own ignorance.[71]
>
> (BhP. X.1.43)

Here, in accord with advaitic understanding, the fear of death is seen as a result of illusory attachment to the body. The meeting and separating of individual beings is ultimately unreal, and the "problem of losing those we love" vanishes along with corporeal identification. Despite his sermon, however, Vasudeva is only able to deter Kaṁsa by promising to hand over his sons to him. Śuka, while describing the behavior and mind of Vasudeva, makes the point that those devoted to Hari are able to part with what is most dear, in this case a son.[72] It seems, then, that the experience of deep loss *(viraha)* is an essential and inevitable aspect of self-knowledge, which leaves one to wonder about the seeming ease with which the "great-souled ones" shake off worldly ties. Could this also be a cultural wish-fulfillment fantasy with the threat of imminent death serving to mirror a deeper phenomenon in worldly experience itself?

Kaṁsa allows the family to return home, remembering that only the eighth son is prophesied to kill him. At this point, however, Nārada intervenes (as he so often does in such situations) and further agitates the mind of Kaṁsa. Kaṁsa then has his sister and brother-in-law jailed, killing every one of their sons at birth. The eighth child (Kṛṣṇa) does survive, needless to say, and is spirited off to Vṛndāvana in the middle of the night.

Thus, "the appearance of the Lord" is shrouded in death, and his childhood, "child-god" pastimes, while played out in an idyllic exile, are surrounded by the prophecy that he will grow up to kill his uncle. The Vṛndāvana *līlā* is a play of the golden age of Indian childhood, while separation and death wait just around the corner. One cannot help but notice similarities to the Oedipus narrative here: a prophecy at the beginning, violent efforts to evade the prophecy, and its inevitable fulfillment. When Kṛṣṇa leaves Vṛndāvana, one of the first things he does is slay Kaṁsa.[73]

The king has been living with the prophecy of his death for years, but immediately before the event he experiences fantastic omens, portents, and strange, uneasy feelings. Kaṁsa experiences these states right after Kṛṣṇa breaks the sacrificial bow in the arena which Kaṁsa has set up. His kingly, masculine power broken, he is all but dead:

> Kaṁsa, however, was struck with terror when he heard
> of the breaking of the bow and of the massacre of its
> keepers and their army, which were the supreme sports
> of Kṛṣṇa and Balarāma. That evil-minded one remained
> sleepless for a long time and while asleep and awake
> saw many evil omens and portents of death. Though his
> reflection was visible, his head was not, and the luminaries
> appeared in double although there was no second one.
> He saw holes in his own shadow and could not hear the sound of
> the vital breath when his ears were closed. The trees appeared as
> gold, and his foot prints were invisible.
> In dreams he saw himself embraced by dead relatives,
> he rode on an ass, swallowed poison, and wandered alone
> with a garland of red flowers, naked, and anointed with oil.
> He perceived these and other scenes in dreams and
> while awake. Anxiety ridden and terribly afraid of death,
> he didn't get any sleep at all.
>
> (BhP. X.41.26–31)

Kaṁsa's death, of course, will be his final liberation for he belongs to a special class of individuals who have the honor of being killed by God. Kaṁsa, Śiśupāla, Hiraṇyākṣa, Hiraṇyakaśipu, and other great villains of the Purāṇa play out great battle-dramas with Kṛṣṇa in which they are inevitably killed. These deaths, however, are seen as "sport." The above-mentioned demons, for example, are said to be former associates of Viṣṇu, his gatekeepers in Vaikuṇṭha, born on the earth as demons, because they were cursed by the four Kumāras for not allowing them into Viṣṇu's realm (the gatekeepers mistook their eternally youthful forms for the forms of children). Commentators insist, however, that the gatekeepers (named Jaya and Vijaya) accepted the curse for the pleasure of being able to fight with Kṛṣṇa, a *līlā* that would not be acceptable in Vaikuṇṭha. The other demon incarnations of Jaya and Vijaya were Dantavakra, Rāvaṇa, and Kumbhakarṇa. Kaṁsa, too, will be killed, but his death will hardly be a resolution to the tenth book; it is just another experience of dying, albeit a central one, which the narrative builds around. Here lies a major difference between Greek tragedy and the Bhāgavata narrative. In both cases, there is a fated inevitability, and the focus is on the youthful slayer (Kṛṣṇa versus Kaṁsa, the son versus the father), but in the Bhāgavata, the prevailing attitude is sport, not guilt. "Good characters," such as Nārada help to move murder and slaughter along without a second thought, since it is all part of the *līlā* anyway. One can argue, of course, that the slaying of an uncle is much different than killing the father and marrying the mother, and to see the uncle as a displaced father figure is quite far-fetched. Nevertheless, the similarities force one to pause, especially when one recognizes the tendency of Epic narrative to operate through displacement, as Robert Goldman and others have shown.[74]

There will be other heroic and ritualistic deaths in the Purāṇa, the dying of heroes and the liberation of demons. What is more, Kṛṣṇa himself will disappear, but unlike the ritualistic death of the other heroes, Kṛṣṇa's departure will create an overwhelming sense of separation. When Kṛṣṇa leaves, he takes his entire dynasty with him; with the dynasty gone, the women commit mass suicide (perhaps this can be another argument for the primacy of the collective in Indian consciousness.). Without Kṛṣṇa, the world itself appears to be devoid of life. In the first book, Arjuna declares that "separation from him, even for a moment, makes the world appear vile like a corpse bereft of its vital spirit."[75] The world suffers in separation from Kṛṣṇa, but such suffering barely approaches the anguish of the cowherd women who had already lost him forever. The intensity of their loss is considered to be more painful than death itself. The ultimate *viraha* of the cowherd women, however, should be seen in relation to other less-exalted instances of love and loss in the Purāṇa. For they form the frame to the all-important tenth book. Moreover, the exaltation of the *gopīs*' anguish will not be congruent with the Purāṇa's more generally stated view of woman. This view must be explored before we can begin to understand the Bhāgavata's elevation of the *gopīs*' loss into its highest form of religion.

5

STRĪ NARAKA DVĀRA— WOMAN AS THE GATEWAY TO HELL

Many Western "students of the East" from Denis de Rougemont to Alan Watts seem to have cherished a naive hope that there would be no spirit/flesh dichotomy in an idealized "East," which included India.[1] The Bhāgavata-Purāṇa more often than not, however, upholds the "normative ideology," be it *dvaita* or *advaita*, that considers the sensate world to be an inferior realm; with physical nature, emotional attachment, and the "feminine" in general viewed as impediments to liberation.[2] The Bhāgavata, buttressed by the rhetoric of renunciation, takes up this issue, not from a frame of good versus evil, but from one of reality versus illusion; and death and dying are clearly part of the realm of illusion.[3] Nevertheless, even when Kapila points out that illusions of attachment can work through men as well as women, "woman" is ultimately to blame:[4]

> One who has attained the Self through my service
> and who aspires to the supreme stage of yoga
> should never associate with women. They say
> that, for him, she is the gateway to hell.
> Woman is *māyā* fashioned by god. She approaches
> gently. Yet, one should regard her as the death
> of the self, like a deep pit covered by grass.
> One who, due to attachment to women, attains the
> female gender, in delusion considers my *māyā* in
> the form of a man, as her husband, the
> bestower of wealth, home, and children.
> He should recognize the illusion of the self
> as having the nature of husband, home, and

> children, one that is death brought about by fate, just as the singing of the hunter is death for the deer.[5]
>
> (BhP. III. 31. 39–42)

A derivative of *pra + mad (pramattah)* was previously used by Śuka to describe deluded householders. Here, another derivative (*pramadā*) is used for "woman," and can be construed as either "young-woman" or "wanton-woman."[6] The use of *pramadā* suggests a link between woman and the word's deeper sense of "madness," and we will frequently see how "woman" serves as a metonym for the "madness" of material desire.[7]

The most frequently used root in the type of description found above, however, is √*muh* which produces the derivative *moha*, "delusion or bewilderment." Whereas the process of attachment, leading to bewilderment and ultimate ruin, is clinically delineated in the second chapter of the Bhagavadgītā,[8] it is portrayed in the Bhāgavata-Purāṇa through a series of conventional and mythic images, along with hyperbolically descriptive narratives. The paradigmatic illustration of this process is found in the Purāṇa's version of the churning of the milky ocean legend (mentioned above) and the subsequent incarnation of Mohinī—Viṣṇu appearing in the form of an enchanting woman to bewilder the enemies of the gods.

When the *asura*s snatch the nectar of immortality in their cosmic tug of war with the gods, Viṣṇu assumes the form of Mohinī (literally, the bewildering woman) who is said to be "beyond definition," *anirdeśyam*. She is ornamentation personified, and succeeds in instantly awakening desire (*kāma)* in the minds of the demonic Daitya generals.[9] Mohinī enchants the minds of the *asura*s while admonishing them:

> How is it that the descendants of the sage Kaśyapa are attached to a wanton woman like me? For the wise never place their trust in a lovely woman.[10]
>
> (BhP. VIII.9.9)

Mohinī compares the friendship of women to that of jackals and states that such relationships are temporary. She then dispenses the nectar, serving the gods first and leaving none for the *asura*s. This leads to another marathon war between the gods and demons in which Viṣṇu intervenes to tip the scales.

The implications here are significant. First, there is the obvious opposition between the *deva*s (divine beings who are attached to the god, Viṣṇu) and the *asura*s whose attachment is to the female form generated by Viṣṇu's *māyā*. The conventional moral is that the gods will attain immortality and defeat the demons, whose attachment to the enchantress is their downfall. Thus, "good," "godly" people will control their impulses and prosper. The characteristic depiction of the *asura* as one who is attached to the feminine can be read in numerous ways. The churning of the milky ocean can be and often is read allegorically, as, for example "the churning of the dualistic mind." We then have a separating of the elements into a model of "lightness" and "darkness." Darkness, illusion, and attachment are all said to be feminine qualities, further evoked by the female form.

Modern commentators on Indian literature, like Aurobindo Ghose, have actually preferred the above vision, declaring the *deva-asura* dichotomy to reflect the battle between the light and dark forces of the psyche. In the tug of war, the ocean of milk—perhaps representative of the creative *citta,* or mind-stuff—is churned by these opposing forces. However, there is more than a mere "sorting out" process happening here; there is a creative process of "value generation" as well. During the churning, many treasures emerge from the ocean, as well as a lethal poison which is drunk by the god Śiva. The churning process, as it is described in the text, is more creative than disruptive. Once again, the underlying metaphor for the dominant process of "churning" seems to be sport as opposed to guilt or pitched battle. Viṣṇu, in his tortoise form, provides the base upon which the ocean is being churned, and his serpent attendant Vāsuki, allows himself to be used as the rope. On the level of polarities, there is a battle between good and evil, but it is always secondary to the sporting of those who exist beyond such dichotomies. The enemies of the gods are described in terms of delusion (as opposed to evil). They are either going after the wrong thing (woman), or going after the right thing in the wrong way (immortality through coercive power).

The inevitable defeat of the *asuras*, however, often engenders in them a wisdom that is lacking in the gods. Thus, while the god Indra triumphs over his greatest enemies, Bali and Vṛtra, in the Bhāgavata, it is Bali and Vṛtra who attain a transcendental wisdom that exceeds heaven. While neither of these *asura*s "falls under the spell of a woman," their wisdom is engendered by defeat and brings up the same issues of attachment, temporality, and illusion. For example, although the *asura*s in the Bali narrative are defeated (and then brought back to life by the life-giving science, *sañjīvanī-vidyā*, of their preceptor, Śukra), their leader Bali does not lament over his defeat. He is *loka-tattva-vicakṣaṇaḥ*, "wise" or more literally "far-seeing to the truth of the world."[11]

Wisdom resulting from defeat often allies itself with imminent separation or death. While Bali loses his conquests, his kingdom, and finally his own body, such loss leads to his taking refuge (*āśraya*) in Viṣṇu, which is the ultimate *telos* (*āśraya*) of the Bhāgavata-Purāṇa. We may also remember that the king of the elephants, Gajendra, began to call to Viṣṇu in desperation when his retinue abandoned him, because the alligator he had been struggling with was about to drag him into the water. Thus, the "defeat" of the ego through loss in one form or another, or through sexuality (which leads to generation, birth, and hence to separation and death), can lead to another kind of knowledge.

To prove its point, the Bhāgavata now has the "bull-bannered god," Śiva, ask Viṣṇu to reveal the form of Mohinī to him. The minute Śiva spies her, he abandons his own consort, the goddess Pārvatī, even as she watches, and runs after the enchantress, "agitated by love," "bereft of shame and robbed by her of good sense."[12] As he chases Mohinī, his "unfailing" seed escapes, like that of "a love-maddened elephant chasing a desiring female," and turns into ores of gold and silver.[13] Śiva follows Mohinī in this manner through rivers, mountains and forests, and "wherever sages lived," as if to instruct the sages, by negative example, on the enchanting power of the female form. When he finally comes to his senses and realizes that he has, in fact, been "stupefied" (*jaḍīkṛtam*) by the *māyā* of the god (*so'paśyad ātmānaṁ deva-māyayā*), he extols the extent of Viṣṇu's power. Interestingly enough, Śiva is described as neither distressed (*aviklavam*) nor ashamed (*avrīdaṁ*) about the incident."[14] Seeing this, Viṣṇu is pleased.

The end of the episode is especially instructive. At the outset it appears that the Bhāgavata repeats the theme we have seen in the Epics and *dharmaśāstras*: a patriarchal element associates woman, sexuality, and the earth with a negative, enslaving, feminine principle. Woman becomes a dangerous sorceress, a fascinating embodiment of powers which cause bewilderment (*moha*) for the masculine, ascending spirit/intellect. Disowned by the culture's dominant values, her denied aspect exerts an even stronger fascination that disrupts the heroic ascent;[15] attachment to her leads to separation and death. Therefore, in the seventh book, in his discourse on the *varṇāśrama-dharma*, Nārada echoes Manu, stating that woman is like fire and man is like a pot of ghee, and that in a secluded place one should even avoid one's own daughter. Furthermore, we remember that in the Bhāgavata's version of an early creation story, the Creator God, Brahmā himself, was bewitched at the sight of his own daughter and shamelessly ran after her in the form of a stag. Nārada goes on to sum this up with the following statement:

> *kalpayitvātmanā yāvad ābhāsam idam īśvaraḥ*
> *dvaitaṁ tāvan na viramet tato hy asya viparyayaḥ*
>
> Until the master, has clearly understood by the self
> [or by himself] that all this [world] is [but] appearance,

> duality will not cease, and thus follows his (*īśvara's*) perversity of the self.
>
> (BhP. VII.12.10)

Commentators have construed this verse with the previous one. Generally it is understood that "master" (*īśvara*) refers either to the *jīva* in full identification with the Absolute, or else to an attainment of perfect mastery over "this" (*idam*), the universe, world, senses, body, and so forth. The idea of "duality that will not cease" is epitomized by woman as an object of enjoyment.

The verse, however, deserves closer consideration. *Īsvara* can be understood in various ways: certainly as a master or controller, but also "a god." There is a suggestion introduced here that whatever *īśvara* may be in this verse, he too can be subject to duality. Such duality is stated to be his *viparyaya*, which can mean "turning," as in the constant revolutions of *saṁsāra*. The word *viparyaya* also has a sense of being "inverted" or "perverse." In the *Bhāminī-vilāsa,* for example, a *viparitā* is a "false or unchaste woman," and the idea of inversion is also applied to inverse sexual intercourse (*viparitā-rata*). *Viparyaya* can also refer to loss, destruction, ruin, and death.[16]

I dwell on the associations here because they suggest an idea which is crucial to the theme of loss and separation: the dualistic attraction, typified by man and woman, is a reversal, a misapprehension, which is nevertheless a reflection (*ābhāsa*) of a certain reality. Happiness, the Bhāgavata says, is the nature of the self (*sukham asyātmano rūpam*), a self that is fundamentally a-social. It is not realized by fulfilling one's *dharma* as Rāma does (a provisional measure at best), nor by chasing after the illusory forms of the world, for both strategies misapprehend the reflection for the real. The world as reflection, allied with a theory of transformation (*pariṇāma*) that we have discussed, is not altogether false, nor sinful. Rather, it is *mohita,* or deluded, in its vision of the one reality.[17]

This delusion becomes evident in the tenth book, which exploits the manifestations of deep-felt loss produced by desire and longing, giving them a positive value. The value judgments center around the axis of illusion and reality and bring us back to the crucial semiotic of the Bhāgavata-Purāṇa: only the word, comparison, or feeling which is in direct relation to the absolute is real. The rest is an *ābhāsa*, a reflection of the reality, and can therefore keep one turning around (*viparyaya)* in the realm of *moha.* It can also catapult one above it through the deep experience of separation and loss.

The narrative makes it clear that Mohinī is the agent of the god. She is none other than Viṣṇu himself, not a separated diabolical force. The silent, ascetic sage may avoid her in the quest for self-knowledge, but there is already an implication here that to suffer from desire and loss may be another path to blessedness. Such experience may purify the self and is discussed, even if didactically, in the narrative of Ajāmila, the fallen son of a *brāhmaṇa,* who regains beatitude by calling out the name of the Lord at the end of his life, while believing himself to be calling his own son.

Rather than allowing things to end well, then, the Bhāgavata, more often than not, opts for disjunction, difference, and inconclusiveness when it adopts and adapts Epic and even Vedic narratives. The Bhāgavata version of the Purūravas and Urvaśī legend is a case in point. The story of the love between the immortal nymph Urvaśī and the human king Purūravas is one of the earliest tales of love and loss in the tradition, and it merits a complete study in its own right.[18] What is most significant for our purpose, however, is how the Purāṇa complicates the ending as it seeks to work through issues of masculinity and femininity, mortality and immortality.

Mortals and Immortals

In the *Ṛg Vedic* version of the story (hymn X.95), which seems to refer to a known, albeit fluid tradition of the tale, Urvaśī refuses to return to her lover, the mortal king, telling him that there can be no friendship with women because they have the hearts of "jackals."[19] The theme of the mortal lover and the immortal woman seen in many myths implies the worldly/other-worldly issue (*laukika-alaukika*). In Bhāgavata terms one can only "marry the immortal" by becoming immortal. In the world this is usually accomplished through progeny, which is the only way that most mortals get a visceral sense of immortality. This theme is found in the *Ṛg Vedic* version where the poet consoles the lamenting king, telling him that since he is a "kinsman of death" his children will offer oblations to the gods, but the king himself will be in heaven.

Later *Brāhmaṇa* texts contain the same basic story retold in the Bhāgavata in which Urvaśī sets down specific conditions for remaining with the king, conditions which the celestials will cause the king to violate.[20] In the Bhāgavata-Purāṇa version, Urvaśī is attracted to the king and approaches him. She asks him to protect her two lambs and to enjoy himself with her, as long as she neither sees him without clothes, nor eats anything except ghee.[21] After enjoying amorous pleasures with him in the gardens of the gods for many years, Indra sends *gandharvas* from heaven to fetch her through a ploy. They steal the lambs, and when Purūravas leaps after them they issue a flash of lightening so Urvaśī sees him naked. The nymph disappears and Purūravas wanders the world searching for her "like a madman." He finally sees her again at Kurukṣetra on the bank of the Sarasvatī river, with five nymph companions. Here, a number of verses are lifted from the conversation between Purūravas and Urvaśī in the *Ṛg Veda* including the verse about Woman having the heart of a jackal (literally jackel-wolf), *kvāpi sakhyaṁ na vai strīṇāṁ vṛkāṇāṁ hṛdayaṁ yathā.*[22] The Bhāgavata narrative goes even further, however, when Urvaśī declares that women are "merciless, cruel and jealous," and that they "will kill their faithful husband or brother over the smallest matter."[23] While the nymph may be immortal, she cautions the king that Woman is associated with death, an association that we have repeatedly seen in the Purāṇa.

The Bhāgavata version follows the *Śatapatha Brāhmaṇa* in reuniting mortal king and immortal nymph, but the reunion is fraught with ambivalence. Urvaśī tells the king that at the end of the year he may be her lord again and enjoy sex for one night only. In this way they can have other children. They meet after a year. The king is initially delighted, but delight turns into affliction over their impending separation. Urvaśī advises him to propitiate the *gandharvas*, who reward him with a fire vessel. The actual word used here is *agnisthālī*, which is a fire-vessel used for worship. Theoretically, he can worship the fire and reach the realm of Urvaśī. The next line, however, says that the king thinks the *agnisthālī* to be Urvaśī. Walking in the forest with it, however, he realizes it is not her. Some commentators, therefore, explain *agnisthālī* as the name of another nymph who is substituted for Urvaśī. The king does not accept a substitute. He returns to his palace and thinks of the nymph.

At this point, the Vedic element enters the narrative. The ages change and knowledge of the Vedic sacrifices reveals itself in the king's mind. He returns to the spot where he has left the *agnisthālī* and finds a tree growing there. He makes "churning sticks," and while rubbing them together thinks of them as Urvaśī and himself and actually chants a mantra, "Purūravas is in the breast of Urvaśī."[24] Thus, the Bhāgavata continues the post-Vedic association of Purūravas and Urvaśī with the sacrificial fire. The friction kindles the Vedic fire which the king worships, desiring to attain Urvaśī's realm, which the text says he ultimately does.

While the Bhāgavata only accepts that union which will take place beyond the mortal world, it does so with an ironic twist. On the one hand, the king is said to attain the heavenly *gandharva* realm because he has accepted the fire as his son. In other words, he has kept the fire burning. This fire can be seen as both the sacrificial fire of *karmakāṇḍa* rites—ceremonial offerings performed for long life, heroic sons, and fame—as well as the burning fire of desire which impels such performance. In this instance, the desired object is a celestial woman, who can lead one to the heavenly realms, but whose pursuit also places one squarely on the ritualistic wheel of death and rebirth, a wheel that the Bhāgavata pejoratively associates with Vedic sacrifice. The image is further reinforced by the sexual suggestiveness of rubbing the kindling sticks.

The final position of the king is discussed in terms of the fall of man through the ages. Formerly, in the Kṛta Age when purity predominated, there was only one Veda: the sacred syllable Om, the basis of all speech. There was one God, Nārāyaṇa, one fire, and one caste.[25] Now that the Tretā Age has arrived, *rajas,* or passion, predominates over purity, and the ritualistic path of Purūravas is said to be a manifestation of this passionate nature of the age. The Bhāgavata thus presents the king as a "devalued" hero, a victim of attachment to Woman, the archetype of illusion. Death will thus remain a problem for him, as it is for the gods.

The Bhāgavata's version of the *Rāmāyaṇa* story corroborates this view. Rāma's own lamentation at the loss of his beloved wife is described in the Bhāgavata as the plight of those attached to women:

> When Sītā was carried away in the woods by
> the lowest of demons, like a wolf,
> Rāma wandered through the forest with his
> brother in the distress of separation,
> showing thus the way of those who are
> attached to women.
>
> (BhP. IX.10.11)

The verb *prathaya*, "showing," is often discussed in commentaries on the verse. It suggests that Rāma himself is not attached but is showing, by example, the plight of those who are. Commentators such as Vijayadhvaja emphatically point this out and conclude that Rāma, as the omnipresent Viṣṇu, could not actually suffer from worldly lamentation.[26]

When Sītā consigns herself to the earth toward the end of the Bhāgavata tale, however, Rāma cannot contain his grief.[27] Śuka comments that

> excessive fondness of men and women
> for each other is always such,
> and brings fear even to powerful souls,
> much more so to a desire-ridden individual
> whose thoughts are bound to household life.[28]

Numerous other narratives repeat the same message that corporeal attachment, most fully expressed in the male-female relationship, leads to an ignorant death. Even the association with those who are fond of women is said to be a doorway to hell.[29]

Just who is this dangerous woman who stupefies men and robs them of their judgment?[30] Is she seen in terms of a Manichaean condemnation of the flesh (understood by some as a characteristically Christian attitude), or as a part of a Luciferian plot to drag angelic beings out of heaven and into matter?[31] Neither perspective is that of the Purāṇa; she is not the devil. To the contrary, Viṣṇu describes her as his own *māyā*:

> Behold the might of my *māyā* in the shape of a woman who by the mere play of her eyebrows treads underfoot even the conquerors of the four quarters.[32]

But she is not an angel either: the text declares that to serve her own ends she will murder her husband, son, or brother.[33] Moreover, it is stated in the sixth book that young women took on a quarter of the curse Indra incurred for killing a brāhmaṇa, and it became a constant sexual urge, clearly perceived in the form of their menstrual discharge.[34]

Now we could title this chapter "Misogyny in the Bhāgavata-Purāṇa," but that would be too simplistic. I would point out that none of the above-mentioned women of the Purāṇa are actually human. Purāṇic narrative, of course, does not generally deal with mere humans; gods and heroes are more their domain. Nevertheless, the male hero is developed as a personality while the woman is not. One could say that the "other-worldly" woman, whether divine or demonic, is a type of Jungian *anima* and usually an undeveloped form at that. Following this line of thinking, then, to marry a celestial, or to "fall" for the delusionary potency of Viṣṇu, is to avoid dealing with a woman as an individual in her own right. The Bhāgavata narrative, then, is dealing in the fantasy images of a male-dominated tradition, and it clearly finds this preferable to dealing with real women, just as Vālmīki's Rāma winds up ruling his kingdom with a golden statue of Sītā beside him. The Epic and Purāṇic tradition in not merely misogynist; it places the female in the realm of the feared and the fantastic and then has to deal with the consequences. In terms of a depth-psychological pattern in which male and female aspects integrate, the Purāṇa is found wanting, which may also be why it eschews any positive form of worldly *polis* (as with the Epics), for all worldly aims are ultimately suspect in this text. And if there is any place in the Purāṇa that would make one stop and ponder the consequences of its ideology, it would be here. In its rejection of the feminine, the household, and ultimately human society itself it leaves the quotidian, natural world behind. One can only wonder, along with G. Morris Carstairs and Sudhir Kakar, if the harsh rhetoric of the Purāṇa in this regard indicates a lack of any mature oedipal resolution—hence, the fear of the feminine. Such a perspective would certainly cause one to consider the interactions between Kṛṣṇa and the cowherd women in another light. But more on this later. In terms of its "harsh rhetoric," when the Bhāgavata does actually address the "real" flesh and blood situation of the household, it does so in the most caustic terms.

Householders and Ascetics

Once one has seen how and why the Bhāgavata is wary of "woman," one can clearly understand the text's repeated condemnations of household life. The householder is the upholder of convention, the only member of the four *varnāśrama* orders that carries a sense of permanence and stability. Therefore, the household itself and the "family value" it represents is a crystallization of a certain kind of delusion (*moha*), and Śuka attacks this realm at the very beginning of his response to Parīkṣit.

The principal problem with the householder, according to Śuka, is that she/he becomes distracted and does not see death approaching.[35] The Bhāgavata does admit at times, however, to the possibility of pious householders attaining liberation and to a licensed sense-enjoyment that does not conflict with the other *puruṣārtha*s (the traditional aims of humanity).[36] The household is, after all, the basic, social unity for the dharmic upholding of religion, but religion, like the political state in the visible *laukika* world, will always disintegrate. Rāma enacts the life of a perfect householder and his kingdom fractures. In the Mahābhārata, grandfather Bhīṣma renounces kingship and householder status in order to preserve family peace, and unknowingly sets into motion the bitter Bhārata war. The Bhāgavata inherits this strong ethos of the futility of all worldly endeavors in the face of impermanence and does not challenge it. It does, however, offer variant perspectives on, and even some new resolutions to, the battle between desire (*kāma*) and duty (*dharma*), and the inevitability of loss.

In the eleventh book, after discussing the evils of excessive attachment to anything or anyone, a *brāhmaṇa* sage gives the conventional bird-and-hunter analogy for human affection and its results in terms of two birds who build a nest and have chicks. The Bhāgavata judgment here is clear:

> With their hearts bound in mutual love, deluded
> by the maya of Viṣṇu, they brought up their
> offspring with anxious care.
>
> (BhP. XI.7.61)

When the birds go out seeking food for their young, a hunter appears and catches the young ones in his net. On her return, the female sees this and, followed by her mate, she rushes towards them and is caught. The sage concludes his discourse as follows:

> Thus, a miserable householder of troubled soul, delighting in the pairs of opposites, like the bird, goes to ruin along with the family he supports. Obtaining a human form in this world is like an open gate to liberation. The wise regard him who remains attached to his household as one who, like the bird, has fallen from a high place.
>
> (BhP. XI.8.73,4)

On the other hand, neither is the convention-spurning path of excess seen as a road to the palace of wisdom. While the mad lover may act like a depraved person, his depravity, in most cases, is looked down upon. As we shall see in the *Rāsapañcādhyāyī,* the tenth book's narrative of Kṛṣṇa and the cowherd women, *kāma* is referred to as *hṛd-rogam* "a disease of the heart."

To return to the story of Ajāmila for a moment, it is significant that he is portrayed as the son of an innocent *brāhmaṇa*, a householder who is properly married. One fateful day, while collecting articles in the forest for his father's worship, he spies a *śūdra* cavorting with a lower-class courtesan (*bhujiṣyā*). Seeing them drunk and singing, the woman with her dress loosened, he becomes *vimohita*, "bewildered." The *brāhmaṇa* tries to control himself by remembering the injunctions of scripture, but his mind is overcome by *madana*, passion personified as *Kāma-deva*. Similar situations occur throughout the text. Wanton sexual desire is often portrayed as something erupting from the lower classes, outside the brahmanical conventions of household life.

Household life can be, and often is, envisioned as a concession to *kāma*, with the purpose of regulating its energy through the normative śāstric injunctions (better to marry than burn). As in the situation in French courts described by Dennis de Rougemont, awakened eros and marriage oppose one another.[37] But even here there are gradations of compromise. Upper-class *brāhmaṇas* maintain respectability, but the lower classes threaten them, just as women threaten men. This situation will be of paramount importance in the tenth *skandha*, when the non-*brāhmaṇa,* Kṛṣṇa, engages in amorous adventures with the wives of others in the middle of the night.

Even the household then, serves as a well-fortified but ultimately precarious protection against the feared power of unbridled eroticism.

The danger of even bearing witness to a sexual act, or anything that reminds the mind of *kāma*, is continuously emphasized in the Bhāgavata. While classic situations appear in the text—of Indra sending down *apsaras* (nymphs) to disturb the meditations of ascetic *yogīs*—there are other situations which are even more piquant because they occur naturally.

The legend of the silent sage Saubhari appears in the ninth book of the Bhāgavata. The *muni*, while meditating under the waters of the Yamunā river, observes the sexual commingling of two fish, and immediately resurfaces into the world to ask the king for a suitable marriage partner. Having attained magical powers by dint of his austerities, the sage is able to convert his body to that of a beautiful youth. He revels with fifty wives in celestial parks and mansions created by his yogic power and begets a hundred sons with each of them. Ultimately, however, he laments his fall from his ascetic position, saying that his judgment had been obscured by infatuation which caused him to look upon the objects of the senses as things worth seeking. Moreover, he laments that he can find no limit to the desires created through conjugal relationships. Disgusted, the sage retires to the forest to purify himself by emaciating his body in the fire of austerity. He attains liberation, along with his fifty wives who follow him, looking upon him as a deity, "even as flames are extinguished with the fire that has cooled down."[38]

Man and Woman

The continual emphasis on "downfall through women" throughout the Purāṇa punctuates an ongoing fear of the feminine as the embodiment of threatening sexual power. The process of *yoga*, after all, is a masculine, martial discipline which centers around the control or even conquest of sexual energies. The image of Śiva burning *Kāma* to ashes for disturbing his meditation with the arrows of desire is never far from Śuka's discourse. The Bhāgavata takes pains to note that Śuka is asexual, unlike his father Vyāsa (the author of the Mahābhārata). When Vyāsa chases after his son, who is leaving home, he is curious as to why a group of women bathing in the river cover themselves up as he passes by, but do not bother to cover themselves when Śuka passes by. The women tell him that Śuka, not being a householder, does not see the duality of male and female whereas Vyāsa does.[39]

While Śuka is said to be beyond the male-female duality, he discusses women as being threatening to men—a perception which has been noted to exist in present day India as well—and makes various remarks about the "weakness of women."[40] While narrating the inauspicious pregnancy of Diti by Kaśyapa, Śuka remarks that, although very learned, Kaśyapa was rendered senseless (*jaḍībhūta*) by the lovely woman. Moreover, being overwhelmed (*vivaśah*) is not so astonishing, because at the dawn of creation, Prajāpati found that all beings were solitary (*ekānta*), and then created woman from half of his body that she might carry away the minds of men.[41]

The further implication here is that the entire creation moves because of the influence of desire, an implication that is more bluntly stated by Ṛṣabha in the fifth book: *puṁsaḥ striyā mithunī-bhāvam etaṁ tayor mitho hṛdaya-granthim āhuḥ*, "they call it the knot of the heart, this state of the male and female becoming coupled to one another."[42] This "knot" (*granthi*) earns its name because it literally binds one to the world. Therefore, the renounced *avadhūta* tells Yadu in the eleventh book that, upon seeing a woman who is *devamāyā* (the illusion of the gods), one who has not conquered his senses becomes seduced by her manner and appearance, and falls into a dark hell like a moth flying into a flame.[43] Even those who opt for the *pravṛtti-mārga,* or the sanctioned path of worldly enjoyment, lament in the end as Yayāti does, complaining that *kāma* is never pacified through enjoyment of desires, but instead flares up anew like a fire fed with ghee.[44] Therefore, Yayāti, who at one time demanded that his sons abandon their youth and offer it to him, now declares that one should without delay give up *tṛṣṇā*, the very thirst for desire.[45]

Here is the Upaniṣadic-Buddhist argument for withdrawal (notice the Buddhist term *tṛṣṇā* here as opposed to *kāma*), a solution offered by the Bhāgavata-Purāṇa as well. When the sage withdraws from the world of wanting, whether through austerity and acts of will, or through the grace of some superintending authority, he abandons the world of *kāma* and thus can no longer suffer. Such a withdrawal could be construed as a symbolic form of death, a "social suicide" of self-imposed chastity that absolves one from the ravaging of desire. It is a strategy of "death to avoid death" if you will. It is also a blanket refusal of the world of desire whose "gifts" of love, home, possessions, friends, and family are seen as forms of delusion, with the wish for them portrayed as a form of insanity, a knot in the heart; there is little sympathy here for the Pauline compromise of marrying rather than burning.

What is at issue is the "central encounter between man and woman" and the concomitant "fall" into marriage and responsibility that literary critics like Leslie Fiedler invoke when they complain about the American novel's avoidance of such situations. Unlike the American narrative of adolescent meandering, however, the Bhāgavata does not avoid this "central encounter." It most consciously and categorically denounces it. And unlike tantric traditions, which visualize absolute reality through the meeting of male and female principles, the encounter between man and woman is seen as the illusion that veils the actual, central encounter of human and divine. Human desire and longing, no matter how inviting, are said to ultimately only generate pain, with no possibility of mortal resolution.

If this were the final message of the Purāṇa, however, there would not be anything new or unusual in terms of reactions to loss, death, and the "fear of falling." The alternative response offered in the Bhāgavata, however, is quite unusual. The "mad-lover" *virahiṇ(ā)* suffers even more acutely from loss than the ordinary being, and it is this fire of *viraha* (separation) which becomes the transformative energy that can take one into the *alaukika* realm. The "central encounter" between man and woman is transposed, transfigured, or transformed (depending upon one's viewpoint) into a different sort of encounter in which loss, and even death, will not be avoided but will actually be cultivated. With all this in mind as background, we are now ready to approach the tenth *skandha* and its *rāsa-līlā*, which inverts many of the paradigms and conventions that we have just discussed.

6

THE RĀSA DANCE AND THE GATEWAY TO HEAVEN

As it expanded into the many alcoves of Indian life, the narrative and attendant imagery of the *rāsa-līlā*, the story of Kṛṣṇa's dancing with the cowherd women of Vṛndāvana, nourished a wide variety of genres of poetry and drama. Indeed, the perspectives, commentaries, and offshoots of this narrative have been innumerable, and it is not within the scope of this volume to deal with many of them. Nevertheless, whether one is looking at the *rāsa-līlā*'s sublime poetry, theological arguments, source materials, or derivative works, one has to acknowledge and contend with the narrative's enduring power. Indeed, the ongoing celebrity of this particular story may very well have something to do with its ability to bring love and death together in an unprecedented manner, and this is therefore where I will focus my investigation.

Is this narrative principally an allegorical or didactic work, a *siddhānta*, or does the text appropriate the "cowherd woman story" as a collective fantasy, reflecting deeper wishes which are utterly at odds with cultural norms (the psychoanalytic reading)?[1] This last idea is a particularly sensitive one, because it raises vociferous objections from partisans and from representatives of disciplic lines (*sampradāyas*) who advocate deep esoteric interpretations of this material, considering its reduction to human terms to be extremely sacriligious.[2] Any judgments about the anagogic experience associated with this text are tenuous to say the least. The esoteric entrance into the *līlā* of Śrī Kṛṣṇa is said to be a religious mystery that is entered through faith and practice as opposed to speculation. Nevertheless, speculation has abounded. We know, for example, that the chapter's "transgressive" material has been quite threatening to Indian reformers like Ram Mohan Roy who spurned the

Bhāgavata. This stands to reason, since some of the most ingrained, cultural paradigms (such as "woman as the gateway to hell") are dramatically inverted in this section of the Purāṇa. The heightened expression of lamentation over loss that is considered a weakness in Śuka's discussion of the *Rāmāyaṇa* becomes an exalted and transformative force in this part of the Bhāgavata. A colleague of mine, who lived as a *sādhu* in India, once remarked that Vṛndāvana contains simultaneously the best and worst of human nature. This statement can well be compared to the responses initiated by the *Rāsapañcādhyāyī*, the five chapters about the *rāsa-līlā* that continue both to inspire profound devotion and to provoke bitter scorn.[3]

The first thing to emphasize here is that the text is presenting ritualized archetypal—as opposed to literal representative—material. The setting, scenes, and characters therefore appear to be "type-cast," symbolic, if you will, and this positioning informs the particulars of the narrative. Except for Kṛṣṇa, there is no individual character study or development. No one else is described or discussed at any great length. The *gopīs*, or cowherd women, are portrayed as a collective body, often as Kṛṣṇa's "ornaments," and always as part of his divinity. And while Kṛṣṇa may be an individual character, he is far from a human one. The text repeatedly emphasizes Kṛṣṇa's divinity in hyperbolic terms, contributing to its fantastic sensibility. This larger than life, material, however, is laden with social and emotional repercussions. Conclusions that have been drawn from, and patterns of living and thinking that have emerged through the *rāsa-līlā* episode can be as disturbing as they are sublime, and this needs to be reckoned with. Although my focus here is more on a literary reading of the text than on its social applications, the text cannot be viewed apart from its pervasive presence in the culture and the possible reasons for it.

The *rāsa* dance, itself—the image of Kṛṣṇa dancing in a circle with the cowherd women—may derive from a specific form noted in the *Nāṭyaśāstra*, in which female dancers move with their hands interlocked in the company of men who have their arms placed around the necks of the women. It may also have been an actual performance tradition of the time.[4] In either case, one sees the operation of elemental images, such as the single and concentric circles, which function on symbolic levels. Whatever else we may have in this configuration, we have a true *maṇḍala*, a "magic circle" that sets boundaries between its interior configuration and the outer world.

This circle, however, does not exist in isolation, but is surrounded by the ornamentation of aesthetic convention. The word *rāsa* is a derivative of *rasa* and expands the meaning of "*rasa*," perhaps suggesting that this defining image in the Bhāgavata is an evolute of the aesthetic principle of *rasa* as codified in the *Nāṭyaśāstra*.[5] As an aesthetic image, then, this figure may be experienced on many levels. Along with the closed circle, one finds the dynamics of meeting, separation, and reunion, fraught with all the multivalent complexity that one might by now have come to expect.

To return to the issue of sexual transgression which has arguably been a major factor of the text's celebrity, the Bhāgavata is all too aware of its controversy and combines the actual *rāsa-līlā* of Kṛṣṇa and the cowherd women with instructive commentary from Śuka to Parīkṣit. This is, after all, in keeping with the ultimate paradox of the text. Passion, as we have seen, has been decried as a sickness and a downfall. Here it becomes glorified after having passed through the fires of loss and separation. It is not the so-called moral issue that will concern us, however, but the centrality of burning passion itself and its relationship to the separation, loss, and ultimately to dying.

Although the Bhāgavata has repeatedly equated passion with death in a pejorative sense, passionate love leading to death will now be exalted. Indeed, in the Western tragic sensibility, this is the logical outcome. De Rougemont speaks of the narrative plot doing all that it can to prevent passion from attaining its completion, thus delaying closure. The narrative may also project a numinous garment around an unattainable union which can only be realized beyond the purview of any worldliness. *Thanatos*, death in its metaphorical sense, becomes the culmination of the most intense passion and can indicate a transformation out of earthly boundaries, as much as it can a preoccupation with one's own "end." The Bhāgavata's narrative, as we have seen, is spoken on a stage of dying. There is no attempt to avoid this ultimate ending, but at a deeper interpretive level, death and dying become subordinated to the non-dualistic vision of the Purāṇa, and passion becomes part of a "purifying ordeal," a penance in the service of a transfiguring death.[6]

This is not, however, the full story in the Bhāgavata, for passion itself is not turned into a hubristic religion personified as *kāma,* but becomes the fulcrum of a transformation as it is transmuted into something else. *Kāma* is both an energy and a god. This dual-role need not be problematic if we acknowledge the personifying ability of the mythic dimension, which suggests much more than the simplistic dismissal of "the gods" as personified psychic processes. If the phenomenology of the psyche can be envisioned as a dramatic narrative, then its multivalent characters may be essential to symbolic communication, offering an enriching dimension to any conceptual abstraction. This takes us back to the power of story, more particularly to the *rāsa-līlā,* which is literally the "divine drama of dance." Nothing here is static. So let us look at the main players.

Kāma is one of the main characters who appears throughout these chapters, as both the state of desire or lust, and as Kāmadeva or "Cupid" (his Greek evolute). He is said to have triumphed over gods as well as humans. The *gopīs*, or cowherd women, are considered by *bhakti* practitioners to be the best of all humankind, exhibiting the highest evolution of devotional sentiment. It should be noted, however, that such heights of devotional sentiment are marked by an extreme sense of servitude. We will return to explore this later. Finally there is Kṛṣṇa, the divinity personified as a cowherd boy, who will replace or displace Kāma, becoming the lover that Rāma has refused to be and that Śiva has annihilated. The energy that binds these characters ranges in a spectrum from desire to "transfigured love." As in a spectrum, it is hard to say where one shade begins and another ends, or what the exact difference is between a dark craving for death and a pull toward the ideal of mystical union. And yet the Bhāgavata will insist that there is a marked difference between levels of desire, and that these differences are most essential. One way of visualizing such subtle difference in the context of the Bhāgavata-Purāṇa is to see that in desire one clings to life, while in love one opens to death. However, this formulation may be premature, because the "love" discussed in this chapter is presented in a very specific way, and it is therefore necessary to have the entire spectrum of desire-energy in mind as our point of reference. In maintaining such a perspective, one can see how the liminal zones of separation, loss, and death function as the crucial junctures in the transformation and rebirth of the god of desire, Kāma, who had previously been labeled as "the great enemy."[7]

There is a traditional reading of these chapters (see Hawley and Shrivatsa Goswami, 1981) that envisions the story as a showdown between *kāma* and *preman*, or "lust" and "love." After all, Kṛṣṇa resides on two battlefields: he takes his place on the battlefield of desire with the *gopīs*, and he joins Arjuna in the Bhagavadgītā on a battlefield of death, declaring himself, in fact, to be death. Life and death, as the Bhāgavata continually contends, cannot easily be separated. Death may be said to be standing in the background while *kāma* takes the foreground, frenzied and unable to see death, as Śuka repeatedly notes.

Occasionally, however, they do meet. Early in the chapter, some of the *gopīs* die of anguish because they are not able to leave their houses for a tryst with Kṛṣṇa. Parīkṣit asks Śuka how it is possible that these *gopīs* could attain freedom from conditioned existence while thinking Kṛṣṇa to be their paramour. Śuka answers by alluding to the King of Cedi (Śiśupāla), who attained perfection simply by hating Kṛṣṇa.[8] Śiśupāla, we may remember, was beheaded when Kṛṣṇa threw his razor-sharp disk at him for questioning Kṛṣṇa's sovereignty. The Bhāgavata describes Śiśupāla's "life-force" as merging into Kṛṣṇa's effulgence immediately upon leaving his body. The common denominator of these narratives is *"bhāvana,"* the constant remembrance of Kṛṣṇa, which is said to lift the mind out of mundane existence. Indeed, Śuka will declare that those who constantly direct desire, anger, or fear, as well as affection, intimacy, or friendship toward Hari (Kṛṣṇa) will attain oneness with him.[9] In this sense the emotions are not to be idealized as much as they are to be focused in a specific way.

I have previously discussed the sensibility of sport under which such deaths occur and the usage of previous lifetimes to explain the narrative action (Śiśupāla's former existence as a gatekeeper in Viṣṇu's realm). Both modes of liberation are corroborated in Viṭṭhala's commentary. Viṭṭhala explains that Kṛṣṇa had graced Śiśupāla with the propensity to hate him because of Śiśupāla's worship of Kṛṣṇa in former lives, the proof of such "grace" being Śiśupāla's liberation.[10] On the explicit level of instruction, Śuka is pointing out that, if remembrance in hatred can lead to liberation, one can only imagine what the *gopīs*' remembrance in pure love can lead to. On the narrative level, however, we have an episode in which love is framed by death (the *gopīs* dying of anguish), and it is associated with another form of death in the Purāṇa, that of being killed by God. Śuka is letting Parīkṣit know that it is somehow fitting that love, remembrance, and death form a triangular equation.

In these chapters the female's position is the *virahiṇī*, separated and suffering. The male position, occupied by Kṛṣṇa as the alluring one, is somewhat unusual: the male God is enticing the female instead of the far more common case of the delusive female potency drawing in the male.[11] Even this position is questioned, however, and becomes somewhat reversed by the end of this chapter, which is characterized by reversals.

The Structure and the Scene

As we further explore the dialectic between love and death in the Purāṇa, let me again underscore the fact that this narrative is told to one who is about to die, and that he is accompanied by an audience of *ṛṣi*s and sages. Moreover, the text has reminded us that the narrator, Śuka, has absolutely no experience with *kāma* (desire).[12] Parīkṣit, as the principal hearer, on the other hand, is represented as the exemplary man of the world and would seemingly be an ideal receiver of Śuka's narrative. Parīkṣit must demonstrate, however, that he is an *adhikārī*—one qualified to hear the *kṛṣṇa-carita,* the most intimate and sacred stories about Kṛṣṇa. When the king first questions the sage, Śuka does not reply. Parīkṣit then cites his lineage as proof of his capacity to hear. This apparently is still not enough, so Parīkṣit reminds those present that he literally shared the same womb as Kṛṣṇa when the latter saved him from Aśvatthāman's burning weapon. Although Parīkṣit praises the narrator, and states that he is a faithful devotee, the qualification that finally permits Śuka to speak is the king's ardent desire to hear *hari kathā* (the discourse of Kṛṣṇa):

> Though I have given up even drinking water in this fast, this unbearable hunger does not torment me since I drink the nectar of Hari's stories flowing from the moon-lotus of your mouth.
>
> (BhP.X.I.13)

Śuka responds by praising the "proper direction" of Parīkṣit's mind and begins by declaring that such inquiry into Vāsudeva-*kathā* purifies all—the reciter, the hearer, and the audience.[13] It is important to keep in mind, then, that the text frames its image of the *rāsa* dance with the substance of *hari kathā*, the narrative itself, as the most potent means of purification, and a fervent desire to hear it as the necessary prerequisite.[14]

The First Meeting

The first chapter of the *Rāsapañcādhyāyī* begins with a reminder, *bhagavān api*, "even though he is Bhagavān," pointing to the incongruity of the Supreme Being reveling and dancing with women in a circle. The opening verse reads as follows:

> *bhagavān api tā rātrīḥ śāradotphulla-mallikāḥ*
> *vīkṣya rantuṁ manaś-cakre yoga-māyām upāśritaḥ*
>
> Even Bhagavān, seeing those autumn nights
> with blossoming jasmine, turned his mind
> toward love-play and resorted to his power
> of creative magic (*yoga-māyā*).[15]
>
> (BhP. X.29.1)

The words *tā rātrīḥ*, "those nights," is in the plural when the text only speaks of one specific night; this fact has inspired numerous commentaries. Some discuss the *rāsa* dance in terms of something that took place frequently, and others speak of many nights passing during that one night. The qualifying "*tāḥ*" is often said to indicate "those" nights that resulted from the promise of the *vastrāharaṇa* episode in which Kṛṣṇa stole the clothes of the cowherd women. The *gopīs* had prayed to the goddess Kātyāyanī that Kṛṣṇa would become their husband, and their prayers were said to be fulfilled when Kṛṣṇa demanded that they come out from the river and approach him if they wished their garments returned. By seeing the *gopīs* without clothes, he is said to automatically become their husband.[16] Whatever the case may be, from the very first verse one is warned that conventional time and space may not apply here, as the plural, *rātrīḥ*, casts doubt on a mimetic or historical night. This will be corroborated by the rest of the verse in which the play of the night has a dream-like quality, even perhaps the quality of a divine dream. Meeting takes place, not only outside conventional, moral bounds, as is often discussed, but more importantly, outside many other contexts of waking reality, even life and death itself.

One may also notice the ingredients for "*rasa*" as an "aesthetic mood" that are included in this first verse: *śāradotphullamallikāḥ*, the night(s) and the autumn blooming jasmine are stimuli (*vibhāva*s) contributing to *rasa,* according to Bharata's dictum on the subject.[17] This leads to the conclusion that even Bhagavān is apparently affected by the ingredients that inspire *rasa*. It may be interesting to consider this verse in light of the *Devī-Bhāgavata's* assertion that Viṣṇu is bewildered by his own *māyā*.[18] The *Devī-Bhāgavata,* of course, is working from its "anti-Vaiṣṇavaite" polemic, but here, even in Bhāgavata theology, whose very foundation is built upon the complete and unequivocal mastery of *īśvara,* there is a hint of a realm where such control is relinquished. Whereas *māyā* itself offers the illusion of control through bodily identification, *yoga-māyā,* offers another form of illusion, one that may be based on a mutual abandonment. Just what is to be willingly relinquished may become the point here.

The next verse, with *tāḥ* in the accusative plural, is part of an elastic construction. It can be construed with *rātrīḥ*, "those nights," or with *śāradotphullamallikāḥ*, "the blossoming jasmine of autumn," or with both together (*śāradotphullamallikāḥ,* being a *bāhuvrīhi* compound, modifying *rātrīḥ*). One could also conceivably take *śārada . . . rātrīḥ* as an accusative of duration, leaving *tāḥ* to refer to the *gopīs*. The blooming, fragrant flowers, inciters of the aesthetic mood, construed with *tāḥ*, can be taken as *gopīs* who bloom like flowers under the influence of the moon as some commentators have done.

In the earlier Bhāgavata narrative, Kṛṣṇa is born on a moonless night in prison and under the threat of execution. Here, the moon infuses the eastern sky with its soothing rays, "like a lover caressing the face of his beloved with cooling saffron after a long absence," again a hint of paradigm reversal.[19] The moon has now emerged and shines beyond the prison house of the conventional, diurnal world. The sight of the moon inspires Kṛṣṇa to play his flute and to enchant the minds of the "lovely-eyed" *gopīs*.

The *rāsa-līlā*, then, is presented as being simultaneously within nature and exterior to it, suggesting the transformative power of the alliance between the aesthetic and devotional principles. The parallel of Sanskrit, aesthetic conventions to such a scene is no surprise. As we have seen, one of the principal modes of discourse in the Bhāgavata is aesthetic and its central modality is play. Thus, Bhagavān makes up his mind (*manaś-cakre*) to play, *rantum* (again from *ram*—to frolic, play, or enjoy sexual delight).

The "making up of the mind" (*manaś-cakre*) invokes the heart as well. Commentators have deemed appropriate here the use of the *ātmanepada* verbal suffix, in which the action of the verb is performed for the subject rather than for another person indicating that the results of all *rasa*s are held by, for, and within Kṛṣṇa.

The pivotal construct here, as mentioned however, is the compound *yoga-māyā*, conceived of by Vaiṣṇava commentators as being the internal potency of the divine, as opposed to *māyā*, the power to create the illusory, phenomenal world. The compound-word *yoga-māyā* appears previously in the *Gītā* in the context of divine opulence, as a synonym for the covering potency of delusion which veils the vision of the unworthy. In the Bhāgavata the "*yoga-māyā*" takes on meanings according to context, but usually refers to the divine powers of Bhagavān as opposed to his more visible powers of creation.[20] In these verses they suggest a magical reversibility; the conventional world of the day, the world of *māyā*, is about to be turned upside down. Therefore, the most unusual, divine opulence will be displayed potentiated by *yoga-māyā*. This term legitimizes the sense of vivid, narrative action as being more than part of the illusory play of the impermanent world.[21] The rather oxymoronic juxtaposition of these words, *yoga* and *māyā*, helps to explain the interpretive energy that has grown up around them. *Yoga* and *māyā* are usually thought of as being in different camps; the *yogī*, after all, is trying to get out of *māyā*.

Yoga-māyā becomes a theological term for the energy under which the *līlā*s of Kṛṣṇa are conducted, as opposed to the *māyā*, or illusion, of the external world. Here, we see again psychology approximating cosmology. Although *yoga-māyā* is a potency, just as *citta*, or mind, is a potency, it is of a different nature. The "*yoga*" component of the compound does not refer to the effacing of mental fluctuations prescribed by the *Yoga-sūtra*s (*cittavṛttinirodhaḥ*), but instead, in the Bhāgavata, it upholds the radical otherness of the divine potency, the fact that it exists wholly beyond the purview of mundane conditions. In any case, we are dealing with an explicit usage. The Bhāgavata wants the reader to know that its upcoming narrative is conducted under a particular power: one that is distinct from *māyā* in its pejorative, illusory sense. This power, it tells us, is related to magic, to the dream, and to "divine illusion" as well, and such a magical sense lends itself to poetic device.[22]

How does the Bhāgavata-Purāṇa incorporate poetic device and aesthetic conventions? Not only does the text dialogue with the terminology and categories of the *Nāṭyaśāstra*. But, in terms of its semiotics, the Bhāgavata presents itself as the heir to both the Epic and aesthetic traditions, situating itself in relationship to both of them.[23] On another level, however, these verses emphasize a ludic dimension. This "ultimate story" is a game as much as it is a ritual celebration. Kṛṣṇa and the cowherd women will dance upon the burning ground of experience, upon birth and death, and thus dissolve the clinging to reward and similar motivations.

As S. Bhattacharya has diagrammed thoroughly, Kṛṣṇa is seen by Vaiṣṇava commentators to be the *ālambana*, "that upon which a *rasa* or sentiment hangs." This position is a full revisioning of the classical *ālaṁkārika* one, which would locate the source of *rasa* in the particulars of style and usage; that is, nonliteral language imbued with deep feeling. The *uddīpana,* or exciting conditions, are the moon, the temperate, autumn nights, the fragrance, and the flowers. The *anubhāva*s, or expressive conditions, will be the gestures of the *gopīs*, and the *sañcāribhāva*s, or accompanying feelings (in this case their sorrow at not being able to meet Kṛṣṇa and their anger when he leaves them).[24] This carefully combined construct of emotions and their causes is said by the *Nāṭyaśāstra*, to produce *rasa*, in sensitive-hearted individuals. However, when Kṛṣṇa is seen as the *ālambana*, the central source of all *rasa* itself, the Bhāgavata-Purāṇa. is rewriting the rules of Sanskrit aesthetics, just as Kṛṣṇa is rewriting conventional, moral codes.

The next verse begins the many plays on the moon in the chapter. The rising moon is compared to the long-awaited sight of a beloved one, setting up the theme of separation and return.[25] This long-awaited *darśana* is, in fact, the climax of a narrative that has continuously reminded us that absence, loss, incompletion, and death are the true signatures of human experience. Thus, true *darśana* or "meeting" must manifest through absence.

As the women of Vraja are attracted by Kṛṣṇa's song, various modes of meeting and separation occur. It is not my purpose here to schematize them. Many ingenious diagrams have been offered by commentators which include categories and even rankings of the various cowherd women, in terms of their response to Kṛṣṇa's flute, or their particular situation within the three *guṇa*s. Here, it will suffice to notice how separation, loss, and even death, figure into the narrative and how the story turns around the fulcrum of desire (*kāma*).

The minds of the women of Vraja are said to be seized by the song which arouses their *kāma*.[26] All worldly activities are suspended, and they leave despite the objection of husbands and relatives:

> Some who were serving food left without serving;
> some nursing their babies set them aside and ran;
> others who were waiting upon their husbands
> suddenly stopped and left; while others who were
> taking their meals set aside their food and departed.
> Some were putting on make-up, others were
> cleansing themselves, others were applying collyrium
> to their eyes, and others were hurriedly putting on
> clothes and ornaments in a confused manner—
> all hastened to Śrī Kṛṣṇa.
>
> (BhP. X.29. 6,7)

Interestingly enough, the text uses the adjective *mohitāḥ* here to describe their condition: *govindāpahṛtātmāno na nyavartanta mohitāḥ* (BhP. X.29.8), "Enchanted, their very selves stolen away by Govinda, they did not turn back." From the beginning, then, these chapters exploit the idea of reversal. *Kāma* and *moha* are present, the same *kāma-moha* that stupefied the *asura*s by the milky ocean. Here, however, there will be exaltation instead of downfall. Beginning with "*yoga-māyā*," there is an intimation that the world of social roles and assigned duties will be left behind, and this intimation crystallizes as the narrative moves into a world of enchantment, of beauty, and of *rasa*, not as an explanatory treatise or allegory, but as a most concentrated experience of tasting *(rasāsvāda)* itself.

At this point Śuka explains that some of the cowherd women cannot manage to leave their homes, or are prevented from leaving by their relatives. Locked into their inner apartments, "merged in their sentiments on Kṛṣṇa," *(kṛṣṇaṁ tad-bhāvanā-yuktāḥ)*, they cast off their mortal bodies and die. Śuka explains their death as follows:

> Their inauspiciousness was washed clean by the intense fire
> of unbearable separation from their most desired one,
> and their auspiciousness was exhausted by the bliss of Kṛṣṇa's
> embrace attained in their meditation upon him. Thinking him to be
> their paramour, although he is the Supreme-Being, they instantly
> dissolved all their karmic bonds and thus cast off their material
> bodies made of the three qualities (*guṇas*).[27]
>
> (BhP. X.29.10–11)

Various commentaries on this verse will discuss the relative merits of these particular cowherd women who seem to "spontaneously combust." Are they higher or lower in "devotional rank" than the *gopīs* who actually "make it to the dance?" Is death by "spontaneous burning" a sign of supreme attainment, an even greater power of devotion than jumping into one's husband's funeral pyre? Leaving devotional issues aside, I would like to point out that the "casting off of the body" here, like the act of *satī,* is most highly valued. In fact, the "death" of Satī, in the Purāṇa, occurs in a somewhat similar manner. In the Bhāgavata's version of the sacrifice of Dakṣa, Satī sits on the ground facing north in yogic posture. Dressed in ceremonial garments, she purifies herself with water, and absorbed in "yogic vision," she moves the vital breaths through her body, meditating upon the fire and air. Thinking of the "nectar of the lotus feet" of her husband, Śiva, who is said to be the "guru of the universe," and seeing all taints of sin destroyed in her body, she immolates herself in a self-generated yogic, fire.[28]

One might note that Satī's "*satī*" differs from the *gopīs* giving up their bodies, in that Satī does so out of anger over the fact that her father, Dakṣa, has insulted her husband Śiva, while the *gopīs* do so out of frustrated yearning. Yet, there are a number of interesting connections between these two. These connections can be made in much the same vein as Śuka citing the death of Śiśupāla in the context of the death of the *gopīs*. In the Bhāgavata version of the myth, Satī specifically states that she is giving up her body due to the shame (*vrīdā*) of having a body produced from a father who has offended the "Great Lord" Śiva.[29] Like the cowherd women, she abandons a conventional relationship for a nonconventional one (Dakṣa's original objection to Śiva is the fact that he does not embrace the norms of brāhmaṇical society). Like the cowherd women, she is ready to let go of family ties, respectability, and even life itself for her worshipful deity (who, in her case happens to be her husband). Both she and the cowherd women who abandon their bodies are given the exalted status of sinlessness before they die. In both cases, death is something of a badge, the offshoot and proof of an exalted, inner process, rather than a sought-after result.

Looking again at the case of the *gopīs*, the agony of their separation is so acute that it removes both good and bad karmic reactions. Its power is such that it propels them into a dimension beyond good or evil. As the ramifications of the Dakṣa story unfold due to the comingling of deep, human, emotional issues with the personhood of a divinity, the Bhāgavata's *rāsa-līlā* episode emphasizes that the power of this deeply erotic situation comes from the cowherd women's particular connection to Bhagavān—*tam eva paramātmānaṁ jāra-buddhyāpi*, "although the Supreme Soul, they thought of him as their paramour."[30]

Śuka continually emphasizes the fundamental incongruity of Kṛṣṇa: the supreme godhead incarnate in the role of a human lover (an incongruity that strongly marks later Vaiṣṇava devotional poems of Sūrdās and others, as Hawley and Bryant have shown). Once again, the divine powers impinge upon the human. Is God the true lover behind the facade of everyone? Is the *gopī*-narrative a variant of the Satī story, in which an incongruous divine lover is the true "husband of the soul," one worth dying for? Is the inherent pathos of desire itself being depicted, in which its frustration is intolerable and in which eternity as its object is a blown-up fantasy compensating for the inevitable loss and nonfulfillment that is the lot of love? In this last sense, one could see the aestheticization and glorification of these beautiful dead women as a most exalted defense against dying. As in *satī,* the belief prevails that one does not really die, but becomes an immortal.

This last possibility must be seriously investigated, for *yoga-māyā* may also be construed as the ultimate energy of denial, a wish-fulfillment scenario of the highest order. "Happy love," De Rougemont ruefully remarks, "has no history."[31] Is the deflection of the basic anguish of a life surrounded by death, for example, the reason for the Bhāgavata's conspicuous and determined exclusion of history, its denigration of society, and its abhorrence of the natural world? Whatever the case may be, in the Purāṇa, the deep anguish of loss remains paramount and must be reckoned with. In fact, it is so intensified that it removes obstacles instead of creating them (a very different picture than de Rougemont's). In this image, which has struck the commentarial as well as religious imagination, death is a welcome by-product of intense longing. For the *gopīs*, devotion is stronger than life, and their death is glorious. They have attained union with the Absolute, even while thinking of him as their lover. One might say that these cowherd women were longing for death itself, but that view would not take the semiotics of the Purāṇa seriously. From the Bhāgavata's viewpoint, what they are longing for is love (Kṛṣṇa), and they get love; not through dying, nor by means of dying, but by means of a desire that mitigates the power of death. As with other "spiritual" deaths in the Purāṇa (Nārada, Dhruva, etc.) their transfer to another state instantaneous.

Of course, the *gopīs*' lover is said to be the Absolute, but what if absolute love turns any lover into the absolute-beloved? This is the *sahajiyā*'s heretical interpretation that sees Kṛṣṇa in every man and the *gopī,* Rādhā, in every woman. Notice, how either way, death and dying pale before the power of intense wanting here, the transfigured desire that moves through the center of desire. Śuka now explains, through the Śiśupāla story, that any emotion directed toward the Supreme leads to eternal oneness with Him, and this is the Bhāgavata's *bhakti* polemic:

intense love for, or focus on, Kṛṣṇa knocks the self off its project of ego-preservation and leads to freedom. Now, previously, the Bhāgavata has stated that intense attachment knocks the self off its center and leads toward regions of darkness. Is the attachment that Bharata felt for the deer in his hermitage fundamentally different than that felt by the *gopīs* for Kṛṣṇa, or are they evolutes or different degrees of one another? The rest of the *rāsa-līlā* moves to construct an answer.

Love as a Battle

Commentators note that the first meeting between Kṛṣṇa and the cowherd women is still within the arena of *kāma*. The conversation in which Kṛṣṇa tells the *gopīs* to return home and in which the *gopīs* respond is filled with the innuendo of games between lovers.[32] Aside from the debated, moral issue of the women leaving their homes and husbands to meet Kṛṣṇa in the night, an essential question of presence and absence is addressed in these passages. The question concerns the exact nature of separation, and whether its "locus" is found through physical proximity or somewhere else.

After a sermon on the contemptibility of adulterous affairs, Kṛṣṇa adds the following argument:

> Deep feeling (*bhāva*) for me comes from hearing, *darśana*, meditation, and glorification, not by physical proximity. So please return home.[33]

The *darśana,* or "vision," of the deity is, here, opposed to physical proximity. This is an underpinning of the idea that the strongest experience of the absolute can occur through separation, and it turns the tables on normative thinking about life and death. The meeting is a fulfillment of desire for the cowherd women. They have practiced austerity, worshiped, and prayed for this moment, and yet, the implication here is that the moment of fulfillment will not yield *āśraya,* ultimate rest. This is Kṛṣṇa's final argument, and its finality supersedes his previous moral sermon.

The cowherd women stammer and cry at the rejection. Although there is to be no meeting, they are persistent and rebut each of Kṛṣṇa's verses with their own teasing and innuendo. In these verses a correlation is made between absence and the practice of *yoga* as "yoking." The cowherd women threaten, "O Friend, with our bodies yoked to the fire born of separation let us go by meditation to the abode of Kṛṣṇa's feet."[34] This is basically what their counterparts who could not leave their rooms did, and it insinuates that death may be preferable to life.

Suicide by *dhyāna* (meditation) not only will lead to union, but separation taken to its ultimate stage of death, will, in this particular case, lead to divine union as well.

The death and dying spoken of here is, of course, much more than a physical event. It is as if the *gopīs* are saying, "if you are going to die, then die the ultimate death." This is not exactly *liebestod* (love-death) since again, death is not an ultimate here. The cowherd women do not will their death; instead it is the result of their deep *bhāva,* or feeling mood. In such a heightened condition there is no possibility of compromise. The conventional world of daylight and language is, itself, the compromise. The cowherd women have given up everything that belongs to that world. They have no other recourse. Their only expressed desire is to become a *dāsī*, a maidservant or slave of Bhagavān, again a position in which there is no compromise.

While the contemporary reader may have difficulty relating to the hyperbole of these passages, they contain the same elements of irrevocable passion and a willingness to choose death over life that are found in the Tristan narrative and its successors. In its all-consuming, burning sense, "passion," or *kāma,* invites death. Indeed, the instinct for self-preservation is criticized by *bhakti* theologians as being present in the desire for liberation, which is why the maidservant relationship to Kṛṣṇa is thought to be superior to that of the accomplished *yogin.*

Śuka interjects epithets reminding us of Kṛṣṇa's position during this encounter. He is called *puruṣabhūṣaṇa*, "jewel or ornament among men" (BhP. X.29.38), and *yogeśvareśvaraḥ,* "master of masters of *yoga*" (BhP. X.29.42). Upon hearing the plea of the *gopīs*, Kṛṣṇa smiles and laughingly agrees to satisfy them although he, himself, is *ātmārāma*—satisfied within himself. Kṛṣṇa again is compared to the moon, "he shone like the deer-marked moon surrounded by stars."[35] The passages here are very much in *kāma*'s province as they speak in detail of Kṛṣṇa's love-sport with the cowherd women and discuss his ability to arouse *kāma* in the women of Vraja.[36] In his commentary on these verses, Vallabha goes so far as to correlate the descriptions here with specific passages in the *Kāma-sūtra.*[37] The frolic is short-lived, however, because as soon as he observes pride in the cowherd women Kṛṣṇa disappears, engendering the great separation:

> *tāsāṁ tat-saubhaga-madaṁ vīkṣya mānaṁ ca keśavaḥ*
> *praśamāya prasādāya tatraivāntaradhīyata*
>
> Seeing the *gopīs* proud and intoxicated by their fortune, the luxuriant-haired Lord, in order to curb their pride and to offer them grace, disappeared right there.
>
> (BhP. X.29.48)

The impending separation here has an apparent twofold purpose. The curbing of pride has been seen before, in the defeat of Bali, for example, and the gift of grace through absence (or through "deprivation" as Mackenzie Brown puts it) has also been part of the narrative pattern, as in the story of Nārada's meditation on Viṣṇu.[38] Here, Śuka connects the two, punctuated by the alliterative connection of the two words, *praśamāya* (for the purpose of ceasing, terminating, extinguishing, as well as curing or healing) and *prasādāya* (for the purpose of grace). These reinforce positive connotations of the disappearance of Kṛṣṇa from the *gopī*'s midst. Scholars such as C. Hospital and C. M. Brown have focused on the idea of "grace through deprivation" here, highlighting the Bhāgavata's polemic of purification through loss and the even stronger notion that the greatest loss is reserved for those who exhibit the greatest devotion.[39] In this sense, one can understand the commentarial tradition's exaltation of the *gopīs* who die before meeting with Kṛṣṇa. For the "grace" of loss, deprivation, and ruin serves to eliminate any other desire than wanting to please God. Such deprivation is indeed the death of all that blocks one's devotion and is welcomed by the likes of Bali and Vṛtra. And thus Kuntī, who has abandoned a son, lost a husband, watched one of her son's (Arjuna) kill the other (Karṇa), and lived through the Epic saga and mass slaughter of the Bhārata war, will ask Kṛṣṇa to remove her "deep ties of affection" for her family members so that her passion love *(rati)* will flow toward him like the Ganges flows toward the sea.[40]

It is the disappearance itself, however, that has attracted most commentarial attention, and for good reason. Of all the words that could have been used for "disappear," *antar-dhā* alone carries corollary suggestions of "merging into" or more literally, to "place within." Dr. Acyut Lal Bhatt, while reading this verse with me in Vṛndāvana, pointed out this verb to me and asked, "Where could he (Kṛṣṇa) have possibly disappeared to?" The text answers, *tatraiva* "right there." He did not go anywhere. Thus, the ensuing separation is not seen uniquely in the context of proximity non-proximity of mundane loss, but rather as a pivotal part of the *līlā*, and Śuka has indicated just how pivotal it is. The idea emphasized in the *Nāṭyaśāstra—na vinā vipralambhena sambhogaḥ puṣṭim aśnute,* "meeting without separation can never achieve fullness"—is turned up an octave, with life and death, loss and reunion each upping the ante, not as an outside agency, but as part of the ongoing intensification of sentiment.[41] The experience of loss becomes the transforming agent, the fire that purifies and intensifies love to its most absolute, the highest degree of self-surrender.

The Great Separation

The disappearance is sudden, and it overwhelms the cowherd women. They begin to exhibit various symptoms and degrees of *viraha*, the first being the imitation of his activities (*tās tā viceṣṭā jagṛhus*) while being fully absorbed (*tad-ātmikāḥ*). In his commentary on these verses Viśvanātha Cakravartī gives the analogy of a man who has just seen a lion in the forest. He is so overwhelmed that he cannot speak and can only imitate with gesture. Speech breaks down. Conventional means are inappropriate to this situation in which the *citta*, the "heart-mind" of the cowherd women, is *ākṣipta*, "overwhelmed," and literally, "cast about."[42] Remember, the separation here is sudden and unexpected, just as the previous "death narratives" have often emphasized its unexpectedness. Furthermore, the disappearance holds a magical quality, as reflected in the word, *"antardhīyata"*; it is a "vanishing act." It may be seen, then, that the first reaction comes from a realm more primal and immediate than thought.

The progression continues. From being "absorbed" in him, the *gopīs* completely identify with him and declare, *asāvaham*, "He is I," or less literally, "It is I who am Kṛṣṇa."[43] This may be seen as the peak of madness, or as a reaction of denial to the undesirable, as in impending death. The actual verse reads as follows:

> The beloved ones imitated the form of their
> beloved in his gait, smiles, glances,
> and words. Those women identified with him,
> and confounded by the play of Kṛṣṇa, declared,
> "I am he."[44]
>
> (BhP. X.30.3)

The progression here is from *pratirūḍha-mūrti*, reflection of form, to identification with another, all in absence. Still, this identification is not satisfying, perhaps reminiscent of the generalized, aesthetic quest of art seeking to capture life embodied in *mūrti,* or form. They must continue to seek.

The seeking now takes on the conventionalized, mad hallucinations of *viraha* in which nature, as a personified landscape, takes an active, participatory role in the separation. The *gopīs* become *unmattakāḥ*, "madwomen," and search through the forest asking various trees, flowers, and animals if they have seen Kṛṣṇa. On the one hand, such behavior is symptomatic of madness, but it is also symptomatic of an animated, inner world where subject and object begin to coalesce. The Bhāgavata is aware of this as it mentions the paradox of the cowherd women seeking for that which is everywhere.[45] Finally, agitated and perplexed from searching, the madwomen again act out the various *līlā*s of Bhagavān. Although, once again, this activity is described by the words *tad-ātmikāḥ*, "fully absorbed in him," commentators like Vallabha point out that in these verses they imitate as opposed to identify and are thus on a lower level.

The *gopīs* imitate the *līlā*s through memory, and their expression of love in separation includes a summary of all the *līlā*s (hardly translatable by the word "game," or "pastime") creating a paradigm for the later practice of *rāgānuga-bhakti*, or spontaneous, devotional remembrance.[46] Ultimately, they come upon Kṛṣṇa's footprints in the forest and see them mixed with those of another women.[47] This marks the end of the "hallucinatory mode" and the return to external perception.

Now, the external search begins, mixed with further fantasy ignited by the sight of two pairs of footprints instead of one. The jealousy expressed here can be seen as being corollary to the experience of loss. The entire dynamic of jealousy presupposes an absence, someone being separated from one's desire. The attainment of that desire by another reminds one of this and amplifies one's lack of fulfillment, leading to emotion, fantasy, or action. This situation has been built into just about every form of love and loss in the Purāṇa. Perhaps this is to be expected, as expected as the love triangle of the "family romance," or as expected as the difference between what we want and what we have, the difference which led Nietzsche to declare humans to be "the sick animal."[48] Nevertheless, the jealousy in this tract is also subsumed into the *līlā*. It is "part of the game," so to speak, and one can only wonder again to what degree the ludic dimension serves to defang real threats of loss. By making the threat of loss into a game, into a great game, into an art form, if you will, it can perhaps be dealt with somewhat more comfortably. However, the nagging question remains about the "illusionism" of the aesthetic dimension (illusionist in D. W. Winnicott's sense of the word in which play and art are seen as useful or positive forms of fantasy) transposing itself onto a theological one. It is no wonder, then, that the "master-narrator," Śuka, offers a full commentary on this scene.

At this point, then, Śuka again interjects with a verse that has caused much scholarly reaction:

> *reme tayā cātma-rata ātmārāmo'py akhaṇḍitaḥ*
> *kāminām darśayan dainyaṁ strīṇāṁ caiva durātmatām*
>
> He, who takes pleasure in his *self*, took pleasure
> with her although he is ever-satisfied and whole,
> showing the miserable state of lustful men
> and the baseness of women.
>
> (BhP. X.30.34)

This verse mirrors the opening of the scene, *bhagavān api* (even Bhagavān). Even though he is satisfied, he takes pleasure in another, yet the pleasure of Bhagavān is declared to be different than that of ordinary men and women. Śuka contends that the activity here is not coming from lack or absence, and thus, the Bhāgavata insists that its own form of erotica is beyond personal desire.[49]

It can be argued that we are witnessing a most outrageous form of sublimation: "abandon your own sexuality which is base and miserable and let God do it. God is 'doing it' in fact to show you just how miserable you are." Moreover, God "doing it" takes all the fear and responsibility of encounter with the other out of human hands. There can be no mistakes or "slip-ups," since the total surrender called for includes giving up the very energy of masculinity which would initiate erotic "action." This is not only the case in Bhāgavatism, where the devotee takes on a female persona, but in Śākta traditions as well, where the devotee, more often than not, becomes a child of the Mother. What seems to be missing in almost every instance of transcendental metaphor is the "integral masculine." How is it that in so idealistic a representation of patriarchy, the male position is abdicated? Kṛṣṇa is said, by the commentarial tradition, to be the only male, while the devotional position is said to be female, not an aggressive or dangerous female, nor even an auspicious fertile female who will renew the earth (to use Marglin's terms), but a maidservant.[50] This verse, often traditionally read as a description of the impending defeat of *kāma*, may also be a narrative reflection of the sublimation process. The collective renunciation of the dominant male position serves to maintain hierarchy, a hierarchy that remains so emphasized in the culture that (as Vasudha Narayanan notes), there is no generic greeting between equals in traditional Indian languages.[51] Does the defeat of *kāma* imply the subjugated resignation of desire, or is this a different sort of transformation? The answer to this question unfolds in the rest of the story.

The *gopīs* continue to envision Kṛṣṇa and his consort. In the vision, it is the consort who believes she has control and is "the best of all women." The dialogue becomes suggestive here as the consort in the vision declares that she can no longer move and that he should "take her wherever his mind goes,"[52] in other words wherever he wishes. Kṛṣṇa invites the woman, the embodiment of *kāma,* to climb on his shoulder, and just when she thinks he has yielded, he disappears. This sequence is often read as the final defeat of *kāma*, for once Kṛṣṇa is gone the desiring mood suddenly changes as the woman falls into "burning remorse." Described anonymously by the phrase, *anayārādhito nūnaṁ bhagavān*," "Bhagavān indeed worshiped by another," this favorite woman is thought by the Caitanya school, through their reading of *ārādhita*, to be a code name for the consort Rādhā.[53] Whoever she may be, she now finds herself alone in the forest with the object of her desire and is unable to possess him. Desire has played its hand, anointing one of the cowherd women in the role of "most intimate" and placing her "on top" (riding on Kṛṣṇa's shoulder). Within this playful energy of *līlā,* the deep frustration of human desire is explored. The urgings of desire bring one to a point of satisfaction that quickly transforms into suffering. It is what happens, next, however, that opens a new and different vision of the question.

At this point, the cowherd women catch up to the lone consort, and their mood changes from jealousy and fantasy to collective lamentation. *Kāma* generally demands privacy, but here separateness and rivalry are abandoned, perhaps an indication that we are moving into a genuinely different arena. The *gopīs* all follow the moon, but cannot penetrate the darkness of the forest and so return to the river bank together meditating on and singing about their beloved:

> Their minds filled with him, speaking of him,
> acting out his gestures, absorbed in him,
> singing about his qualities, they did not
> remember their own homes.[54]

In deep *viraha,* in deep loss, there is another kind of dying, the complete dying to the conventional self-absorbed posture. The intense emotionality of the cowherd women is beyond any form of personal calculation, and their lamentation takes on an exalted status as the singing cowherd women wait for his arrival. It is expressed in this verse through progressive meditations—speaking, acting, absorption—on Kṛṣṇa coupled with *nātmāgārāṇī sasmaruḥ,* forgetting their own homes. The exact sequence delineated is, *manaska* (mind), *ālāpa* (speech), *viceṣṭā* (action), and finally *ātmikā* (absorption of the self). This "dying to the world" is correlative to the desire for the mysterious other and is read by commentators as the ultimate sign of devotional love. To "forget your own home," is after all, no small feat. To be freed from any sense of belonging is so fearful to the conditioned being, that it is often thought of as synonymous with madness. Or else, it is viewed guardedly, often with a disbelieving cynicism that would see the merging into an absent, or absolute other as a projection, created to escape an untenable home situation. There is, in fact, the somewhat obliquely related precedent in the Indian cultural tradition of Rāma living with a statue of Sītā as opposed to her physical person. It can be argued however, that this is done to insure stability in his realm since Rāma's focus is on *rāja-dharma*, "the political-social arena." The cowherd women, however, have completely abandoned this area of life. According to Śuka and the commentarial traditions, their abandonment of the world and forgetting of their homes is supremely exalted. Indeed, their gestures and actions lead them further and further away from the quotidian in any form and into a world informed by deep longing and enacted through gesture and song.

The Bhāgavata appears in history long before the ascent of romantic love to a preeminent position in human society, whether it be expressed through the troubadours of the twelfth century or the musical television videos of the twentieth. The Bhāgavata employs romance and seduction as metaphors and as models; this fact makes its point even more emphatic: passion and love are the most powerful modalities of human experience. But are passion and love identical, opposites (sexual love founded on spiritual hate as Blake suggested), or different degrees of the same energy? What is the relationship between Kṛṣṇa and Kāma?

Songs of the Cowherd Women

The "*gopī-gītā*," the songs of the *gopīs* that follow, are the most celebrated and repeated passages of the *Rāsapañcādhyāyī* and also the most aesthetically self-conscious. The first and seventh syllables of these verses begin with the same consonants as do the second syllables of each *pāda,* or quadrant, of one verse.[55] Thus, the cowherd women explain that "for your sake we maintain our lives." The *gopīs* do not die of separation, but survive by listening to *hari kathā*. The subject matter of the songs spans the entire spectrum of feeling and is not uniquely centered around the *gopīs*' "sensual experience" of Kṛṣṇa, as some contend.[56]

The expression of the experience of separation and loss can be rather perplexing. While previously the cowherd women have asked Kṛṣṇa to place his hands on their burning breasts, they now demand that his lotus-feet be placed on their breasts in order to sever *kāma* from their hearts.[57] Kāma is given the epithet *hṛcchaya*, "the one who lies in the heart." In the context of the verse, in which Kṛṣṇa's feet destroy the sins of surrendered souls, the cowherd women are asking for the death of *kāma*, a death which can only be located in Kṛṣṇa's ultimate satisfaction.[58]

This lends a fascinating perspective on the death of mortal life as opposed to the death of desire. From the Bhāgavata's viewpoint, literal death is not death at all, but is part of the dualistic revolutions of *saṁsāra*. The "authentic death," if you will, is the ending of desire, or rather its transformation, and there is a major difference between the two. The appeal of the Bhāgavata over conventional Buddhist or Advaitic discourse on the subject is also its problematic: the existence of and need for a personal God, a holy or wholly other, through whom desire is transfigured into another dimension. The problematic, of course, is the inherent absolutism involved, the privileging of a higher world above this one. By "leaving their own homes" are the cowherd women not leaving an unredeemed world as well?

The cowherd women also ask for their life to be revived, remarking that *hari-kathā* is the "life for those afflicted with *tapas*,"[59] the burning fire of both desire and loss. The cowherd women constantly shift their focus between physical and metaphysical. They return to memories of Kṛṣṇa's smile and loving glances while calling him a *kuhaka*, a deceiver, the very same word used in the first verse of the Purāṇa where the absolute is described as being *nirasta-kuhaka*, completely free from deceit.[60] Here is another sign of inversion. *Kāma* becomes something other than *kāma*, as does deceit and trickery, a sort of negative capability, or perhaps more accurately a homeopathic sensibility, in which the disease is somehow the cure: it takes fire to put out fire. In this extreme condition the *gopīs* abandon all shame and again implore Kṛṣṇa to love them:

> O Hero, please spread the nectar of your lips among us.
> That nectar by which men forget other passions increases
> our longing and destroys our sorrow beautifully kissed
> by your flute as it produces tones.[61]

The next verse offers the image of a moment in time appearing like a millennium to the cowherd women. This image is frequently employed in Sanskrit drama, but *bhakti* commentators like Jīvā Gosvāmī see it as indicating the most elevated form of spiritualized emotion, known as *mahābhāva*, in which the intensity of feeling completely obliterates time and space, and hence, life and death. The *gopīs* go further, however, declaring that the creator of the eyes has erred, since blinking eyelids hinder their contemplation of Kṛṣṇa's face. The eye is paired with the ultimate object of vision, and it is this ultimate nature of Bhagavān which is said to transform the mundane into the sublime.[62] The rest of the chapter continues to pair images of "above" (Kṛṣṇa as *acyuta,* or infallible) with "below," (Kṛṣṇa as a *kitava,* or cheater), of "rising desire" (*hṛc-chayodaya*, literally "rise of what lies in the heart") with "the slaying of desire that breaks the heart" (*hṛd-rujāṁ yan niṣūdanam*).[63]

The last verse of the songs mirrors the plea in the earlier part of the narrative. Here, however, after asking for relief, the *gopīs* show more concern for the state of Kṛṣṇa's feet than for the burning of their breasts. This indicates the decisive transformation of self-centered desire, and this is where the Bhāgavata distinguishes between wanting and caring. One may argue that there is still a deep double-bind here. How can wanting transform into a purified caring when wanting to care is still wanting? This is where separation and loss come into play. The Bhāgavata insists that it is by grace instilled through the fire of loss and the pain of being abandoned that the clinging ego is transformed. Now, and only now, is true meeting possible.

The Return

When Kṛṣṇa reappears, he is described with an epithet related to Kāma, *manmatha-manmathaḥ*, literally, "the bewilderer or agitator of the mind of he who bewilders the mind," or the "Cupid of Cupids."[64] This is the first time such an epithet is used in these chapters and suggests that Kṛṣṇa has become the new cupid.

Notice that, once again, Kṛṣṇa does not appear from outside but becomes manifest *(āvir+√bhū)* or reappears from among them. The correlation between extreme separation and death continues in a decidedly extra-mundane context when their eyes are described as blooming like flowers and their inanimate bodies are said to be standing again with their life-breath returned as at the end of a creation cycle.[65] Even in this meeting sequence, *tapas* is mentioned twice, as the burning fever of separation lingers on before disappearing.[66]

Kṛṣṇa's subsequent discourse on love is one way in which the text reflects upon the experience of loss. While explaining various categories of love and reciprocity, Kṛṣṇa declares that he does not respond to living beings right away in order to intensify their love:

> Even when living beings worship me, O friends,
> in order to induce their following, I do not respond.
> In the same way a poor man who has gained
> wealth and lost it is so fixated upon the object
> of (his) thoughts that he does know anything else.[67]

This verse becomes puzzling upon close examination. The obvious association, noted by many commentaries, would be from the *Gītā* (IV.11), "As they seek refuge in me, I respond to them."[68] In characteristic fashion, the tenth book, inverts this equation. Here, Bhagavān does not reciprocate human desire. Rather, he provokes separation, loss, and even ruin "in order to induce them to follow him." He has orchestrated the separation for this purpose and explains that, while hidden, he was actually reciprocating. One may reasonably argue here that such "reciprocation" appears to be rather sadistic at times, and that going to the extreme of denying all of one's relations and even destroying one's life to love God is not love at all, but an exaggerated form of divinely coated slavery (with slavery to a husband and a social order being displaced with slavery to God). But the Bhāgavata-Purāṇa does not trade in reason. I do believe, however, that the issues of "love" and "devotion" deserve extended critical attention. Are love and devotion the same thing? Can there be love without mutuality and equality?

When one does consider the possible social contexts of these passages, it is not difficult to unearth reasons for the development of such divine ideals which have nothing to do with devotion. A love-struck maidservant will not bother to challenge an unjust or oppressive social order, nor will she quibble about individual rights; a love-struck maidservant will preserve religious hierarchies, and as aesthetically minded as the Bhāgavata-Purāṇa may be, it does maintain hierarchy: Kṛṣṇa is always in the center and, his actions are always justified. In fact, when Parīkṣit questions Śuka about the righteousness of Kṛṣṇa's actions, Śuka immediately counters with the response that the status of the "powerful controllers" or "gods" (*īśvarāṇām*) can never be harmed by apparent transgressions of *dharma*.[69] This position is never questioned, and the ancillary position of the cowherd women is taken for granted. Moreover, by relegating the historical world to a fantasy *(māyā)* the cowherd women are able to retreat into their own fantasy. The social function of the *rāsa-līlā* may then be to offer a safe, fantasy outlet for the earthly passions of women who have literally been cooped up in their homes and cannot get out. Or they may perhaps provide religiously sanctioned fantasy images for "cooped up" men, who have little or no erotic access to women. And while social orders, individual rights, and collective hierarchies all seem to fade in the face of death, and although reason can offer no satisfaction in the face of such a finality, the fact remains that while Kṛṣṇa and the *gopīs* sing and dance, other people run the world. In many ways, the cowherd women serve as prototypes of the female saint who rejects earthly marriage (like Āṇṭāḷ and Mira), adored and glorified by mothers who would nevertheless be horrified if their daughters wanted to follow such a path of divine deprivation.

The Kṛṣṇa of the Bhāgavata, in any case, insists that God withholds reciprocation in order to strengthen the love of the devotee, claiming a parallel with the poor man who obtains a treasure, loses it, and then has no thought other than regaining it.[70] Perhaps one perspective need not cancel out the other, but whether or not there may be a causal relationship between the two is a disturbing question indeed.

At this final point, however, while extolling the *gopī's* love, Bhagavān, himself, is at a loss:

> Even in a lifetime of the gods, I could not
> repay my debt to you who are faultless.
> Loving me, you have severed the difficult chains
> of your homes. May your reward be your own
> goodness.[71]

Here, the mood of the cowherd women overcomes Kṛṣṇa. Their love is so strong that he cannot fully reciprocate. The concept of a reward is no longer applicable. Thus, Kṛṣṇa, himself, is "defeated" by the power of devotion; he cannot reciprocate fully, and one is left with the transforming power of dying to one's self as its own glory.

The dynamic of this transforming power focuses on the cowherd women leaving their homes and all that "home" signifies. By making the *gopīs* not only women but wives and mothers, the Bhāgavata radically moves beyond the gripping power of convention and respectability. By depicting the cowherd women as having abandoned all shame, the texts seems to cast aside traditionally valued female qualities, such as modesty and self-restraint. But respectability is maintained through the focus on the *yoga-māyā* aspect of the *līlā,* on the theological insistence that it takes place out of time and out of mind. Although the *gopīs* have committed adultery and Kṛṣṇa is a seducer and a deceiver, their relationship is not envisioned as a mere surrender to passion. It is rather understood by the devotional tradition as a decisive movement away from human nature (in terms of sexuality), from social convention, and even from the solace of the known.

The woman who was previously described as the "gateway to hell" is here an exalted paramour. Her love, instead of dragging one down into the "dark well" of household existence, continues the metaphor of breaking free of the home. Previously, in the tradition, leaving home and/or exile from home has been a requisite to gaining a higher vision, as well as a socially disruptive factor leading to death. In this case, the "exile" is actively encouraged. One should get away from "the difficult chains" of one's home. The separation of Rāma, one could say, who never extricates himself from the social order nor from the matrix of the feminine, is not complete. By inverting the script and having women instead of men leave their home, the Bhāgavata glorifies the most extreme spurning of social convention. What could be worse for society than a woman, who is not kidnaped like Sītā, but who leaves home of her own accord (and in a sexual frenzy to boot)? The fact that the *gopīs* are seduced and goaded on by God himself legitimizes all of this and perhaps applies a strong counterbalance to a confining social order. The fact that the cowherd women are never represented as women, that is, as real individuals, may encourage the reading of this section as an escapist fantasy. On the other hand, one could understand this passage to be declaring that, when the female principle frees itself from entrapment by following the divine call of the flute (the higher imaginative capacity) no matter what the cost, then and only then is freedom found. This may be a noble ideal, but one that still leaves the world to its own fate.

The Bhāgavata, in any case, directs its attention to the disruptive process from the very beginning. Parīkṣit, as the kingly man, as the remaining representative of the Pāṇḍu dynasty, as the emblem of the ego, has everything to lose by being cursed to die. The king, then, must become a *gopī*. Rather than interpreting this literally, as theologians have done, by saying that the soul is female and God is male, I would offer the reading that the soul must turn to its feeling function in order to overcome its "kingly dilemma." In later Vaiṣṇava narratives, it will be said that when Śiva wants to join in the *rāsa*-dance he is told that he must become a *gopī* in order to participate, and indeed "following in the footsteps of the *gopīs*" will become the major *sādhana,* or spiritual practice, in some Vaiṣṇava communities. Whatever, this transformation may entail, and on whatever level one views the "feminization of *bhakti,*" it does include the valuing of the potential for feeling and of the feminine in general, and it is seen as necessary to create the *rāsa-maṇḍala*, the circle dance that transcends time.

The *Rāsa* Dance

The image of the dance itself is one of fulfillment. The text introduces the dance through Śuka's declaration that the cowherd women abandoned their burning distress born of loss, their hopes now fulfilled through his limbs.[72] Then and there (*tatra*) the dance begins, referred to as *rāsa-krīḍā*, the play of Govinda with the "faithful" and "loving" women. All the worldly impediments of desire have been done away with, which leads to the mutuality of play.

The dance celebration commences with a circle of decorated *gopīs*, as Kṛṣṇa, the master of *yoga*, appears between each one of them. It should be noted here that the point of focus is the dance, not Kṛṣṇa. The women here, who were unadorned during their experience of *viraha*, are richly dressed (*maṇḍitāḥ*). We are dealing with an archetypal circle image here, an aesthetic image of fulfillment and ornamentation, with Kṛṣṇa appearing as "an emerald amidst golden ornaments."[73] To complete the aesthetic image, an audience is also necessary, and the celestials are happy to fulfill this role:

> At that time, the sky was filled with
> hundreds of aerial cars of the celestials
> and their consorts who were overwhelmed
> with eager longing.
>
> (BhP. X.33.3)

Then comes pure aesthetic descriptions where sight and sound merge:

> By the steps of their feet, the gestures of their hands,
> their smiling, and playful movements of their eyebrows,
> with their bending waists, swaying breasts and clothes, and
> earrings rolling on their cheeks, the consorts of Kṛṣṇa,
> who had perspiring faces and loosened braids of hair and
> girdles, sang of him, shining like lightning in a circle
> of clouds.[74]
>
> (BhP. X.33.7)

Just as the lightning cannot live without the cloud, the *gopīs*, whether in union or separation, cannot live without Kṛṣṇa because they are his *śakti* (his own energy). One can conceive of this as a reversal of the Sāṅkhya image in which the male *puruṣa* is bewildered by the dance of the female *prakṛti* and thus becomes entangled. Here, the female *śakti* is enthralled by the dance of the male *śaktimān* and fully participates in it, a reversal of the "Mohinī equation" discussed previously, where the male god Śiva chases the female form. Indeed, entrapment becomes transformed into play as Kṛṣṇa is said to enjoy love with the beautiful women of Vraja just as a child plays with his own reflection.[75] The *śakti-śaktimān* relationship is thus described in terms of an image and its reflection, they are both one and many, intertwined and inseparable. Therefore, the image of a dance, along with all of its enjoyments, becomes extraordinarily effective as the "pure-aesthetic" is exalted. Indeed, the singing of the cowherd women is said to pervade the universe.[76]

As mentioned before, however, "pure aesthetic images" may also be suspect, for the image remains just that, an image, wholly removed from mundane concerns. And, it could be argued that the cowherd women remain as images, perpetuating a sense of voyeuristic, male enjoyment. Whether the *gopīs* are eternally perfected beings (as some commentators contend) or not, they are never human. Their voice is collective and the descriptions of them are primarily physical: they are "young women of Vraja," "lovers," "ladies with beautiful eyes," "beautiful-waisted ones," "slender," "jewel-like women," and of course "maidservants." The Bhāgavata never gives them names or personalities. They are literally aesthetic ornaments, adorned around Kṛṣṇa for the viewing pleasure of a celestial audience. And they are quite elite ornaments as well: there are only a few *gopīs*, everyone else is in the supporting cast. Human beings, who will grow old and die, have little place in this circle, as it brilliantly shines from above.

After dancing, a fatigued Kṛṣṇa enters the water "like the lord of elephants along with his female consorts having broken through the dam" (BhP. X.33.22). The word *setuḥ* can mean a dam, as in a paddy field where elephants might frolic, or a formal limitation or injunction. The suggestion of course is that all limits have now been broken.

The *līlā* ends and the *siddhānta,* or instruction, begins with the following verse:

> In this way, he whose desire is true and
> whose passion is self-contained, to whom
> the bevy of passionate women were so deeply
> attached, enjoyed those moonlit nights,
> which are the basis of *rasa* for the
> narratives and poetry of autumn.[77]

Śuka invokes the *aiśvarya*, or majestic aspect of Bhagavān, speaking of him as *satyakāma*, an expression which Śrīdhara glosses as *icchāśakti*, "one who has total free will." The text points out the incongruity between Kṛṣṇa's position of extreme majesty and the role in which the *gopīs* see him, as their lover, *kānta,* and not as a god. Just as love can transform one out of the kingly role, it can transform a monarch-divinity into a lover.

The instruction and metaphysical explanations of Bhagavān's seeming transgressions continue. There is no point in going into them here except to note how fully the text is aware of its own transgressive content.[78] The value of these explanations lies in their suggestion that the *rāsa-līlā* itself is magical and belongs to the realm of *yoga-māyā*. Therefore, Śuka ends his *siddhānta* by stating, *brahma-rātra upāvṛtte*, which can indicate either a particular hour of the night—the dawn when the *gopīs* would have to return to their homes—or else an entire night of Brahmā, eons of time. What we are dealing with here is not simply an altered time-space frame, but one that is superimposed upon conventional time and space. This has been the magical meeting that at once took place (for Kṛṣṇa and the cowherd women under the energy of *yoga-māyā*) and did not take place (for the husbands of the cowherd women who are described as being "bewildered by his (Kṛṣṇa's) *māyā*" into thinking that their wives spent the whole night by their sides). Therefore, although there was a meeting, a separation, and a final meeting, the end result is still ambiguous. However, in the wider context of the narrative the purported end result is made clear in the final *phala-śruti* verse which declares that one who hears this account with faith obtains *bhakti* and quickly throws off *kāma*, the "disease of the heart" (*hṛd-rogam*).[79]

The Place of *Viraha* in the *Rāsa-līlā*

Upon first consideration, we may be satisfied to see the separation sequence here as one of purification, and as a necessary aspect of the meeting. Whether faced with imminent loss or imminent death, a reevaluation of cherished desires is often in order. One has to wonder, however, about the placement of these chapters. While generally viewed as the culmination of the Bhāgavata, these chapters do not end the work in either a structural or narrative sense. Rather, they are bound by the life-cycle narrative of the Kṛṣṇa *līlā*. This particular *līlā* still belongs to his youth, and there are many more worlds to conquer. Perhaps, and this may be one reason for the Purāṇa's popularity, they represent that brief but magical moment of awakening to the romantic other before social conventions assume their power. This moment is duly glorified in the narrative.

In the text itself, however, there is a curious epilogue to these chapters. In chapter thirty-five, just one chapter after the end of the dance, we again find the *gopīs* singing in separation. This time, however, their singing takes place in broad daylight with no *yoga-māyā*. Kṛṣṇa has returned to "work," his caste-appointed work of tending the cows, and the cowherd women have returned to the state of separateness and duality, as well as to the socioeconomic appointed drudgery that will rule their mortal existence. What was the dance of the night world, the sudden disappearance and the visionary union of the *rāsa-līlā*? What was the energy of *yoga-māyā* then? Clearly it was not of the daytime world, the world of convention where the basic condition is one of separation and inevitable death. Perhaps the *rāsa-līlā* does portray a state that one can only wish for, or a truly divine state that can only be approximated by the dance of lovers. One wonders if this state is one of transcendent ecstasy, mytho-poetic fantasy, or a combination of both. What is the relationship of the night to the day, of unabashed free expression to strict forms of social convention, of timeless flight to the constant wearing-down process of mortal existence? The dance, as emblematic of union, appears in a glorious, visionary dream, and has moved poets, theologians, and devotees to dizzying heights of contemplation. Surely, there is one thing that is clear and certain: when the *līlā* ends, the text again turns back to separation as the basic condition of the world we know and live in.

7

FINAL PARTINGS

"All men are defeated, the poet only in a grander way."

—attributed to Ezra Pound

Separation and union manifest not only as different sensibilities of loving, but also as different poses in the face of dying. Union corresponds to the "great peace which passeth all understanding," *śānta-rasa*. William James might have seen its workings as a hallmark of the "healthy soul" sheltered in "the pure calm of infinity."[1] (According to de Rougemont, ". . . if the soul is able to achieve union with God, then the soul's love of God is a happy one").[2]

The metaphor of union, however, also mimics death, or at least certain images of death, appearing as stasis and ultimate finality as it draws one away from the realm of human experience. It may also appear as the *āśrayam*, the final and ultimate refuge, the resting place from the throes of desire and *suffering*. Advaitic and other monistic schools of spiritual thought and practice, therefore, have offered various "metaphors of dying" for realization of the Supreme. From the *Chāndogya Upaniṣad's* melting of salt in water, to descriptions of heroes and *yogins* divesting themselves of the various *koṣas*, or external sheaths, to practices of *laya-yoga* (the *yoga* of dissolution), dying is often envisioned as a movement toward unification on a greater plane of existence.

Separation, on the other hand, begets activity, frustration, longing, and painful discontinuity. In this sense, it acts as a form of "soul-making" different from union. The intensity of love in this form heightens through repeated impediments, and finalities of any sort would not serve its design. Hence, meetings tend to occur in concealment (as Bharata notes in the *Nāṭyaśāstra*), in the other-worldly realm, or not at all.[3]

The literary and aesthetic sensibility aligns itself with meeting in the romantic and with separation in the tragic. In either instance, the action of "plot" serves as a "prolonging device," postponing the moment of its own dissolution. Endings, in fact, are rarely satisfying or ultimate. Thus, variants and multirecensions abound in Indian literature.

In the Bhāgavata, however, one can make the argument that union and separation cannot exist without one another, despite arguments made for each as ultimate reality in different areas of the text. Advaitic readings, for example, refuse to consider separation as substantial in any ultimate sense, and turn their back on worldly form and its inevitable tragedy. Dvaitic readings, in their various forms, refuse the inconceivable extinguishing of difference between self and other, and seek their own creative resolutions.

The Bhāgavata, as we have seen, continually discourses on the very real anguish of the dualistic experience, while rationalizing it through its purgative possibilities, or by suggesting that the "fatal desire for mystical union" can be surpassed through another form of illumination.[4] Just what this illumination might be is depicted in a variety of different ways, but usually involves the hint of an eternal relationship with a "wholly other" (to use Otto's term).

Moreover, befitting its nature as a collection of stories, the Bhāgavata represents illumination or beatitude through its tableaus of devotion and processions of paradigmatic characters. In a narrative, "truth" or "meaning" cannot be directly disclosed. That would place it in the province of philosophy, mathematics, or science. Story, on the other hand, fuels itself with the proposition that truth cannot be signified as much as it may be embodied. In advaitic understanding, there can be no ultimate body, just pure essence of principle. In narrative traditions, however, embodiment and form are crucial and even ultimate.

What is fascinating about the Purāṇic project, here, is its pastiche-like nature which oscillates between didactic-philosophical and narrative modes. The Bhāgavata's stories do not follow one another in sequential fashion, but are interspersed between teachings on cosmology and the nature of reality. On the other hand, the *kṛṣṇa-carita* of the Purāṇa does respect the sequential stages of Kṛṣṇa's childhood, boyhood, youth, and beyond, although the narrative digresses, leaps forward, and reflects backward and even "sideways" on occasion. In a way, a Purāṇa is itself a microcosmic universe: anything that exists is represented, and singular perspectives are etched against an overwhelmingly pluralistic super-structure.

The Continuation of the Story

After the *rāsa* dance, the *gopīs* pass their days following Kṛṣṇa in thought as they remember "his deeds," sing about his activities, and engage in an extended meditation upon their beloved's attributes and exploits.[5] The daytime-world has returned, but through *hari-smaraṇa*, the practice of divine remembrance, the fire of separation continues to fuel both the hope and memory of meeting. In the text, Kṛṣṇa and his brother Balarāma even return to dance and enjoy with the *gopīs* one more time. Thus, the play of union and separation, *sambhoga* and *vipralambha*, continues. Final separation on the physical-social level, however, is heralded by the intrusive arrival in Vṛndāvana of Kṛṣṇa's uncle Akrūra, threatening the idyllic nature of these playful games.

Akrūra: Messenger of Separation

Akrūra's arrival is precipitated by fate. He is sent by Kaṁsa, Kṛṣṇa's evil uncle, to bring Kṛṣṇa back to Mathurā, where the king has plans to kill him. Kaṁsa, like Sophocles' Laius, is bent on avoiding his own fate. A prophecy has stated that the eighth son of Devakī (Kṛṣṇa) will kill him. Here, the Bhāgavata contrasts two very different responses toward impending death by focusing on the behavior of the two kings. Kaṁsa rails against fate and death, seeking to destroy it before it destroys him. He ardently resists the demise of his earthly kingdom, and is thus dragged down. Parīkṣit, on the other hand, accepts his situation. He even hastens the process by divesting himself of his kingdom and its accoutrements in order to hear *hari kathā*, much as the *gopīs* abandon their homes and families to meet Kṛṣṇa in the forest.

Throughout the Bhāgavata, in fact, one could say that character is revealed by the way one meets loss. The true heroes of the Purāṇa—Nārada, Bali, Prahlāda, Parīkṣit, and others—are all faced with stark situations of separation from the known, and they respond with acceptance and trust (as opposed to the fear and recoil of Kaṁsa).

Akrūra, although employed by Kaṁsa, is a devotee of Kṛṣṇa as well as a trusted relative. While on the way to Vṛndāvana, he muses upon his coming good fortune of having the *darśana* of the Lord, citing Kṛṣṇa as "one who has dispelled the confusion of difference and darkness through his shining splendor" (a description that is quite ironic considering the circumstances that are about to occur). Here we have the reversal of a long-standing messenger theme in South Asian literary traditions. The *dūta*, or messenger, like Hanumān in the *Rāmāyaṇa* of Vālmīki, or various *gopīs* in later versions of the *kṛṣṇa-carita*, usually brings separated parties together. Here, the messenger is coming, not to engage separate parties in a possible reconciliation, but to disrupt an ongoing union. It is this disruption that makes the Bhāgavata-Purāṇa what it is: a work glorifying the mood of *viraha* as the ultimate attainment of the living being.

The cowherd women are extremely distressed when they learn that Akrūra has come to take Kṛṣṇa away, and they manifest strong symptoms of separation. The text begins with physical symptoms—burning hearts, sighing, and turning pale[6]—and then moves into terminology reminiscent of the *Yoga-sūtra*s as it describes the state of the *gopīs*:

> *anyāś ca tad-anudhyāna nivṛttāśeṣa-vṛttayaḥ*
> *nābhyajānann imaṁ lokam ātma-lokaṁ gatā iva*
>
> And for others, deeply meditating on him, all the sensory functions were turned inward. They were oblivious to this world, as if they had gone to the world of the *self*.
>
> (BhP. X.39.15)

In the above verse, the *gopīs* are equated with *yoga* practitioners who strive to halt all fluctuations of thought as described by Patañjali (*yogaś citta-vṛtti-nirodhaḥ*).[7] The power of their mood is likewise equated with the purifying power of *yoga*; both bring the mind to a one-pointed focus. The cowherd women, however, do not seek to escape the world or to attain any superior state. Rather, they are pulled by their anguish and their sense of impending absence, an anguish born of their striking experience of Kṛṣṇa's beauty.

It is Kṛṣṇa who embodies the beautiful. He has been presented as the ultimate aesthetic principle, the repository of all *rasa*. This idea corresponds to one of the suggested etymological derivations of the word *kṛṣṇa*, from the root kṛṣ, to "draw" or "drag" like a plow and hence to attract.[8] The minds of the *gopīs* are dragged to one-pointedness by their attraction to a beauty that is departing. Their situation mirrors that of Nārada's in the first *skandha*, in which he loses the vision of Viṣṇu and spends the rest of his life looking for it.

The *gopīs'* situation might also be said to reflect the loss of an idyllic state of youth. Kṛṣṇa's life with the *gopīs* in Vṛndāvana has been one of sport and frolic. Moreover, following Kurtz's analysis here, the *gopīs* (who are all older than Kṛṣṇa), along with Yaśodā and possibly others, may be evocative of the many comforting maternal elements present in the life of a Hindu child. There comes a moment of separation, however (as Carstairs, Kakar, and Roland discuss extensively), when the male child is taken from this maternal enclave and abruptly brought into the male socialization process. While this occurrence is usually said to take place at an earlier age (from five to eight), there is a similar sense of irrevocability here. It is almost as if the *gopīs* intuitively sense that Kṛṣṇa will never return, and that the idyllic state they have enjoyed, monumentalized though it may be through the *rāsa-līlā*, will be gone forever.

Frightened by the impending separation, the cowherd women gather together and decry providence. They inveigh against the "arranger of the world," for callously bringing people together and then pulling them apart, an image that the Bhāgavata employs in a variety of situations. In Kṛṣṇa's teaching to Uddhava, for example, companionship and connection with one's children, wives, and relatives are compared to a momentary meeting of travelers at a roadside source of drinking water. With the change of body at death, they are said to "part company like a dream that disappears with sleep."[9] Kṛṣṇa's teaching is meant to engender dispassion in Uddhava. The *gopīs*, who are considered to be the most exalted devotees, however, are anything but dispassionate:

> O Providence, you have no mercy. Having
> brought people together through friendship
> and love, you senselessly separate them while
> their aims are still unfulfilled. Your play
> is just like that of a whimsical child.[10]
>
> (BhP. X.39.19)

The *gopīs* continue their complaint, punning upon the name of Akrūra (not cruel), the messenger coming upon them to bestow the cruellest fate of all. The cowherd women also upbraid Kṛṣṇa for leaving them in order to seek new lovers, while they have given up everything for him. They wonder if Kṛṣṇa, falling under the spell of the sophisticated women of Mathurā, will ever want to return to the simple scene of his pastoral play.

Kṛṣṇa, described as "hardhearted" (*anārdra-dhīḥ*—[literally, dry-minded]), climbs upon the chariot and is whisked away. The cowherd women clamor after him, declaring that fate has turned against them this day, and wondering "how they will cross over the long darkness of his absence," since they cannot bear to be separate from him for the time it takes to "bat an eyelash."[11]

Bereft of all shame, they cry out after their beloved, but the chariot begins to move away. The *gopīs* follow after the chariot, hoping for some message or instruction, and Kṛṣṇa consoles them sending the words "I shall return"(*āyāsye*) through a messenger. The women remain motionless as painted figures, their minds following the chariot, and finally they turn back "without hope" to pass their days "singing of the activities of their beloved."[12]

Akrūra stops at the Kālindī river and goes to take his bath, while Kṛṣṇa and his brother Balarāma remain seated on the chariot by a grove of trees. While bathing, Akrūra has a vision of the brothers before him. He wonders how this can be and returns to the chariot to find them seated there as well. He wonders if his vision in the water was an illusion and returns to the river where he has a vision of the *aiśvarya,* or majestic aspect, of Bhagavān in the form of Viṣṇu, reclining upon the thousand-headed serpent, Anantaśeṣa. The scene is similar to the theophany of Arjuna in the Bhagavadgītā and is repeated a number of times in the Purāṇa when, at crucial moments, the divine breaks into the mundane realm (as when Yaśodā sees the universe in Kṛṣṇa's mouth while looking for evidence of her child swallowing mud).[13] The oxymoron of juxtaposing the mortal child and immortal god is characteristic of the Bhāgavata's strategy; its emphasis upon the wonder of divine play and aesthetics is predicated upon the active awareness of inconceivability. This phenomenon has been subject to extensive analysis by Ken E. Bryant in the later poems of Sūrdās.[14] In the Bhāgavata-Purāṇa, however, it is important to note that this vision occurs at the text's most drastic moment of separation (much as the theophany of the *Gītā* occurs at a moment of impending mass destruction). As Kṛṣṇa leaves Vṛndāvana forever, the text offers its theophany, showing that even the most intense and undesirable loss is contained within the ever-existing form of the Supreme Person. In this way, the Bhāgavata undercuts and undermines any absolute vision of loss. All contradictions and contradistinctions of appearance and disappearance are contained within the inconceivable play of the divine. Akrūra thus exclaims:

> The worlds, together with their divine protectors
> and teeming crowds of living beings, are
> situated in You, the basis of mind, the
> Supreme Spirit, O Ever-Existing Self, just as
> schools of fish move in water or tiny
> insects within the *udumbara* fruit.[15]

The Bhāgavata thus seeks to illustrate the inconceivable paradox of separation and death within a non-dual field that is forever whole. One wonders to what degree the tradition is contending with itself here, when we consider that at the most painful moments of the narrative, this non-dualistic vision seems to be offered as a revelatory consolation. Is this tale about the irrevocable impossibility of earthly love, about the intensification of love and its transformation into a higher order? Or does the narrative, in Hamlet-like fashion, reflect a tradition that cannot decide between loss and recompense, leading to a strange mixture of both? Is the repeated frustration of the cowherd women the consummate way to represent an encounter with the inconceivable, or is the tradition unable to decide upon an immanent or transcendent reality? On the other hand, one can argue that the very oscillation of the text is truly mimetic, representing a vision of reality that cannot be "completed" or located within a single overarching image. Instead, there is ongoing dismemberment juxtaposed upon an ongoing sense of wholeness.

Kṛṣṇa, in the Bhāgavata's seminal version of the story, never returns to Vṛndāvana, and the cowherd women are obliged to spend the rest of their mortal lives in broken-hearted remembrance of him. Commentators, like Jīva Gosvāmī, could not tolerate this and have gone so far as to insist that Kṛṣṇa secretly lamented his separation from the *gopīs*, inferring that, like Rāma, he is placing *rāja-dharma*, kingly duties, over personal preferences.[16] This does not seem to be very plausible, however, because Kṛṣṇa, in the text, is repeatedly identified with providence. He has orchestrated the separation and has encouraged the practice of *hari-smaraṇa*, of placing absence over presence.

The idyllic, pastoral scene and the dancing that took place during the autumn nights will now be available only through memory (*smaraṇa*), through singing of his activities, and through *hari kathā*. By preferring *kathā*, the narrative, over any romantic or comic resolution, the Bhāgavata foreshadows Abhinavagupta and the aestheticians in seeing removal from the field of space and time as an essential step toward the real.[17] Just as the dominant emotion (*sthāyibhāva*) in Sanskrit Aesthetic theory is transformed (*pariṇata*) into the "other-worldly" state (*alaukikāvasthā*) of *rasa* through detached contemplation, the "distancing effect" of loss transforms immediate emotions into constant remembrance.[18]

One could say that Kṛṣṇa himself is the distancing effect. The text is very clear on this. While God himself creates separation that appears to be cruel, senseless, or capricious, it is a separation that produces a detached yet intense inner state equated with the ultimate human attainment. Now whether or not this "state" is actually a narcissistic defense against the risk of human mutuality and its inevitable disappointments may be open for debate. What is clear, however, is that understanding the phenomenon of loss involves more than seeing it as the disinterested, playful expression of the illusory world of *māyā*. The emotions of loss and anguish are heartfelt and real, but they exist within a greater context. One must wonder if this "greater context" is but another version of the appeasement of existential anguish offered by religious mythologies the world over; that is the comforting notion of absolutism.

While I would not deny that the Bhāgavata's vision smacks of absolutism, I would argue that there is another dimension present as well. This other dimension is the exaltation of anguish and the amplification of human helplessness in the face of death as a purifying, even transcendent factor. This is a step beyond the idea of "grace by deprivation" because it is the deprivation itself that becomes grace. The anguish of the cowherd women overrides their fear of death, and Parīkṣit's listening to Śuka's ongoing discourse enables him to die nobly, not because he will be saved afterwards, but because he transcends the dualistic vision while in his very body.

Thus, while the Bhāgavata offers a world-denying transcendent vision, it also simultaneously offers a "narrative vision" that embraces and then greatly expands the idea of personality and character as the locus of experience. Śuka hardly ever refers to Parīkṣit's immediate situation. Instead, he explores multiple storylines around loss and devotion within a context of cosmological history, widening the field of discourse in a way that seems similar to James Joyce's single character Humphrey Chimpden Earwicker of *Finnegans Wake*, becoming "Here Comes Everybody." The visions of monism and pluralism dance around and interpenetrate one another in many incongruous ways throughout the Purāṇa, but they finally encounter one another head on through the meeting of Uddhava with the *gopīs*.

Uddhava: Messenger of "Union"

In the Bhāgavata version, although Kṛṣṇa never returns to Vṛndāvana, he does send his messenger Uddhava to ease the anguish of the cowherd women. Uddhava is a key figure in the *kṛṣṇa-carita*. He plays the role of Kṛṣṇa's confidant, brother, and student. Since we have, in the Viṣṇu-Purāṇa, the example of Kṛṣṇa's brother Balarāma being sent to appease the *gopīs*, we may see Uddhava as a substitute sibling. As with Lakṣmaṇa and Rāma, in Vālmīki's *Rāmāyaṇa*, Uddhava will be the last person to leave Kṛṣṇa. Uddhava is sent to Vraja as a messenger by Kṛṣṇa, who speaks of the pain of the *gopīs*' suffering from his absence:

> Myself, their most beloved, being away
> at a distant place, the women of Vraja
> always brood over me and are overwhelmed by
> deep longing due to separation from me; they
> have thus become oblivious to all else, dear friend.
> With their minds absorbed in me, the cowherd
> women are sustaining their lives with great difficulty,
> by clinging to the message of my
> promised return.[19]

One of the verbs used to qualify the *gopīs*' anguish is √*muh*, "be stupified," the same verbal root that yields the derivative *moha*, a noun signifying the bewilderment of the demons during the tug-of-war at the milky ocean. Is the text implying that even this heartfelt agony is a form of conditioned and illusory *moha*? The cowherd women, however, being bereft of all else, have taken separation to almost its final stage, death. The *gopīs* do not fear transgressing *dharma*. That has already been done. Vālmīki's witnessing of an unjust and unforeseen separation caused him to utter the first poem. The cowherd women live their poem. Discourse on the *līlās* of Hari has become their principal activity, and the business of living and dying has become a secondary affair.

Uddhava arrives in Vṛndāvana where he is received by Kṛṣṇa's foster parents, Nanda and Yaśodā, who cannot stop remembering their divine son. Uddhava is impressed by their mood of love, and praises them. Then he repeats the promise of Kṛṣṇa that he will return to Vṛndāvana. On the one hand, he comforts them, telling them not to grieve, since their son will soon be with them again. One the other hand, he puts forth bits of advaitic reasoning declaring that in fact "he dwells within all hearts like fire in wood," and that he, in truth, has "neither father, nor mother, nor son."[20] Uddhava, then, repeats the semiotic polemic of the Purāṇa:

> No subject, seen or heard, that has happened
> and that will happen, still or moving, great
> or small, is worth speaking of without Him.
> He alone is everything. He is the "highest truth."[21]

The compound *paramārthabhūtaḥ*, translated here as "the highest truth," literally means "one whose being is ultimate meaning." (Since all meaning, *artha*, is only validated through Bhagavān.)

Uddhava then meets the cowherd women, who are churning curd and singing their stories of Kṛṣṇa. The women of Vraja recognize him as an emissary of Kṛṣṇa, and begin to speak about the "travesty of love." In these and other verses, the Bhāgavata's distinction between love and pleasure, a distinction that will figure so greatly in later Vaiṣṇava philosophy, is made explicit through the discourse of the cowherd women:

> Friendship with others made for one's
> own interest is a mockery. A man treats
> a woman as a bee does the flower.[22]

The *gopīs* go on with a litany, observing how prostitutes abandon destitute clients, subjects leave an incapable king, students, having learned what they wanted, leave their teachers, and animals leave a burnt forest.[23]

The complaints soon give way to swoons of separation, however, along with the constant recall and recitation of the *kṛṣṇa-carita*.

Seeing a black bee (literally, the one who sucks honey), one *gopī* addresses herself to the bee, assuming that it too is a messenger from Kṛṣṇa, and recounts the pain of her separation. She rebukes Kṛṣṇa for his treatment of women, interestingly enough referring to Rāma's mutilation of Śūrpaṇakhā and slaying of Vālin as proof of his hardhearted nature.[24] Again, the rebukes turn into sighs as she finally asks if "he still remembers us," and "when will he return?"

Uddhava, although he has come to Vraja as an "emissary of union," is overwhelmed by the *gopīs*' love which he attributes to their loss, stating that through separation the cowherd women have claimed the *self* of all.[25] He then conveys Kṛṣṇa's puzzling message in which it is said that separation from him is, in fact, impossible.[26] The heart of this message is the ultimate discourse on love and loss in the Purāṇa because, as far as the commentarial and devotional traditions are concerned, the Lord himself is explaining it. After discussing his all-pervading, absolute nature, Bhagavān states (as he did right before the *rāsa* dance) that his purpose in disappearing was to draw the minds of the cowherd women closer to him. Thus, the Bhāgavata echoes the sentiment of the poets (Amaru, for example) and the *Nāṭyaśāstra*, in seeing separation as the impeller of a stronger and more complete union, albeit a nonmaterial one. As the text repeats this idea, the message is much like that of the Gītā: "by focusing your mind upon me, you will come to me." In fact, Kṛṣṇa states that the cowherd women who were not able to come and dance with him during the nights in Vraja attained him by thinking about him.[27]

One may be tempted to read these chapters as a struggle, with an attempted reconciliation, not only between immanent and transcendent possibilities, but also between the sensual "anti-normative" sensibility of the South Indian poetic tradition (according to Hardy), and the established, brāhmaṇical polemic of detachment and renunciation. Perhaps on some level it can be seen as such, but the overriding project of the Purāṇa, from its very first verse, would be more accurately described as mutation than as synthesis. Whereas the very sensual theme of love-in-separation has existed in "brāhmaṇical" Sanskrit literature from the Epic, through *kāvya*, and onwards, only the Bhāgavata seeks to make a "religion" out of the "poem," establishing the narrative song of the maddened lover as an alternative to the silence of the *brahman*-realized *yogin*.

The *gopīs* remain "in character" after hearing the message. They ask if Kṛṣṇa "remembers those nights" when he is among the women of Mathurā. They cannot forget him, and wonder if he will ever return to infuse new life into them by the touch of his limbs, as Indra does to a forest with clouds of rain.[28] Their talk becomes more maddened and hysterical in its anxiety and finally ends with an invocation:

> O Lord, O Lord of the Goddess of Fortune,
> O Lord of Vraja, O Reliever of Agony,
> O Protector of the Cows, Lift Gokula out of
> the ocean of grief into which it has sunk.
>
> (BhP. X.47.52)

Uddhava remains with the cowherd women for some months in order to help alleviate their agony. Together they enjoy Vṛndāvana by "singing the stories of the Kṛṣṇa *līlās*." The text declares that as long as Uddhava remained there, the days passed like moments, in talks of Kṛṣṇa.[29] Thus, *hari kathā* (discourse on Hari) shares the sense of timelessness with which the experience of deep anguish due to loss is so often associated. Both separation, and the visionary experience of *hari kathā*, take one out of conventional time and thought.

Uddhava is a friend and a messenger, but he is also a "brother" of sorts. Not only does Uddhava play the role of Kṛṣṇa's surrogate brother, but he also plays the brother to the *gopīs* as well. He is an asexual, male presence supporting the cowherd women in light of what could be construed as a difficult, if not abusive, situation, a role similar to that played by a brother for his sister who has gone to another household and only gets to return once a year to air her grievances with her familial confidant.[30] In any case, Uddhava is so delighted by the state of being he experiences in the presence of the cowherd women, that he prays to be reborn as a shrub, creeper, or blade of grass in Vṛndāvana. There he will receive bliss from the *gopīs*' presence, while saluting "the dust of their feet that sanctifies the three worlds."[31]

Here, again, the Bhāgavata offers a series of mixed messages. Uddhava, it can be argued, was dispatched by Kṛṣṇa in order to relieve the *gopī's* distress by instructing them about the non-dual reality. And yet it is Uddhava, supposedly situated in the oneness of the absolute, who is affected by the cowherd women and now wishes to join them. Just as Akrūra is confused by the bilocation of Kṛṣṇa and Balarāma, Uddhava is confused and deeply impressed by the power of the *gopī*'s *bhāva*, because their constant remembrance of Kṛṣṇa creates an even stronger presence in his absence.

In this sense, one could argue, along with Freud and others of his persuasion, that the practice of *hari kathā* is something that makes mundane life bearable. The singing and glorifying of the absent Lord may be a metonymic consolation, much in the way Kenneth Burke considers the

Medusa myth to be an analogy for poetry itself; the narrative acts like the mirror of Perseus, enabling one to confront brutal facts through the protection of poetic indirection.[32] On the other hand, as we have seen, the poem itself more than substitutes for the absent event, it amplifies and sanctifies it. "Life exists," said Stéphane Mallarmé, "to be written in a book!"

As Uddhava prepares to leave, Nanda and the other residents of Vraja ask that the movements of their minds be focused on the feet of Kṛṣṇa, that their speech may utter his name alone, that their bodies may be prostrated before him, and that, wherever they may go due to their particular *karmas*, their *rati* (loving desire) may always be found in Kṛṣṇa. The text makes its polemic clear: "focus on Kṛṣṇa, on Viṣvaksena (the all-pervading), as opposed to your own life and times." This focus, however, is neither reductive nor "singular" as one might imagine, since Viṣvaksena appears in a myriad of forms and situations encompassing the full flow of Purāṇic cosmic-history. The universe of the Bhāgavata is a pluralistic one, and its shared images and scenarios allow for an identification with a mythic dimension that breaks beyond individual personality, locality, and history, as opposed to the type of reflection found in historical and psychoanalytic readings.

Kurukṣetra

Kṛṣṇa never returns to Vṛndāvana, but he does meet the cowherd women once more at the pilgrimage site of Kurukṣetra. The occasion is a total eclipse of the sun, the kind which may portend the dissolution of the world. People thus gather "from everywhere" to gain religious merit and ward off calamity.

The Bhāgavata chooses Kurukṣetra as the site of its most poignant scene of union and separation. As the Bhagavadgītā in the Mahābhārata pays tribute to the "field of *dharma*," the Bhāgavata acknowledges its source and then goes on to rewrite it.[33] The text has all its major characters convene on a site of pilgrimage which has been a site of slaughter as well as instruction (and one can only notice the powerful connection between the two).[34] In the Epic, it is here that the final battle takes place. In the Bhāgavata-Purāṇa, it is here that we will have the final meeting between Kṛṣṇa and his lovers.

The initial scene is one of reunion. Kṛṣṇa, now a grown-up ruler, enters with his sixteen thousand queens and huge entourage. People hug one another and are filled with joy. There is much nostalgia at this great meeting, but when queen Kuntī sees her long-lost family she tells her elder brother, Vasudeva, that "none of her desires have been fulfilled."

Because of her experience of loss, particularly the death of her first-born son Karṇa, she is convinced that friends, brothers, and even parents will not remember their own relatives if "fate is against them."

Nanda and the residents of Vṛndāvana are also present at this assembly, and there are heartfelt scenes of reunion between Kṛṣṇa and his foster parents. Thus, the Bhāgavata places its portrait of loss within the context of a reunion, much as the commentator Jīva Gosvāmī argues that, philosophically speaking, separation can only exist if union does as well. This sets the stage for the meeting between Kṛṣṇa and the cowherd women, who have been entranced in meditation upon him. They embrace him mentally, take him into their hearts through their eyes, and merge into him, "a task that is difficult even for *yogīs* who cultivate absolute oneness."[35] Seeing them in that state, Bhagavān meets with them privately. The commentaries become very creative here, and sometimes construe this verse to mean that Kṛṣṇa expanded himself as he did during the *rāsa* dance to meet with each *gopī* privately. The text only says that he saw them in an isolated place, embraced them, questioned them, and smilingly spoke to them. Kṛṣṇa then offers the cowherd women a lukewarm apology, asking them not to think ill of him, since his absence was caused by providence. In a discourse similar to that of Uddhava's—and this is his final instruction—he repeats a verse that appears many times in the Purāṇa, placing the burden of *viraha* upon the will of God:

> Like the wind that brings together and
> disperses clouds, blades of grass, cotton
> particles, and dust, the Creator unites
> or disunites beings carried by him.
>
> (BhP. X.82.47)

The only difference here is that the Creator happens to be himself. He is the cause of separation.

Kṛṣṇa goes on to explain his absolute nature, declaring that the devotion of the *gopīs* has brought them to the state of immortality. He explains his divine nature by echoing the sensibility of the very first verse of the Purāṇa. He states that he alone is the beginning, middle, and end of all phenomena, permeating the sky, water, wind, and fire, that the *self* exists apart from material phenomena, and that he alone is the *self* of all. Śuka then comments that by contemplating the instructions of Kṛṣṇa, the *gopīs* let go of their material coverings and merged into him.[36] Thus, on a holy field of death where the great *Bhārata* war was fought, the women of Vraja enter into the inconceivable. On the physical plane, however, separation remains the order of the day. When the cowherd women do leave Kurukṣetra, they find that they are unable to withdraw their hearts from Śrī Kṛṣṇa. They leave, but they leave their hearts behind.

The text, then, offers no conventional resolution, no happy ending in the narrative sense, and yet no tragic ending either. Rather, in its extended tale of days of yore, the Purāṇa revels in the inconceivable interfacing of multiplicity and unity. In some narrative traditions, which actually speak of Kṛṣṇa inviting the cowherd women to return to Dvārakā with him as his queens, they refuse, preferring to remember him with them in their youth under the autumn moon of Vṛndāvana.

Multiplicity and multivalence live alongside monistic nondifferentiation as the Bhāgavata offers the inconceivable nature of its reality and extends an invitation to that reality. The price of admission is paid by going through the experience of death—the separation from one's beloved in any form—even when the coating of the experience is sweetened with poetic beauty and wonder. Nevertheless, the harshness of Kṛṣṇa's absence was often as unpalatable to the subsequent tradition as Rāma's rejection of Sītā. Later texts offered alternate resolutions. Jīva Gosvāmī's *Gopāla-Campū*, for example, has Kṛṣṇa returning to Vṛndāvana, as does Viśvanātha Cakravartī. The Vaiṣṇava theology evolved here much in the same way as it did through the *Rāmāyaṇa* tradition. Just as Sītā is later said to have never really left Rāma, Kṛṣṇa is said to never really leave Vṛndāvana.[37] What is suggested in the Bhāgavata is told in the Padma Purāṇa, which offers a *kṛṣṇa-carita* in which Kṛṣṇa returns to Vṛndāvana. Once again, the tradition is ambivalent. In Vṛndāvana one can, to this very day, frequent temples that either focus on the mood of separation or on the mood of union in their respective liturgies.

Uddhava's *Viraha*

One can ascribe any number of motives to the Bhāgavata's efforts to accommodate the reality of impermanence to its other-worldly vision of the Absolute. One important point, however, is that the Purāṇa does not postulate a promised, eternal reality as a panacea for the suffering of the here and now. While there is an absolute realm that devotees such as Bali and Prahlāda attain, the Bhāgavata simultaneously exalts worldly suffering through its treatment of *viraha*, seeking, perhaps, to give it meaning or positive value. The depth of separation is hence seen as an index of the intensity of one's love. Because of this fact, suffering does not necessarily end with the world, but is transformed and universalized in the same way that *rasa* is said to be.

The Bhāgavata is also very clear about the *śāpa*, the often-used device of a curse as an explanatory mode for disruptive intrusions. In the eleventh book, Kṛṣṇa himself instigates the curse that will destroy his own dynasty (as opposed to his receiving the curse from Gāndhārī in the Epic). Once again, God—the supreme power—is the agent of separation and death.

As with Rāma, Kṛṣṇa is visited by the gods and asked to return to his eternal abode, and as in the *Rāmāyaṇa* of Vālmīki, the person who remains until the end is another male, in this case, Uddhava. Uddhava guesses Kṛṣṇa's intentions and approaches him, saying that he cannot bear separation from him for even half a moment. He asks Kṛṣṇa to allow him to come with him. Uddhava is referred to both as Kṛṣṇa's beloved, and his devoted servant, and as his intimate friend. As with Arjuna in the Epic, who was perplexed by the imminent disappearance of his relatives and friends, Kṛṣṇa instructs him. This part of the Purāṇa has, in fact, become known as the "*Uddhava-Gītā*," because of its striking similarity to the Bhagavadgītā in the Mahābhārata. More pointedly, Kṛṣṇa tells Uddhava how to overcome the pangs of loss, since he will leave Uddhava, just as he has left the cowherd women. Kṛṣṇa tells his devotee that his mission is complete and that his own kinsmen will soon be annihilated. He advises Uddhava to give up all attachments and sentiments for friends, and to attain equanimity. Throughout the episode, Kṛṣṇa insists that the concept of difference is an illusion:

> Whatever is perceived by the mind,
> speech, eyes, and ears, know that to be
> transient, a product of the illusory mind.
> The notion of difference is the misapprehension
> of a scattered and wandering mind partaking
> of good and evil consequences.[38]

After receiving a catechism on the virtues of dispassion, Uddhava fears that such renunciation will be too difficult for him. He voices his fear and receives another series of narratives within narratives, all illustrating the futility of material attachment. The main narrator is a stark renunciate (*avadhūta*) who continually stresses the futility of desire.[39] The *Uddhava-Gītā* continues to assert the polemic of renunciation, repeating the dictum of the *Chāndogya Upaniṣad* about the "one substance alone being real" (XI.28.17–20). Kṛṣṇa instructs Uddhava in *yoga* and devotion, and finally dispatches his now self-realized servant to Badarikāśrama. Still feeling separation, Uddhava asks for and receives Kṛṣṇa's sandals to take with him.

Just as Rāma can disappear only after Lakṣmaṇa has been banished, Kṛṣṇa cannot disappear until Uddhava is gone. Kṛṣṇa's dynasty, the entire Yadu clan, annihilates itself in a drunken brawl. The women commit mass *satī*, throwing themselves upon the funeral pyres of their burning husbands, the "fire" of separation from their spouses being greater than the pain of physical fire. Kṛṣṇa's "real" brother, Balarāma, enters into meditation and leaves the mortal world behind. Kṛṣṇa then sits "quietly" under a tree and assumes his four-armed form of Viṣṇu. A hunter, mistaking his foot for the open mouth of a deer, pierces him with an arrow. We have come full circle. Whereas the hunter comes upon Kṛṣṇa as Daśaratha came upon the *brāhmaṇa* boy in the *Vālmīki-Rāmāyaṇa*, here, there is no curse, no anger, and no disruption. Kṛṣṇa tells the hunter to have no fear. What has been done was willed by himself.[40]

The hunter as the agent of "the death of God" is significant. Not only in the *Vālmīki-Rāmāyaṇa*, but throughout the Bhāgavata, the low-caste, "evil-minded" hunter has been portrayed as the agent of doom. In this final image, the hunter meets the hunted. God meets himself. There is no quarrel. The lowest, most vile agent is seen to also be a part of the divine *līlā*, and is accepted. Separation, be it through violent death, suicide, or other circumstances is not thought of as evil. It is, rather, the direct manifestation of the maker of the cosmic drama. Separation is disruptive and fearsome, but it is to be met ultimately by everyone, even God, as the disappearance of Kṛṣṇa from the earth illustrates.[41]

The Death of Parīkṣit

The appearance and disappearance of God, and the play of his activities, has been narrated, but a human being must still face the very physical, existential fact of death, and it is perhaps significant that the Bhāgavata does not end with the "death of God" but rather with the death of Parīkṣit and the continuation of his line. Parīkṣit has been intently listening to the long string of narratives, and now his time has come. The narrative of the Bhāgavata-Purāṇa does not seek to deter this event, for it has been preparing for it.

Śuka summarizes the text as the glorification of the Almighty, soul of all, Bhagavān, the all-pervading *self*.[42] He then commands Parīkṣit to give up the "animal intelligence" that thinks it will die, explaining that the king has never been nonexistent, and will not be destroyed like the body.

Śuka asserts the distinction of the *self* (*ātman*) from matter, a separation that is crucial to the project of the Purāṇa. Separation and loss can be seen, then, as I have previously mentioned, as working like homeopathic medicine, evoking symptoms of the disease which will be cured. The identification with the body/mind and with the contents of consciousness is the *paśubuddhi* (animal intelligence), and coming face-to-face with its ending is the cure. Śuka asserts:

> *ahaṁ brahma paraṁ dhāma brahmāhaṃ paramaṁ padam*
> *evaṁ samīkṣya cātmānam ātmany ādhāya niṣkale*
> *daśantaṁ takṣakaṁ pāde lelihānaṁ viṣānanaiḥ*
> *na drakṣyasi śarīraṁ ca viśvaṁ ca pṛthag ātmanaḥ*
>
> I am the absolute, the supreme abode.
> I am the absolute, the supreme resting place.
> Thinking thus and placing the *self* in the *self*
> free of time, you will not notice the snake-bird,
> Takṣaka, with its mouth full of poison on your
> foot, nor will you see your body or the universe
> as separate from your*self*.
>
> (BhP. XII.5.11–12)

There is a pun here on the word *pada*. The supreme abode is contrasted with the mortal foot, as *pada* is synonymous for both (the same foot by which Kṛṣṇa himself leaves the world). We may remember that *pada* also means verse. The supreme abode, *brahma*, is the ultimate language in which signifier and signified are non-different (*ahaṁ brahma*/"I am *brahman*, the absolute"), and death strikes only at mortal verse.

The *phala* or fruit of the Purāṇa is then spoken by Parīkṣit:

> My Lord, I fear neither the snake-bird nor
> any other being. Having been given the vision
> by you, I have entered the supreme, absolute,
> infinite state and have thus become fearless.
>
> (BhP. XII.6.5)

The king settles his mind, meditates upon the supreme, and becomes as still as a tree. He is bitten by the snake-bird as both lamentation and praise ring in the heavens.[43]

The Alaukika World

The importance of the Bhāgavata-Purāṇa for the future of "Kṛṣṇaism" and the *bhakti* movement, as well as the general life of India, has been well-documented.[44] Perhaps, a greater awareness of the Bhāgavata's vision may also serve as an impetus for intercultural dialogues on death as well. There could be many aspects to this dialogue. One that intrigues me is "to what degree is the fear of death correlative to the polemic of renunciation," and "to what degree is the rhetoric of renunciation related to power imbalances in constructs of gender?" Is the harsh world-denying rhetoric in this text part of a defense against inevitable loss and pain? On the other hand, is "the noble truth of suffering" a phenomenon that needs to be enacted and experienced as a conscious sacrifice rather than transcended? And, if this may be so, do the characters of the Bhāgavata-Purāṇa offer any fresh perspectives on this? And finally, does the text's celebrated experience of the intensity of loss champion a masochistic polarity to the stoicism of the hero in the face of death? Or can the anguished lover open death's door in another way?

In any case, discourse around the elemental issue of meeting death is surely worthy of more sustained attention, and if "to philosophize is to learn to die," as Montaigne declared, then the Purāṇa, through its confrontation with loss in so many forms, does this well. In its meditation on the ending of things, *viraha* is indeed exalted, and through it the Bhāgavata deals with both the emotional bondage that arises from duality—the illusion of separateness from Bhagavān—as well as with the exaltation that arises from the inability to achieve a state of union, as its attendant frustration becomes a source of ecstasy. That is, the longing for communion is preferred to its attainment. In the *Nārada Bhakti-sūtra*, then, separation is given first place as the highest form of devotion, and for the Gosvāmīs of Vṛndāvana, *līlā-smaraṇa* (the practice of remembrance) was the last word in the devotional experience. Rather than meet in union, one should sit in a solitary bower (*kuñja*) and remember.[45]

The sign or symbol embodies its own absence, and thus union or God can never be adequately expressed in language as we generally know it. In a similar sense, the signs and situations of loss point to another form of presence that is experienced through the characters who had the closest connection to separation and dying—Kṛṣṇa's foster parents, Nanda and Yaśodā, his friend and confidant Uddhava, and the cowherd women. The natural order allows for only the symbolic presence of Kṛṣṇa, but the *alaukika* order may allow for his living presence.

If the distance of separation existed only to more fully elevate the state of union, there would be no finality to the *viraha*. To create obstacles, to suspend ecstasy in time, as in *tantra*, is a very different approach.[46] The Bhāgavata asserts that *viraha* is final. There is no compromise: Saubhari Muni's meditation is broken, the creation of the Vedas leads to despondency, and the entire universe moves towards recurrent dissolution. For the Bhāgavata, separation breaks the hold of the visible world and allows for the revelation of the true nature of things. But the world remains. The *gopīs* churn butter and Parīkṣit dies. And the poetic creation, the fabric of the text, issues forth as a response to incompleteness and to dying, and perhaps this is where the power of loss is to be found. In its acknowledgment of the defeat of the human, it becomes the most exalted sentiment of all.

NOTES

Introduction: Many Ways of Dying

1. *MBh.* II.311 (Southern Recension).

2. Sigmund Freud, "Our Attitude towards Death," in *Thoughts for the Times on War and Death* and in *Civilization, Society, and Religion*, vol. 12 (1915; reprint, The Pelican Freud Library; Harmondsworth: Penguin, 1985).

3. I cite Wendy Doniger's introduction to *The Laws of Manu*: "For it is the privilege of the Orientalist (and I use the word in a non-pejorative sense, in the hope of restoring some of its faded dignity) to reopen a text that the native commentators have closed. *The Laws of Manu* (New York: Penguin Books, 1991).

4. *svamate tu acintyabhedābhedam eva acintyaśaktimayatvād iti //* Jīva Gosvāmī, in Radhagobinda Natha, *Gauḍīya Vaiṣṇava Darśana* (Calcutta: Pracyavani Mandir, 1957), 1:139.

5. There are instances in the Bhāgavata-Purāṇa where human beings are brought back from the dead, but they are often given an ironic twist (see chapter 4 of this volume).

6. See Friedhelm Hardy, *Viraha-Bhakti* (Delhi: Oxford University Press, 1983); and Ludo Rocher, *The Purāṇas* (Weisbaden: Otto Harrassowitz, 1986), for a discussion of the dating of the Bhāgavata. Based on the Purāṇa's appropriation of the poetry of the Alvārs, Hardy dates the Purāṇa from the ninth to tenth century. E. W. Hopkins dates the text between 850–900 C.E. M. A. Winternitz, *A History of Indian Literature*, vol. 1:2 (Calcutta: Calcutta University, 1971). He declares that it "bears the stamp of a unified composition," while Surendranath Dasgupta, *A History of Indian Philosophy* (Cambridge: Cambridge University Press, 1949) calls it "a collection of accretions from different trends at different times and not a systematic whole." Let me mention, once again here, that extrinsic authorship and dating, as fascinating and problematic as they may be, are not the concern of this volume.

7. Along with its other polarity—Hebraic evolving into Judaeo Christian. See James Hillman, *Revisioning Psychology* (New York: Harper and Row, 1975).

8. *Bhagavadgītā* VIII.5,

anta-kāle ca mām eva smaran muktvā kalevaram
yaḥ prayāti sa mad-bhāvam yāti nāstyatra saṁśayaḥ

9. Note the difference in this focus from that of the *Gītā*, in which the narrative grows out of an encounter with the possibility of warfare, and more specifically, with the seemingly senseless death of others.

10. A. S. Biswas, *Bhāgavata-Purāṇa* (Dibrugarh: Vishveshvaranand Book Agency, 1968; Friedhelm Hardy, *Viraha-Bhakti* (Delhi: Oxford University Press, 1983); R. C. Hazra, *Studies in the Puranic Records on Hindu Rites and Customs* (Delhi: Motilal Banarsidass, 1974); Ludo Rocher, *The Purāṇas* (Weisbaden: Otto Harrassowitz, 1986); S. Bhattacharya, *The Philosophy of the Śrīmad Bhāgavatam* (Santiniketan: Visva Bharati, 1960).

11. I credit James Hillman with exposing me to this idea. See Hillman, *Revisioning Psychology*, 1975.

12. See Philip Lutgendorf, "Rāmāyan: The Video," in *Drama Review* 34, no. 2 (Summer, 1990).

13. A. K. Ramanujan, interview by author, New York, NY, 1989, Personal Communication, 1992. The religious-devotional cult aspect is, of course, absent in *Ulysses*, though some may want to argue this point.

14. BhP. I.19.37.

15. BhP. I.3.46,

kṛṣṇe svadhāmopagate dharma-jñānādibhiḥ saha
kalau naṣṭa-dṛśām eṣa purāṇārko' dhunoditaḥ

See BhP. XII.2.1 for a discussion on the length of life declining due to the strong force of the Kaliyuga. "Indeed," says the text, "the life-span will gradually be reduced to twenty to thirty years."

16. Hazra, *The Purāṇas*, 246–247. Hazra continues with "sacraments, customs, pacification of unfavorable planets, dedication of wells, tanks, gardens of worship, and so forth.

17. There are a number of possible working definitions of myth that I would accept here, although I suspect that definition could too easily demythologize myth. As Wendy Doniger notes in *Other Peoples' Myths* (New York and London: Macmillan, 1988), "the desecration of the word 'myth' to mean 'lie' began with Plato." Doniger speaks of myth as "a story that is sacred to and shared by a group of people who find their most important meanings in it . . ." Antonio De Nicolas speaks of myth as "an explanatory mode." Antonio De Nicolas, *Four Dimensional Man* (Stony Brook, NY: N. Hays, 1976); Sudhir Ka-

kar, *The Inner World* (Delhi: Oxford University Press, 1978) refers to myth-making as dreaming on a cultural level; and Dennis Tedlock, *Spoken Word and Work of Interpretation* (Philadelphia: University of Pennsylvania Press, 1983), discussing narrative as ritual, describes it as "a complex ceremony in miniature."

18. Biswas, *Bhāgavata-Purāṇa,* 1968; J. A. B. van Buitenen, "On the Archaism of the Bhāgavata-Purāṇa, in *Krishna: Myths, Rites and Attitudes*, by Milton Singer (Honolulu: East-West Center Press, 1966).

19. Thomas C. Coburn, *Devī Māhātmya* (Delhi: Motilal Banarsidass, 1984), p. 24 discusses the *Śatapatha Brāhmaṇa* declaration that "The *Veda* is indeed the declaration of the *Purāṇa*," *tān upadiśati purāṇam vedaḥ soyam iti kiṁcit purāṇam ācakṣita.*

20. Camile Paglia, *Sexual Personae: Art and Decadence from Nefertiti to Emily Dickenson* (New York, Harmondsworth: Penguin, 1992), 12.

21. *Similia similibus curantur*, "like is cured by like."

22. James A. Fruehling, ed., "A New Definition of Death," in *Sourcebook on Death and Dying*, 1st ed. (Chicago: Marquis Professional Publications, 1982). An interesting alternative definition of death, "the inability of the organism to adapt to its environment," was offered by Michael K. Bartelos, chairperson of the Columbia University Seminar on Death and Dying, at a panel on death and dying given at the Society of Fellows in the Humanities at Columbia University in 1992.

23. BhP. III.31.44–46.

24. BG II.27.

25. BhP. I.15.41–43. Also note the following verse: "The same immortal Lord who, as the time spirit, puts an end to the world, though endless himself, is the first maker though himself without beginning. It is he who creates the universe by begetting one individual through another and dissolves the same by destroying the destroyer through death." Also note BhP. IV. 11. 19–21, and VI.5.15, "razor sharp time destroys all creation," and in X.1.7, "who dwelling as time in the form of the inner controller meets out death and immortality."

26. The metaphor appears again in BhP. V.8.26, "death approached Mahārāja Bharata like a serpent approaching the hole of a rat."

27. BhP. III.29.26,

ātmanaśca parasyāpi yaḥ karotyantarodaram
tasya bhinnadṛśo mṛtyurvidadhe bhayamulbaṇam

28. BhP. III.31.40,

yopayati śanairmāyā yoṣid devavinirmitā
tamīkṣetātmano mṛtyuṁ tṛṇaiḥ kūpamivāvṛtam

29. BhP. III.31.42.

30. BhP. III.31.42. I have taken the phrase "advaitic theism" from Dan P. Sheridan's work on the Bhāgavata, 1986.

31. BhP. IV.11.24.

32. BhP. IV.28.20–30.

33. BhP. III.29.38.

34. For an anthropological discussion of the cycle of seeding the Gaṅgā with the ashes of the dead, see Jonathan Parry, *Death in Banaras* (Cambridge, New York: Cambridge University Press, 1994)

35. Notice the root of *yajña*, to consecrate, hallow, or offer (*yaj*) and thus "to make sacred" in a very hermetic way. The broken sacrifice is an oft-repeated theme, see J. C. Heesterman, *The Broken World of Sacrifice* (Chicago: University of Chicago Press, 1993). Moreover, the idea that all culture is founded upon murder and expiation has been explored by Sigmund Freud, *Totem and Taboo* (New York: Knopf, 1918); and Renee Girard, *Des Choses Cachees Dipus La Foundation du Monde* (Paris: Grasset, 1978).

36. BhP. IV.24.56.

Chapter 1: Examinations of the Past

1. See Rocher, *The Purāṇas*, p. 24, who cites Wilson, *The Vishnu Purana: A System of Hindu Mythology and Tradition* (London: J. Murray, 1840). Also see the early Burnouf edition, *Le Bhāgavata Purāṇa ou histoire poétique de Krichna*, traduit et publié par E. Burnouf, vols. 1–3, Paris, 1840–1847; publé par M. Haunette-Besnault et P. Roussell, vol. 4, Paris, 1884, 1898. The disparity between the listing of "five Purāṇic characteristics" and their actual content has led scholars to speculate on the Purāṇas being partial or later interpolated versions of the "old" or "original" *Purāṇas* (see Ramachandra Dikshitar 1950, and Mehendale 1970 cited in Rocher). Thomas Hopkins, *The Social Teaching of the Bhāgavata-Purāṇa*, pp. 1–23, 1966 (in Singer's *Krishna: Myths, Rites, and Attitudes*) refers to the *purāṇa-pañcalakṣaṇa* as a "literary myth" but does not elaborate or discuss their function in terms of the text itself.

The five characteristics are given in the *Matsya Purāṇa* as: *sarga* (creation), *pratisarga* (secondary creation), *vaṁśa* (lineage), *manvantara* (periods of time presided over by Manu), and *vaṁśānucarita* (dynastic lineage):

Matsya II.10.1,

> *sargaśca pratisargaśca vaṁśo manvantarāṇi ca*
> *vaṁśānucaritaṁ caiva purāṇaṁ pañcalakṣaṇam*

The Bhāgavata-Purāṇa defines ten *lakṣaṇa*s instead of the usual five. These characteristics are differently enumerated in two different parts of the text (BhP. II.10.2–7, XII 7.11–20). Such variants, far from being considered unusual, are the norm in Purāṇic lore where differing narrative episodes contribute to an overall thematic mosaic. (See O'Flaherty, *Asceticism and Eroticism in the Mythology of Śiva* (London: Oxford University Press, 1973), 16–21, for a discussion of the configuration of myth in Indian texts. In this sense, then, when we speak of the *pañca* or *daśa-lakṣaṇa*s we are, in fact, discussing a myth of content which the tradition bestows upon the Purāṇa and which the Bhāgavata holds to in its effort to integrate itself firmly within this tradition.

In the second *skandha* the *lakṣaṇa*s are enumerated as follows: *sarga* (creation), *visarga* (secondary creation), *sthāna* (law and order), *poṣaṇa* (welfare and protection), *manvantara* (the lineage of the earth rulers), *ūti* (enjoyment), *īśānukathā* (stories of the Lord), *nirodha* (annihilation), *mukti* (liberation), and *āśraya* (ultimate refuge). The Bhāgavata, in this *skandha*, declares *āśraya* to take precedence over the others.

BhP. II.10.2,

> *daśamasya viśuddhyarthaṁ navānām iha lakṣaṇam*
> *varṇayanti mahātmānaḥ śrutenārthena cāñjasā*
>
> By their meaning as heard in scripture and by
> their connotation as well, the great souled ones
> have explained that these nine characteristics
> are given in order to clearly ascertain the tenth.

This verse emphasizes the significance of the tenth *skandha* which sets the Bhāgavata apart from most Purāṇas and which has awarded it enduring fame. (The tenth *skandha* is said to be concerned with *āśraya*, "ultimate refuge," by almost all the commentators on the text.)

In the twelfth *skandha*'s listing of the *lakṣaṇa*s, *vṛtti* is substituted for *sthāna, rakṣa* for *poṣaṇa, vaṁśa* for *ūti, vaṁśānucarita* for *iśānukathā, saṁsthā* for *nirodha*, and *hetu* for *mukti*.The difference in order leads one to wonder about Winternitz's claim that the Bhāgavata has the "stamp of a unified composition." M. A. Winternitz, *A History of Indian Literature*, 1971, translated from *Geschichte der Indischen Litteratur* (Leipzig: Amelangs Verlag, 1907).

These *lakṣaṇa*s are said by many Indian commentators to correspond to particular *skandha*s of the Purāṇa although there are major disagreements over the particulars of correspondence.

2. Willibald Kirfel in his *Das Purāṇa Pañcalakṣaṇa*, versuch einer Textgeschichte (Bonn: Kurt Schroeder, 1927), concludes that out of about four hundred thousand verses in the Purāṇas, only about ten thousand or less than 3 percent, are concerned with *pañcalakṣaṇa* material. Cited by Thomas C. Coburn in *Devī Māhātmya: The Crystallization of the Goddess Tradition* (Delhi and Columbia, MO: Motilal Banarsidass and South Asia Books, 1985).

3. Both the *Matsya* (53.63) and *Vāyu Purāṇas* (I.123) declare that they are older than the *Veda*. See Madeleine Biardeau, "Some More Considerations about Textual Criticism," *Purāṇa* 10 (1968), 123; Upadhyaya, *Purāṇa-vimarśa* (Varanasi: Chowkamba Vidyabhawan, 1978), 2–36. On the age of the Purāṇas, see Georg Bühler, cited in Rocher, *The Purāṇas*, and in Jan Gonda, ed., *A History of Indian Literature* (Wiesbaden: Otto Harrassowitz, 1986), 24.

4. See Sudhir Kakar's discussion of the transformation of the Gandhi narrative from history to myth in *The Inner World: A Psychoanalytic Study of Childhood and Society in India* (Delhi: Oxford University Press, 1978).

5. Friedhelm Hardy, *Viraha-Bhakti: The Early History of Kṛṣṇa Devotion in South India* (Delhi: Oxford University Press, 1983).

6. Formed from the etymology of "*pari*" and "*īkṣ*" (to look towards).

7. As far as I know, the "we versus I" self was first articulated by Alan Roland, *In Search of Self in India and Japan: Toward A Cross-Cultural Psychology* (Princeton: Princeton University Press, 1988).

8. The Vedas and Upaniṣads seem to be cognizant of the Purāṇas as well. According to Coburn, the *Śatapatha Brāhmaṇa* (13.4.3.13) states that the Adhvaryu should instruct those who have assembled saying, "the *Purāṇa* is the *Veda*; this is it," and should then "recite some *Purāṇa*," the BU 2.4.10 envisions the *Vedas, Itihāsas, and Purāṇas* as the breath of the Great Being (*mahad bhūtam*).

9. BhP. I.1.3. The use of the word *nigama* is puzzling here. Perhaps it is to distinguish the *Bhāgavata-pañcarātra* tradition from the *āgama* tradition. Vallabha in this regard says:

> *nitarāṃ gamayati brahma bodhayatīti paramopaniṣat nigamah sa eva kalpataruḥ sarvadānasamarthaḥ.*
>
> That by which *brahma* is known, the highest Upanishad, that is *nigamaḥ;* indeed it is the desire tree capable of fulfilling all endeavors.

10. BhP. I.5.21.

11. *Evaṁ vā are'sya mahato bhūtasya niḥśvasitam etad yad ṛg-vedo yajur-vedaḥ sāma-vedo 'tharvāṇgirasa itihāsa-purāṇam* (BU. 2.4.10.). Thus, the Ṛg Veda, Yajurveda, Sāmaveda, the Atharva-Angirasa, itihāsa, and purāṇas—all this has been exhaled from the Great Being.

Itihāsa-purāṇāni pañcamaṁ vedam īśvaraḥ sarvebhya eva vakrebhyaḥ sasṛje sarva-darśanaḥ. Then, from his mouths, the Lord created the fifth Veda, the Purāṇas and histories, altogether since he had all-pervading vision. (Bh.P 1.12.39.)

12. This is the case regardless of the reason for its Vedic appropriations. I am thinking of van Buitenen's argument ("On the Archaism of the Bhāgavata-Purāṇa" in *Krishna: Myths, Rites, and Attitudes*, ed. Milton Singer (Honolulu: East-West Press, 1966, 23–40) that the Bhāgavata adopts this linguistic stance to legitimize itself in the potentially hostile area of Tamil Nadu.

13. See Wendy Doniger's definition of myth in *Other Peoples' Myths* (New York: Collier Macmillan, 1988), p. 27. Doniger cites Husserl's definition of a "tradition" as a "forgetting of the origin."

14. One example of seeing the Bhāgavata-Purāṇa as an extrinsic synthesis is Hardy's assertion that the Bhāgavata is an attempt to harmonize northern and

southern cultures, with South Indian culture characterized by "emotional religion and aesthetic sensibility" and the northern culture oriented towards a *varṇāśrama* social system and a Vedantic ideology. See Hardy, *Viraha Bhakti*, 1983.

15. BhP. I.3.43,

> *kṛṣṇe svadhāmopagate dharma-jñānādibhiḥ saha*
> *kalau naṣṭa-dṛśām eṣa purāṇārko 'dhunoditaḥ*
>
> Now that Kṛṣṇa has returned to his abode
> accompanied by *dharma* and *jñāna*, the light
> of this Purāṇa has now arisen for those who have
> lost their vision in this age of Kali.

16. *raso vai saḥ*, "He (the Absolute) is Aesthetic Rapture (*rasa*)," *Taittirīya Upaniṣad* II.7.1.

17. The two Gauḍīya Vaiṣṇava commentators that I have mentioned are not the only ones who view the Purāṇa in this way. Commentators from both the Nimbārka and Vallabha schools also employ the classical Aesthetic terminologies of dominant and complimentary *rasa*s in their discussion of the Bhāgavata.

18. See Viśvanātha Cakravartī in his *Sārārtha-darśinī-ṭīkā* on BhP. I.1.1

19. See James Hillman, *Revisioning Psychology* (New York: Harper and Row, 1975).

20. The "right audience" is often spoken of in the text as one made up of *rasika*s—those who are familiar with the breadth of the tradition and its intertextual references and innuendos, and who can thus "taste" the *rasa*—the "aesthetic flavor" of the narrative. See BhP. I.1.3.

21. By "pathological," I am referring to the various hyperbolic and sometimes rather grotesque Purāṇic stories, such as the sixth *skandha*'s narrative of King Citraketu who had ten thousand wives and no heir. When he finally produces a son through the intervention of the sage Aṅgiras, the child is immediately poisoned by the King's nine thousand nine hundred and ninety-nine jealous cowives and dies. The distraught king demands that the sage return his son to him. The sage, beside the wailing mother and father, asks the son to return to his body, to which the son replies: "To which set of parents? I have been incarnated so many times, that I don't know who you are speaking of." The king finally "understands" his true situation, renounces the world, and goes off to the mountains to meditate. These "narratives of renunciation" will be discussed in full in chapter 4 (See BhP. VI.16).

22. Northrop Frye, *The Critical Path: An Essay on the Social Context of Literary Criticism* (Bloomington, IN: Indiana University Press, 1973).

23. The two variant episodes of the *Varāha-līlā* will be discussed in chapter 2.

24. See BhP. I.1.3:

> *nigama-kalpa-taror galitaṁ phalaṁ*
> *śuka-mukhād amṛta-drava-saṁyutam /*
> *pibata bhāgavataṁ rasam ālayam*
> *muhur aho rasikā bhuvi bhāvukāḥ //*

In his commentary on this verse, Viśvanātha Cakravartī says: *galitam iti vṛkṣa-pakvatayā svayam eva patitaṁ, na tu balāt patitam iti*, that the fruit is not picked from the tree by force, but falls from its own power of ripeness. Having been tasted by Śuka, the fruit of the Bhāgavata becomes more sweet (*svāditatvād atimadhuram*). The name of Śuka, the principal narrator of the tale, also means "parrot."

25. BhP. I.4.13,

> *tat sarvaṁ naḥ samācakṣva pṛṣṭoyad iha kiñcana*
> *manye tvāṁ viṣaye vācāṁ snātam anyatra chāndasāt.*

> We think you to be bathed
> In the discourse of (all) subjects
> With the exception of some of the
> Vedas. Therefore, explain to us
> All that we have inquired (of you).

26. BhP. I.4.13. See David Dean Shulman "Toward a Historical Poetics of the Sanskrit Epics," *Journal of South Asian Literature*, 4, no. 2 (1991), and Tzvetan Todorov "Recherches Sémantiques," Langages 1 (1966).

27. J. L. Mehta, "Dvaipāyana, Poet of Being and Becoming," paper presented at International Seminar on the Mahābhārata, February 17–20, 1987, at Sahitya Akademi, New Delhi.

28. I am specifically referring to the end of the Mahābhārata in which the Pāṇḍavas are forced to experience hell while seeing their evil archenemies enjoying the delights of heaven. Even if this vision is later proven to be illusory, the actual postmortem situation of the Pāṇḍava brothers is never clearly resolved in the Epic.

29. BhP. I.2.11,

> *vadanti tat tattva-vidas tattvaṁ yaj jñānam advayam*
> *brahmeti paramātmeti bhagavān iti śabdyate*

> Knowers of the truth call this Absolute-Non-Dual
> Knowledge—"Truth." It is also spoken of as Brahman,
> Paramātman, and Bhagavān.

30. See the list of twenty-one *avatāras* in BhP. I.3.6–25, followed by BhP. I.3.28,

> *ete cāṁśa-kalāḥ puṁsaḥ kṛṣṇas tu bhagavān svayam*
> *indrāri-vyākulaṁ lokaṁ mṛḍayanti yuge yuge*

All these are parts and portions of the Supreme Being,
but Kṛṣṇa is himself the Supreme Being himself, who graces
The world in every age when it is troubled by the enemies of Indra.

31. *Mbh.* I (5) 38–40.

32. Eugene G. D'Aquili and Charles D. Laughlin Jr., "The Neurobiology of Myth and Ritual," in *The Spectrum of Ritual: A Biogenetic Structural Analysis* (New York: Columbia University Press, 1979); reprinted in *Readings in Ritual Studies*, ed. Ronald Grimes (New Jersey: Prentice Hall, 1995). "The matrix usually takes the form of a myth in nonindustrial societies and a blend of myth and science in Western societies" (136).

33. Michael Stone, ed., *Jewish Writings of the Second Temple Period: Apocrypha, Pseudepigrapha, Qumran, Sectarian Writings, Philo, Josephus* (Philadelphia: Fortress Press, 1984).

34. Hillman, *Revisioning Psychology*, p. 111.

35. Harold North Fowler, trans., "Phaedo," in Plato I (Cambridge: Harvard University Press, 1914).

36. Cervantes, *Don Quixote*, cited in Weir, ed., *Death in Literature* (New York: Columbia University Press, 1980), 75–80.

37. Philip Aries, *Western Attitudes Toward Death*, trans. Patricia Ranum (Baltimore: The Johns Hopkins University Press, 1974), 6–9.

38. Umberto Eco, *A Theory of Semiotics* (Bloomington, IN: Indiana University Press, 1979), 66.

39. The Gītā's great theophany, for example, occurs when Kṛṣṇa reveals himself to be the true slayer of all (*kālo 'smi loka-kṣaya-kṛt pravṛddho*). Bhagavadgītā, XI, 32.

40. BhP. I.6.28–29.

Chapter 2: The Semiotics of Separation

1. Kakar, Sudhir, *The Inner World*, 1978.

2. See Apte, *The Practical Sanskrit-English Dictionary*, reprinted from the Revised and Enlarged Edition, Poona, 1957, ed. in Chief, P. K. Gode and C. G. Kurve, Kyoto, Rinsen Book Co., 1986, p. 1210.

3. BhP. I.3.28, *ete cāṁśa-kalāḥ puṁsaḥ kṛṣṇas tu bhagavān svayam*. Jīva Gosvāmī, in the *Krama-sandarbha*, declares this verse to be the *mahāvākya* or "ultimate declaration" of the Purāṇa. Vallabha also highlights this verse in his commentary on the BhP., the *Subodhinī*.

4. See *Chāndogya* VI.1.4, the "one substance" in the cited verse is clay. Other examples used are copper-gold, and a nail pairer of iron.

5. *Taittirīya Upaniṣad* II.4.1,

yato vāco nivartante / aprāpya manasā saha

Wherefore speech turns back with the mind,
not having attained it.

6. See Karl Potter, *Presuppositions of India's Philosophies* (Englewood Cliffs: Prentice Hall, 1963), and S. C. Chatterjee and D. M. Datta, *An Introduction to Indian Philosophy* (Calcutta: University of Calcutta, 1950) for discussions on the *pramāṇas*. Jīva Gosvāmī, in his *Tattva-sandarbha*, upholds *śabda* as the only *pramāṇa* capable of revealing the transcendental object (*veda evāsmākaṁsarvātīta-sarvāśraya-sarvācintyāścāryasvabhāvaṃ vastu vividiṣatāṁ pramāṇam*).

7. BhP. X.87. 1–41,"Oh Brāhmaṇa sage! How is it possible for the Vedas, conditioned as they are by the *guṇa*s and their products, to carry out their function directly with reference to the Supreme Brahman which is beyond specific indication and hence indefinable, devoid of qualities, and beyond cause and effect?"

8. The *puruṣārtha*s or "aims of humanity" are traditionally categorized as *dharma* (religious duty), *artha* (economic and political power), *kāma* (pleasure), and *mokṣa* (liberation). I am translating the word *loka* as realm, one could equally say "world." The discussion in question is said to have taken place on Janaloka, the fifth of seven divisions (some would like to say planetary systems) of the universe according to the Bhāgavata.

9. BhP. X.87.16

10. BhP. X.87.18

11. D. P. Sheridan, *The Advaitic Theism of the Bhāgavata Purāṇa* (Delhi: Motilal Bonarsidass, 1986).

12. BhP. X.87.26–28

13. In the twelfth *skandha*, Śuka gives his own encapsulation of the *Upaniṣads* on the matter.
BhP. XII.4.28–30,

Whatever is perceived as a cause or effect is
an illusion as the two are mutually interdependent.
That which has a beginning and an end is unreal.

Although apparent as a transformed manifestation
this phenomenal world cannot at all be explained
independently of the self. Otherwise it would be
the same as the conscious self.

There is no diversity in the real. If an ignorant
person thinks so, it is as like the distinction
between the air, the sun, or empty space.

14. *na cāsya kaścin nipuṇena dhātur avaiti jantuh kumanīṣa ūtīḥ*
nāmāni rūpāṇi mano-vacobhiḥ santanvato nata-cāryām ivājñaḥ

15. See Hardy, *Viraha-Bhakti*, p. 16: "It follows from this that the emotions placed below the mind and ego and in fact directly involved via sense impressions . . . were equally suspect. Any spiritual exercise must start by suppressing them. Nor could objects to which they refer such as natural beauty, artistic creation, or the attraction of the female form, be accepted in any positive sense." See pp. 12–17 for further discussion of the "normative ideology."

The attributing of certain devotional hymns to Śaṅkara does not depend upon authorial authenticity. What is at issue here is the reception of the work by a culture. See P. Hacker, "Relations of Early Advaitins to Vaiṣṇavism" (Vienna, *WZKSA*, 1965), vol. 9: 147–54. on the Śaṅkara problem.

16. Sheridan (1986) describes the Bhāgavata's "redirective" project as "searching for metaphors and concepts to describe its ineffable vision of the relation of the Absolute with the created world." Here, the semiotic problem is stated in the terminology of religious studies. In addressing the Bhāgavata-Purāṇa, however, one cannot separate the linguistic, social, or religious fabrics of the work without shredding the garment. The ineffable experience can only be communicated through that language which is the legacy of an entire tradition. The Bhāgavata, as a Purāṇa, must therefore navigate an all-inclusive course. Thus, Sheridan refers to its "Advaitic Theism," a necessary oxymoron when trying to approach this text philosophically.

17. The BhP.'s employment of Vedic verbal forms and meters has been duly noted by J. A. B. van Buitenen, who referred to it as the "literary Purāṇa." Meier's work on Vedic roots in the BhP. is referred to by J. A. B. van Buitenen, "On the Archaism of the Bhāgavata-Purāṇa, in *Krishna: Myths, Rites, and Attitudes*, ed., Milton Singer (Chicago: University of Chicago Press, 1968). Also see A. S. Biswas, *Bhāgavata-Purāṇa: A Linguistic Study* (Dibrugarh: Vishvesh varanand Book Agency, 1968).

18. Śrīdhara,

gāyatryā prārambheṇa brahmavidyā-rūpam etat purāṇam iti darśitam.

19. BhP. III.12.39, in this verse, as one of many examples, the Bhāgavata claims its status as the fifth Veda emanating from the mouth of Brahmā.

20. See R. C. Hazra, *Studies in the Puranic Records on Hindu Rites and Customs*, Dacca University, 1940, reprint, Delhi Motilal Banarsidass, 1975. P. V. Kane, *History of Dharmasastra: Ancient and Medieval Religious and Civil Law in India*. Poona: Bhandarkar Oriental Research Institute, Vol. I, The Puranas, 1930, Origin and Development of Purana Literature, Vol. V.2, 1962.

21. See Vans Kennedy, *Researches into the Nature and Affinity of Ancient and Hindu Mythology* (London: Longman, 1831).

22. See van Buitenen, "On the Archaism of the Bhāgavata-Purāṇa."

23. *Nāṭyaśāstra* VI.32.

24. Different aestheticians have propounded variant theories on *rasa*. For Bhaṭṭa Lollaṭa, for example, *rasa* was an intensification of the *sthāyibhāva* or dominant emotion. See Raniero Gnoli, *The Aesthetic Experience According to Abhinavagupta* (Rome: Instituto Italiano pari Medio ed Estremo Oriente, 1956); and Gerow, "Rasa as a Category of Literary Criticism," in *Sanskrit Dramatic Performance*, ed. Rachel Van M. Baumer and James Brandon (Honolulu: University of Hawaii Press, 1981). This is also stated in *NŚ* VII.29.

25. For Bhaṭṭa Nāyaka the aesthetic experience, while free from personal interest, is still marked by temporality as it is dependent upon mental constructs. The similarities and differences between aesthetic and meditative experience are discussed in J. Moussaieff, J. L. Masson, and M. V. Patwardan's *Śāntarasa and Abhinavagupta's Philosophy of Aesthetics*, Bhandarkar Oriental Series, no. 9 (Poona: Bhandarkar Oriental Research Institute, 1969), 161–64.

26. Out of forty-one psychological states (*bhāvas*), eight were classified as durable emotional states (*sthāyī*): *rati* (love), *krodha* (anger), *śoka* (sorrow), *hāsya* (mirth), *utsāha* (enthusiasm), *vismaya* (wonder), *jugupsā* (disgust), and *bhaya* (fear). The Aesthetic tradition generally recognized eight principle *rasas*: *śṛṅgāra* (erotic), *hāsya* (the comic), *raudra* (the furious), *karuṇa* (the compassionate), *vīra* (the heroic), *adbhūta* (the wonderful), *bibhatsā* (the disgustful), and *bhayānaka* (the fearful).

27. *Śakuntalā,* V. 2, trans. B. S. Miller, 1984, in *Theater of Memory: The Plays of Kālidāsa* (New York: Columbia University Press, 1984),

> *ramyāṇi vīkṣya madurāṁśca niśamya śabdān*
> *paryutsukībhavati yatsukhito 'pi jantuḥ /*
> *tac-cetasā smarati nūnamabodhapūrvaṁ*
> *bhāvasthirāṇi jananāntarasauhṛdāni //*

28. Robert Thurman, trans. *The Holy Teachings of Vimalakīrti* (Pennsylvania: Pennsylvania State University Press, 1981), 78.

29. Hardy, *Viraha-Bhakti* (1983), p. 490.

30. See James Hillman's contention here in *Healing Fiction* (Dallas: Spring Publications Press, 1978).

31. *parabrahmāsvādasavidhena bhogena paraṁ bhujyata iti* (*Abhinavabharati*).

32. *Taittirīya Upaniṣad* II.7, *raso vai saḥ rasam hy evāyaṁ labdhvā'nandī bhavati*, "that is *rasa*; for only upon attaining *rasa* does one attain bliss," cited by Śrīdhara, Jīva Gosvāmī, Viśvanātha Cakravartī, and others on BhP. I.1.3. Since the *Upaniṣads* are considered to be part of the Vedic tradition, this verse gives Vedic legitimacy. Sanātana Gosvāmī, a sixteenth-century disciple of Caitanya (one of the principal canonizers of the Bhāgavata) has even written an entire commentary on Kālidāsa's *Meghadūta*, the *Tātparya Dīpikā*. It is quite

unusual for a theologian to "stoop" to discuss a non-religious *kāvya*, and the fact that Sanātana Gosvāmī, an avid propounder of the Bhāgavata, does so is a further indication of the importance of the poetic project for the development of Vaiṣṇava theology.

33. Beyond the Bhāgavata the Bengali Vaiṣṇavas adapt this poetic theory to their concept of religious realization in such works as Rūpa Gosvāmī's *Bhakti-rasāmṛtasindhu* and *Ujjvalanīlamaṇi*. For them, *bhāva* is the worshipful attitude that the devotee assumes toward Kṛṣṇa, and *rasa* is the experience of pure bliss in the love relationship between the two. However, one can see the main elements of this equation already present in the Bhāgavata. See E. Dimock, *Place of the Hidden Moon* (Chicago: University of Chicago Press, 1966).

34. See C. Hospital, "Līlā in the *Bhāgavata-Purāṇa,*" *Purāṇa* 22, no. 1 (January, 1980). The idea of a "parade" is quite consistent with later theological discussions in which *līlā* is said to be both *prakaṭa* and *aprakaṭa*, that is, it appears in a certain place and time almost like a road show, while simultaneously existing in the absolute realm.

35. "In my opinion, the BhP., in spite of its lyricism and artistry, remains an academic and hybrid work when compared with some of the sophisticated and yet strikingly intense and passionate emotional songs of Nammālvār or Antal." Hardy, *Viraha-Bhakti* (1983), p. 245.

36. Hardy, 1983.

37. BhP. I.1.16.

38. BhP. I.2.17.

39. Lit. *gam* "to go," and *ni*—affirmative prefix—*nigama* "by which one goes,"

Vijayadhv. I.1.3, *nigamayati nitarāṃ jñāpayati apekṣitāśeṣa-puruṣārtham iti nigamo vedaḥ.*

40. In *Pāṇini*, the word is even identified with *rasa* itself, and the two words also appear together in the *Śiśupālavadha*, referring to the moonbeams as shedding ambrosia. *Pāṇini* VI.I. 21, *Śiśupālavadha* IX.36.

41. Śrīdhara,

tac ca tanmukhād bhuvi galitaṁ śisya-praśiṣyādirūpa-pallava-param-parayā śanair akhaṇḍam evāvatīrṇam

> This ripened fruit fallen to earth from
> the mouth of Śuka thus is handed down gently,
> unbroken, through the branches of disciplic succession
> from teacher to student.

42. Śrīdhara notes *aho bhuvi galitam iti alabhya-lābhoktiḥ*, "Ah! The ripened fruit (fallen) on earth is the rare attainment of the unattainable." The alternate meaning of *galita* was first pointed out to me by Shrivatsa Goswami in

a personal communication. Viśvanātha Cakravartī, relates *galita* to the tree being so ripe that the fruit falls by itself and not by force. The "falling" fruit, then, cannot be seized. It is only received through grace.

43. Śrīdhara rhetorically asks "How can it be drunk?" "Because," he answers, "it is *rasa* and a liquid where even pit, rind, and pulp are ripened." The whole body of the text is thus turned into *rasa*.

44. BhP. I.1.19,

vayaṁ tu na vitṛpyāma uttama-śloka-vikrame
yac-chṛṇvatāṁ rasa-jñānāṁ svādu svādu pade pade

Chapter 3: Narratives of Absence

1. J. L. Mehta, "Dvaipāyana, The Poet of Being and Becoming," paper presented at the *International Seminar On The Mahābhārata*, Delhi, Sahitya Akademi, 1987, p. 5: "The central theme of the epic, in this sense, is the human state as governed by desire, by the pursuit of the means of attaining these, and by man's subservience to rule and principle, to an over-arching law, as the necessary condition for gaining his ends."

2. In terms of the ideology behind myths of authorship, the son, in the Bhāgavata, clearly surpasses the father. Śuka is said to be superior to Vyāsa, although he is but the narrator of the text which his father has compiled.

3. BhP. I.2.8,

dharmaḥ svanuṣṭhitaḥ puṁsāṁ viṣvaksena-kathāsu yaḥ
notpādayed yadi ratiṁ śrama eva hi kevalam

4. Sūta, capitalized, denotes Ugraśravas, the son of Romaharṣaṇa, who is one of the principal narrators of the text, while *sūta* denotes the title of "bard" or Purāṇic reciter.

A Purāṇic *sūta* is traditionally the offspring of a *kṣatriya* by a *brāhmaṇa* woman. While this *sūta* is usually taken as the Ugraśravas of the Mahābhārata, the *Kūrma-Purāṇa* gives a different genealogy, explaining that Hari/Nārāyaṇa sprang as Sūta from a sacrifice of Brahmā (the self-born) with full scriptural knowledge and the ability to expound upon the ancient lore.

5. See Rocher, *The Purāṇas*, pp. 53–9, for a discussion of the Sūta in the Purāṇas. The Bhāgavata is ambiguous as to whether or not the *sūta* belongs to a mixed caste. Balarāma, in the tenth *skandha*, must atone for killing a brāhmaṇa when he kills Romaharṣaṇa Sūta. However, the BhP. does indicate that Sūta, the narrator, cannot recite certain portions of the Veda (I.4.13, *manye tvāṃ viṣaye vācāṁ snātam anyatra chāndasāt*). And, as E. W. Hopkins (in Singer, 1966) points out, Sūta does seem to confirm his mixed origin in I.18.18,

aho vayaṁ janmabhṛto 'dya hāsma
vṛddhānuvṛttyāpi vilomajātāḥ

> Even though we were born into
> a mixed caste we have achieved the
> object of our life through service to our elders.

Either Romaharṣaṇa or his son Ugraśravas is the narrator of nearly all the Purāṇas.

6. Mehta, "Dvaipāyana, Poet of Being and Becoming," paper presented at International Seminar on the *Mahābhārata*, February 17–20, 1987, Sahitya Akademi, New Delhi, p. 2.

7. See R. K. Narayan, *Gods, Demons, and Others* (New York: Viking Press, 1964), for a description of current bardic recitations. Also see Milton Singer, *When A Great Tradition Modernizes: An Anthropological Approach To Indian Civilization* (New York, Washington, London: Praeger Publishers, 1972).

8. BhP. I.1.9, *puṁsām ekāntataḥ śreyas tan naḥ śaṁsitum arhasi.*

9. My translation of *pravrajantam* as "recluse" here comes from the relationship of *pravraj (pra + vraj)* with the renunciate (see *Manusmṛti* VI.38.8).

10. *taṁ sarva-bhūta-hṛdayaṁ munim*

11. There are a number of intertexts to this "Śuka-story." In the Mahābhārata XII. 320.20–26, Śuka flies into the sun leaving his father behind and becomes "one with all beings." When Vyāsa wails for his son in this text, the entire creation responds "bhoḥ!," "Alas!." Śrīdhara says that Śuka answered "in the form of the trees" in order to quell his father's affection, since he is now one with all beings:

> *tadā tanmayatayā śukarūpatayā taravo' bhineduḥ pratyuttaram uktavantaḥ pituḥ snehānubandha-parihārāya yo vṛkṣarūpeṇottaraṁ dattavān ityarthaḥ.*

One of the most creative commentaries on this verse is that of Viśvanātha Cakravartī who says that the trees' answer was an echo (*pratyuttaram*), thus echoing Vyāsa's misapprehension that he is the father and Śuka is the son. If Vyāsa cries out "O son," and the trees respond in the exact same manner, "O son," then Śuka is indirectly saying, "If I am the son, then you are also my son. Who is the father, son, etc. of whom? Delusion is the cause of this! The trees' response suggests "aren't you (Vyāsa) deluded, not knowing the truth?"

Yadi tavāhaṁ putras tadā tvam api me putra ityata kasya ke pitṛputrādya moha eva hi kāraṇam iti tattvam avijñāya kim iti muhyasīti vyañjayāmāsuḥ. Since Śuka has become one with all beings, he no longer lives by such distinctions. For a discussion of the Śuka-story in the Mahābhārata, see Wendy Doniger, "Echoes of the Mahābhārata: Why is a Parrot the Narrator of the *Bhāgavata Purāṇa* and the *Devībhāgavata Purāṇa?*," in *Purāṇa Perennis: Reciprocity and Transformation in Hindu and Jaina Texts* (Albany: The State University of New York Press, 1993).

12. *āsīnam urvyāṁ bhagavantam ādyaṁ*
saṅkarṣaṇaṁ devam akuṇṭha-sattvam /
vivitsavas tattvam ataḥ parasya
kumāra-mukhyā munayo' nvapṛcchan //

13. This is confirmed by the Purāṇic tradition which sees Vyāsa as a generic title. See BhP. XI.16.28 where Kṛṣṇa states that he is Dvaipāyana Vyāsa among the Vyāsas (*dvaipāyano'smi vyāsānām*). This verse is noted by Rūpa Gosvāmī in his discussion of the *Vyāsāvatāra* in *Laghubhāgavatāmṛta* 1.82. He cites *Viṣṇu-Purāṇa* III.4.5. as one example (Nārāyaṇa is said to be the author) and the *Śānti Parvan* III.46.11. Where Vyāsa is said to be Nārāyaṇa himself. The Bhāgavata also lists Vyāsa as an *avatāra* in I.3.21.

14. *tataḥ saptadaśe jātaḥ satyavatyāṁ parāśarāt*
cakre veda-taroḥ śākhā dṛṣṭvā puṁso'lpa-medhasaḥ

Then, as the seventeenth incarnation, born of Satyavatī through Parāśara, He (Vyāsa) created the branches of the Vedic tree, seeing the debilitated intelligence of humanity.

15. *smayanniva*. See Gītā II.10 where Kṛṣṇa appears to Arjuna "as if smiling" (*prahasanniva)*. In the *Vālmīki-Rāmāyaṇa*, Nārada appears in a similar manner to allay Vālmīki's anxiety.

16. See *Dhvanyāloka* III, 41–42.

17. BhP. I,5,13, *urukramasyākhila-bandha-muktaye samādhinānusmara tad-viceṣṭitam*
BhP. I.5.14,

tato'nyathā kiñcana yad vivakṣataḥ
pṛthag-dṛśas tat-kṛta-rūpa-nāmabhiḥ /
na karhicit kvāpi ca duḥsthitā matir
labheta vātāhata-naur ivāspadam //

Since you were desiring to describe something
whose vision is separate from this, your mind,
which has become agitated by names and forms,
like a boat swept away by the wind,
will never anywhere achieve stability.

18. One could make the argument, of course, that to perceive the world in a dualistic manner is murder of sorts, or inversely, that thinking oneself the "slayer" or the "slain" is a hallmark of the dualistic mind. One could also perhaps claim, more accurately, that the cardinal sin in Vālmīki's *Rāmāyaṇa* is not murder per se, but is the causing of *viraha*. The "murder" is in fact accidental. What is significant is the forced separation from one's beloved. While the *Rāmāyaṇa* employs the conventional device of a curse to move the plot along, the Bhāgavata takes a more introverted (and perhaps in this case, philosophical) approach.

19. BhP. I.6.1–38.

20. Śrīdhara glosses *uttama-śloka* as "he whose fame (*śloka*) is such that from it *tamas* disappears." *Bhāvārtha-dīpikā* I.1.19, *udgacchati tamo yasmāt sa uttamastathābhūtaḥ śloko yaśo yasya.*

21. See, for example, BhP. X.10.38, "May our speech be engaged in your qualities, our ears in your stories, our hands in your work, our minds in the thought of your feet . . ."

Chapter 4: The Dominion of Death

1. The Bhāgavata does not refer to "sexuality" through one particular term, but speaks of desire (*kāma*), and often uses "woman" (*strī*) as a metonym for sexuality, especially when related to the word *māyā* as illusion.

2. Sudhir Kakar, *The Inner World* (Delhi: Oxford University Press, 1978), 34–35. Psychologically speaking, a pervasive fear of death betrays either the fear of loss of a love object or the fear of loss of individuality in fusion with the object." The quality of this fear is determined by imagination and dependence. . . . The fear of death, then, contains these two elements: the fear of dependence and obliteration as an individual in the state of fusion, and the fear of unimaginable loneliness, emptiness, and desolation in the state of separation. Both fears are rooted in early infancy when they are first and most directly experienced."

3. BhP. II.1.2–4.

4. *dehāpatya-kalatrādiṣvātma-sainyeṣvasatsvapi*
teṣāṁ pramatto nidhanaṁ paśyann api na paśyati.

5. John Weir Perry, *Lord of the Four Quarters: Myths of the Royal Father* (New York: George Braziller, 1966).

6. In the Indian epic imagination, the search for a homeland is not the top priority that it is in the Greek and Latin epics. In both the *Vālmīki-Rāmāyaṇa* and the Mahābhārata, the concept of an earthly resting place is fraught with ambivalence. While kingdoms are ultimately established, they fade before the specter of the "next world." Note the difference between the journeys of Rāma and Lakṣmaṇa and the Pāṇḍavas, which end in dissolution, and those of Odysseus and Aeneas, which involve brief excursions into the underworld, but which are primarily concerned with establishing or re-establishing their earthly domains. It is only relatively recently with the politicization of the Indian epic and the advent of Indian nationalism that the "homeland" takes on a similar charge.

7. BhP. I.19.37–38.

8. I am tempted to see the *Vālmīki-Rāmāyaṇa* as an intertext here and to ask if there is any connection in dying by a hunter's arrow and being *kāmamo-*

hitam, "bewildered by desire." Kṛṣṇa, of course, is not said to be "bewildered by desire." In fact, he is the one who bewilders desire itself, but he does act out his human role. On the other hand, the theme of "bewilderment by desire" is extensive throughout the Epic and Purāṇic literatures.

9. BhP. VI.17.28.

10. I am specifically referring to the beginning of the Gītā here. The Gītā and the Bhāgavata also share a poetic sensibility within which philosophical positions are presented, always from the platform of infallible authority.

11. BhP. III.26.57,

retas tasmād āpa āsan nirabhidyata vai gudam
gudād apāno'pānācca mṛtyur loka-bhayaṅkaraḥ

12. *BG* II.27,

jātasya hi dhruvo mṛtyur dhruvaṁ janma mṛtasya ca /
tasmād aparibarye' rthe na tvaṁ śocitum arhasi //.

13. BhP. IX.13.4.

14. *dehaṁ nāvarurutse' haṁ duḥkha-śoka-bhayāvaham*
sarvatrāsya yato mṛtyur matsyānām udake yathā.

15. *Tibetan Book of the Dead*, Chogyam Trungpa and Francesca Freemantle, trans. (Boston: Shambhala, 1987).

16. Robert Goldman, "Fathers, Sons, and Gurus: Oedipal Conflict in the Sanskrit Epics," in *Journal of Indian Philosophy* 6: 325–392.

17. Stephen Batchelor, *Buddhism without Beliefs* (London: n.p., 1998).

18. BhP. III.31.20–24.

19. BhP. X.45, and BhP. X. 85.

20. For discussions on narratives of beheading see Wendy Doniger, *Karma and Rebirth in Classical Indian Traditions* (Berkeley: University of California Press, 1980), *Other People's Myths: The Cave of Echoes* (New York: Macmillan; London: Collier Macmillan, 1988); and Doniger and Howard Eilberg Schwartz, editors, *Off with Her Head: The Denial of Women's Identity in Myth, Religion, and Culture* (Berkeley, Los Angeles: University of Calfornia Press, 1995).

21. BG XI.32, *kālo'smi loka-kṣayakṛt pravṛddho lokān samāhartum iha pravṛttaḥ*.

22. BhP. *V.14.29*, VI.9.20, X.1.7.

23. BhP. III.29.45,

so'nanto'nta-karaḥ kālo' nādir ādi-kṛd avyayaḥ
janaṁ janena janayan mārayan mṛtyunāntakam

A similar sermon on God as time is spoken to a lamenting Dhruva by Manu in BhP. IV.11.19–21.

24. BhP. III.14.5,

yayottānapadaḥ putro muninā gītayārbhakaḥ
mṛtyoḥ kṛtvaiva mūrdhny aṅghrim āruroha hareḥ padam

25. See Apte, 1986, p. 959.

26. BhP. III.14.5,6.

27. See, for example, BhP. X.1.37.

28. BhP. IV.11.24.

29. BhP. III.29.38.

30. BhP. VI.5.15.

31. BhP. X.52.2 To be accurate, Mucukunda doesn't awake, but is awakened by a ruse of Kṛṣṇa's, and immediately upon rising burns to ashes Kālayavana, the person who actually woke him.

32. The Sanskrit word for "son," *putra*, has been analyzed in the *Manusmṛti* 9.138 in terms of a deliverer (*tṛ* to cross) from the hell known as *put*, the hell where childless persons are sent to. The *śrāddha* ritual ceremonies, in which the eldest son makes a series of offerings to the deceased to insure his or her promotion to the status of an ancestor, are delineated in greatest detail in sections of the *Garuḍa-Purāṇa*.

33. *paritapyamānā / tadārudad-bāṣpakalākulākṣī.*

34. BhP. I.7.15.

35. BhP. I.8.4, *bhūteṣu kālasya gatiṁ darśayann na pratikriyām.*

36. *antaḥsthaḥ sarva-bhūtānām ātmā yogeśvaro hariḥ*
sva-māyayāvṛṇod garbhaṁ vairāṭyāḥ kuru-tantave

37. BhP. I.6.6,

ekātmajā me jananī yoṣin mūḍhā ca kiṅkarī
mayyātmaje'nanya-gatau cakre snehānubandhanam

This situation may actually mirror an important dynamic in the Indian family, the mother's strong attachment to the son who validates her social existence, and the son's subsequent attachment and aversion towards the mother. We will see the BhP. alternately embrace and repudiate the mother just as it accepts and rejects union.

38. BhP. I.6.9,

ekadā nirgatāṁ gehād duhantīṁ niśi gāṁ pathi
sarpo' daśat padā spṛṣṭaḥ kṛpaṇāṁ kāla-coditaḥ

39. See Apte (1986), p. 717. Śrīdhara construes *spṛṣṭah* as "slightly trod upon" (*padenāspṛṣṭa īṣad-ākrāntaḥ*). Thus, I have translated it as "grazed" emphasizing its relationship with the mother as innocent and/or helpless before her ordained destiny.

40. David Aberbach, *Surviving Trauma: Loss, Literature, and Psychoanalysis* (New Haven: Yale University Press, 1989).

41. Ibid.

42. *rūpaṁ bhagavato yat tan manaḥ-kāntaṁ śucāpaham*
apaśyan sahasottasthe vaiklavyād durmanā iva

43. See *The Bhāgavata-Purāṇa,* translated and annotated by G. V. Tagare (Delhi: Motilal Banarsidas, 1976), 7:52.

44. BhP. I.6.30

45. While the "negative" "split-off" woman is evident in the *Rāmāyaṇa,* one may wonder about the other epic here. I would see Ambā as the "victim" split-off female in the Mahābhārata, since she brings to the fore the conflict caused by Bhīṣma's "terrible vow" of chastity. The vow, made to enable his father King Śantanu's indulgence in the pursuit of pleasure, has ongoing consequences, not the least of which is Bhīṣma's own death. The "split-off" woman, portrayed as an instrument of death and destruction, is the woman who does not play a conventional marital and/or maternal role. Ambā's sisters, Ambikā and Ambālikā, both give birth to "defective" children due to their reactions of repulsion to Vyāsa during intercourse. Even Kuntī and the divine Gaṅgā, by rejecting their children (Kuntī sets Karṇa in a basket and leaves him floating down river, Gaṅgā drowns her first seven children), become instruments of later unresolvable problems in the Epic. In the Bhāgavata, we see the ultimate emblem of this group, the demoness Pūtanā, who offers the child Kṛṣṇa her poisoned breast milk to drink.

46. BhP. VI.14.11.

47. BhP. VI.15.20.

48. BhP. VI.16.4

49. *bandhu-jñāty-ari-madhyastha-mitrodāsīna-vidviṣaḥ*
sarva eva hi sarveṣāṁ bhavanti kramaśo mithaḥ.

50. BhP. VI.16.15.

51. BhP. X.45. 37–50.

52. This sort of juxtaposition is very similar to the "child-god" juxtaposition that Ken Bryant notes in the poems of Sūr Dās which are based on the Bhāgavata-Purāṇa narratives. See Kenneth E. Bryant, *Poems To The Child God* (Berkeley: University of California Press, 1978).

53. BhP. V.8.15.

54. Gītā, VIII.6,

yaṁ yaṁ vāpi smaran bhāvam tyajatyante kalevaram
taṁ taṁ evaiti kaunteya sadā tadbhāva-bhāvitaḥ

55. BhP. V.8.30–32.

56. The other archetype, that of the "mad lover," will be discussed in chapter 6 of this volume.

57. See A. K. Ramanujan, "On Woman Saints," in *The Divine Consort: Rādhā and the Goddesses of India*, John Stratton Hawley and D. M. Wulff, eds. (Boston: Beacon Press, 1986). Also see Kakar, *The Inner World*, pp. 160–182.

58. BhP. VII.2.23.

59. In the epic, the Pāṇḍavas die and are revived by a poisoned pool of water. The poisoned pool also appears in the tenth *skandha* narrative of Kṛṣṇa's dancing on the heads of the serpent Kāliya. The association of water with the feminine is clear in Sanskrit as well as in Indian religious imagery. I would like to go further and see the pool of water as representing the "unconscious" (derived from the many instances in which reflection in water is associated with the illusory world of *māyā*).

60. In BhP. VIII.2.27, following traditional astrological symbolism, the foot is related to the unconscious through the sign of Pisces, its ruler. One thinks of the deaths of Kṛṣṇa and Achilles here, but more interesting in this regard may be the extraordinarily detailed descriptions of the specific marks on the soles of Kṛṣṇa's feet given in the tenth *skandha.*

61. BhP. VIII.2.33,

yaḥ kaścaneśo balino'ntakoragāt pracaṇḍa-vegād
abhidhāvato'bhṛśam / bhītaṁ prapannaṁ paripāti
yad-bhayān mṛtyuḥ pradhāvaty araṇaṁ tam īmahi //

62. BhP. *I.9.43–46, I.15.39–42, IV.23.13–26*

63. *ātmanyagnīn samāropya saṁnyasyāhaṁmamātmatām*
kāraṇeṣu nyaset samyak saṅghātaṁ tu yathārhataḥ
khe khāni vāyau niśvāsāṁs tejaḥsūṣmāṇam ātmavān
apsvasṛk-śleṣma-pūyāni kṣitau śeṣam yathodbhavam
vācamagnau savaktavyāmindre śilpaṁ karāvapi
padāni gatyā vayasi ratyopasthaṁ prajāpatau
mṛtyau pāyuṁ visargaṁ ca yathāsthānaṁ vinirdiśet
dikṣu śrotraṁ sanādena sparśenādhyātmani tvacam
rūpāṇi cakṣuṣā rājan jyotiṣyabhiniveśayet
apsu pracetasā jihvāṁ ghreyairghrāṇaṁ kṣitau nyaset
mano manorathaiścandre buddhiṁ bodhyaiḥ kavau pare
karmāṇyadhyātmanā rudre yadahaṁmamatākriyā
sattvena cittaṁ kṣetrajñe guṇairvaikārikaṁ pare
apsu kṣitimapo jyotiṣyado vāyau nabhasyamum

kūṭasthe tacca mahati tadavyakte'kṣare ca tat
ityakṣaratayātmānaṁ cinmātramavaśesitam
jñātvādvayo'tha viramed dagdhayonirivānalaḥ

When, because of disease or advanced age, one is neither able to perform one's duties, study philosophy, or pursue spiritual knowledge, one should begin to fast. Properly placing the fires (of the body) within oneself and relinquishing the notion of "I" and "mine," one should then completely merge the aggregate elements into their causes. The knower of the self (should merge) the apertures of the body into space, the vital airs into the air, the heat into fire, the blood, phlegm, and pus into water, and the rest into earth, from whence they came. One should place one's speech and subject matter of speaking into Agni, the two hands and their crafting capacity into Indra, the feet and their power of movement into Viṣṇu, the Spirit of time, the genitals and sexual enjoyment into Prajāpati, the anus and its power of evacuation into Mṛtyu, directing each into their proper place. One should merge the sense of hearing, along with sound, in the directions, tactility with the sense of touch into the wind, and form along with vision, O King, into the sun. One should merge the tongue, along with the sense of taste, into water, and fragrance, along with the sense of smell, into the earth. Mind, along with its desires unto the Moon, intelligence along with its objects to the supreme seer (Brahmā), actions and self-awareness to Rudra, from who proceeds the action of egotism and self-interest, existence and thought into the individual (knower of the field) and the individual along with the qualities of nature into the Supreme. Earth in water, water in fire, the latter in air, that into space, that into the ego, and the latter into the totality of matter, that into the unmanifest, and that into the undying, imperishable. Thus, knowing the remaining imperishable self to be made of consciousness without a second, one should come to an end. like a fire that has devoured its own origins.

BhP. *VII, 12,24–31.*

64. BhP. *IV.23.22.*

65. BhP.*VI.11.27.*

66. BhP. *VI.12.35.*

67. In the seventh *skandha* one finds *ajagara* and *mahāsarpa* apparently used interchangeably. In the eleventh *skandha* we find *ajagara* and *mahāhi.*

68. *rājataś corataḥ śatroh sva-janāt paśu-pakṣitaḥ*
arthibhyaḥ kālataḥ svasmān nityaṁ prāṇārthavad bhayam

69. Quoted in *the Caitanya-caritāmṛta* of Kṛṣṇadāsa Kavirāja: *Antya* V.20,

na dhanaṁ na janaṁ na sundarīṁ kavitāṁ vā jagadīśa kāmaye
mama janmani janmanīśvare bhavatād bhaktir ahaitukī tvayi

70. BhP. X.1.34.

71. *jyotir yathaivodakapārthiveṣv adaḥ samīra-vegānugataṁ vibhāvyate*
evaṁ svamāyā-raciteṣv asau pumān guṇeṣu rāgānugato vimuhyati

72. "What is difficult to endure for the wise? What do they require? And what will the sinful not do? And what sacrifices are too difficult for the firm minded?" (BhP. X.1.58) *Dhṛtātmā*, "firm-minded," is also a common epithet for Viṣṇu, and thus extends to the devotees of Viṣṇu in this verse (see Śrīdhara's gloss). This is contrasted with the word *vijitātman*, "one who has an agitated mind," which is used two verses later to describe Vasudeva's appraisal of Kaṁsa.

73. The actual journey from Vṛndāvana, leading to the breaking of the bow, the wrestling match, and the death of Kaṁsa, is filled with wondrous and archetypal events that would be fascinating to study in terms of myth and narrative structure.

74. See Goldman, "Fathers, Sons, and Gurus: Oedipal Conflict in the Sanskrit Epics," in *Journal of Indian Philosophy* 6:325–92.

75. BhP. I.15.6.

Chapter 5: Strī Naraka Dvāra—Woman as the Gateway to Hell

1. See Dennis de Rougemont, *Love Declared*, trans. Richard Howard, (New York: Pantheon Books, 1963), 3. De Rougemont goes on to say that "only in Europe have religious morality and eroticism reached a state of permanent conflict. The categorical (and strongly mythic) separation of "East and West" is repeated by Joseph Campbell in *Myths To Live By* (New York: Bantam Books, 1973).

2. See Hardy, *Viraha-Bhakti*, p. 16.

3. See Karl Potter, *Presuppositions of Indian Philosophies* (Englewood Cliffs: Prentice Hall, 1963), 4. Potter points out that the key words in Indian philosophy are neither morality nor restraint. More clearly, they are control and *freedom*, or control for the sake of freedom.

4. BhP. III.31.34.

5. *saṅgaṁ na kuryāt pramadāsu jātu yogasya pāraṁ param ārurukṣuḥ*
mat-sevayā pratilabdhātma-lābho vadanti yā niraya-dvāram asya
yopayāti śanair māyā yoṣid deva-vinirmitā
tām īkṣetātmano mṛtyuṁ tṛṇaiḥ kūpam ivāvṛtam
yāṁ manyate patiṁ mohān man-māyām ṛṣabhāyatīm
strītvam strī-saṅgataḥ prāpto vittāpatya-gṛha-pradam
tām ātmano vijānīyāt paty-apatya-gṛhātmakam
daivopasāditaṁ mṛtyuṁ mṛgayor gāyanaṁ yathā

6. See *Apte* (1986), p. 1100, and *MW* (1899–1981), p. 685.

7. One remembers the opening verse of the *Meghadūta*, where the Yakṣa is described as *pramattaḥ* or "negligent" in the performance of his duty, as well as Śuka's opening monologue in the second *skandha* of the BhP., where those who do not see the truth of the self (*apaśyatām ātma-tattvam*) are referred to as *pramatta* (BhP. II.2.2–12).

8. *BG* II.62–63,

dhyāyato viṣayān puṁsaḥ saṅgas teṣūpajāyate
saṅgāt sañjāyate kāmaḥ kāmāt krodho'bhijāyate
krodhād bhavati sammohaḥ sammohāt smṛti-vibhramaḥ
smṛti-bhraṁśād buddhi-nāśo buddhi-nāśāt praṇaśyati—

For a man meditating on the sense objects, attachment to
them is created; from attachment desire is born;
from desire anger arises.
From anger comes bewilderment;
from bewilderment memory lapses;
from faltering memory understanding is lost;
from loss of understanding one is ruined.

9. BhP. VIII.8.46.

10. The *Arthaśāstra* contains similar declarations: *viśvāso naiva kartavyaḥ strīṣu rāja-kuleṣu ca*, "One should not put one's faith in a woman or a politician."

11. See the narratives of Vṛtra in BhP. VI.10–13 and Bali in BhP. IX.15–19. Other characters, such as Yayāti and Saubhari, also suffer "defeat" in succumbing to their desires, and eventually lament their ways and renounce the world.

12. BhP. VIII.12. 25,

tayāpahṛta-vijñānas tat-kṛta-smara-vihvalaḥ
bhavānyā api paśyantyā gata-hrīs tat padaṁ yayau

13. BhP. VIII.12.32–34.

14. BhP. VIII.12.37

15. See Erich Neumann "Fear of the Feminine," in *Quadrant* (New York: Journal of the C. J. Jung Foundation for Analytical Psychology, spring 1986).

16. See Apte (1986), p. 1450, and MW (1899,1981), p. 974.

17. BhP. VII.13.27,

sukham asyātmano rūpaṁ sarvehoparatis tanuḥ
manaḥ-saṁsparśajān dṛṣṭvā bhogān svapsyāmi saṁviśan

This verse is spoken to Prahlāda by the "python" sage who recommends withdrawal from all action.

18. See A. B. Keith, "The Birth of Purūravāḥ," *JRAS* (January, 1913): 412–417; K. R. Srīnivāsa Iyengar, "Urvaśī," *Sri Aurobindo Mandir Annual*

(August 15, 1949); D. D. Kosambi, "Urvaśī and Purūravāḥ," *JB(B)RS* 27 (1951): 1–30; and Wendy Doniger, *The Rig Veda* (Harmondsworth, Middlesex, England: Penguin Books, 1981), 252–256. I am tempted to read this myth as an inverse "Eros and Psyche" story with fullness and individuation at issue.

19. *Ṛg Veda* X.95.15. The jackal will later become a symbol of an unfaithful woman.

20. See Bṛhaddevatā XII.140–47, *Vedārthadīpikā*, and the *Śatapatha Brāhmaṇa* V.102.

21. BhP. IX.14.20–22.

22. *Ṛg Veda* X.95. 1, 14, and 15 all appear in this BhP. version.

23. The text goes on to state that women are wanton and unchaste and that they abandon men of taste to seek new lovers.

24. BhP. IX.14.45, *urvaśyām urasi purūravaḥ.*

25. BhP. IX.14.48,

eka eva purā vedaḥ praṇavaḥ sarva-vāṅmayaḥ
devo nārāyaṇo nānya eko 'gnir varṇa eva ca

26. See G. V. Tagare, trans., Bhāgavata-Purāṇa (Delhi: Motilal Banarsidass, 1976), 1170, n. 1. According to Viśvanātha Cakravartī, since Rāma is *parabrahman* possessing a pure spiritual and blissful body, sorrow is not possible for him:

cidānandādyo mano-buddhīndriyaśarīrasya parabrahmaṇas tasya duḥkha-sambhāvanāpi śāstra-yukti-pratikulā.

27. Vijayadhvaja actually drops this particular verse (IX.11.16) from his text.

28. BhP. IX.11.17,

strī-puṁ-prasaṅga etādṛk sarvatra trāsam-āvahaḥ
apīśvarāṇāṁ kim uta grāmyasya gṛha-cetasaḥ

29. *tamo-dvāraṁ yositāṁ saṅgi-saṅgam*—instructed by Ṛṣabha (BhP. V.5.2).

30. BhP. VI.18.28–30, "such stupefaction of men by women indeed is no wonder. Finding men unattached at the dawn of creation, Brahmā converted one half of his body into the female sex which robbed men of their judgment" (Kaśyapa to Diti).

31. See Dennis De Rougemont, *Love in the Western World* (New York: Pantheon Books, 1956), 78–81.

32. BhP. III.31.38.

33. BhP. VI.18.42.

34. BhP. VI.9.9.

35. See BhP. II.1.1–5.

36. See BhP. III.22.34.

37. Marriage, in Indian society is not a question of *kāma,* which disrupts the social order, but rather of *dharma*, the foundation of the social order. Kakar, *The Inner World,* p. 74. He remarks: "Any signs of a developing attachment and tenderness within the [newly married] couple are discouraged by the elder family members."

38. BhP. IX.7.55.

39. BhP. I.6.5.

40. See Kakar, *The Inner World,* p. 95. Śuka sees Satī as weak in the BhP. version of the Dakṣa myth (IV.4.3.), and refers to "the sin of women's sexual urge being clearly visible in the form of their menstrual discharge" (BhP. VI.9.9).

41. BhP. VI. 18.29–30,

> *evaṁ striyā jaḍībhūto vidvān api manojñayā*
> *bāḍham ity āha vivaśo na tac citraṁ hi yoṣiti*
> *vilokyaikānta-bhūtāni bhūtāny ādau prajāpatiḥ*
> *striyaṁ cakre sva-dehārdhaṁ yayā puṁsāṁ matir hṛtā*

42. BhP. V.5.8. The verse goes on to say that this knot bewilders one with regard to home, sons, relatives, and wealth, leading one to believe that they are one's own. See BhP. V.14.28 as well.

43. BhP. XI.8.7,

> *dṛṣṭā striyaṁ devamāyāṁ tadbhāvair ajitendriyaḥ*
> *pralobhitaḥ pataty andhe tamasy agnau pataṅgavat*

The polemic continues as follows:

> *yoṣidd-hiraṇyābharaṇāmbarādi-dravyeṣu māyā-raciteṣu*
> *mūḍhaḥ / pralobhitātmā hy-upabhoga-buddhyā*
> *pataṅgavan naśyati naṣṭa-dṛṣṭiḥ //*

A fool whose self is thus seduced, allured by a woman's golden ornaments, clothes, and other things, while enjoying these creations of *māyā* loses his insight and is destroyed like the moth. (BhP. XI.8.7)

The Avadhūta goes on to say that a mendicant should not even touch with his foot a wooden woman, for he would be "bound like an elephant with the she elephant." (BhP. XI.8.12).

44. BhP. IX.19.14,

> *na jātu kāmaḥ kāmānām upabhogena śāmyati*
> *haviṣā kṛṣṇa-vartmeva bhūya evābhivardhate*

45. BhP. IX.19.16,

tāṁ tṛṣṇāṁ duḥkha-nivahāṁ śarma-kāmo drutaṁ tyajet.

Chapter 6: The Rāsa Dance and the Gateway to Heaven

1. See Sudhir Kakar and John Munder Ross, *Tales of Love, Sex, and Danger* (New York: Basil Blackwell, 1987), 9. The *kṛṣṇa-carita* and other Purāṇic works have been subject to much psychoanalytic study recently. See O'Flaherty, *Asceticism and Eroticism*, 1973; Volvin Hein, "Comments: Radha and the Erotic Community," in *The Divine Consort*, eds., John Stratton Hawley and Donna M. Wulff (Berkeley: Berkeley Religious Study Series, 1982); John Stratton Hawley, *Krishna* (Princeton: Princeton University Press, 1983).

2. Before Dr. Acyut Lal Bhatt would consent to read these *Rāsa-Līlā* chapters with me, he felt it necessary to warn me that a "misreading" would land me in hell.

3. Bitter scorn: for an example of the scorn both within the Indian and colonial community, see David Haberman's "On Trial: the Love of the Sixteen Thousand Gopees." *History of Religions* 33, no. 1 (1993).

4. Sanātana Gosvāmī cites the *Nāṭyaśāstra*:

naṭair gṛhīta-kaṇṭhīnām anyānyāttakara-śriyām
nartakīnāṁ bhaved rāso maṇḍalībhūya nartatām

(cited in Tagare, 1976, Vol. 10, p. 1458). Hardy, *Viraha-Bhakti*, pp. 600–605, believes it derives from a South Indian performance tradition.

5. See John Stratton Hawley, *At Play with Krishna* (Princeton: Princeton University Press, 1981), 162. "It was supposed that the name of the dance itself, *rās*, is but a permutation of this more encompassing term. Grammatically this is possible. One noun can be derived from another noun by the use of *taddhita* affixes. These create secondary derivatives which rely on a phonetic change termed process called "increase" or *vṛddhi*; and the meaning of *rāsa* (with a long *a*) is semantically connected with or derived from *rasa*.

6. "Passionate love, the longing for what sears and annihilates us in its triumph—there is the secret which Europe has never allowed to be given away; a secret it has always repressed—and preserved! Hardly anything could be more tragic; and the way passion has persisted through the centuries should cause us to look to the future with deep despondency." De Rougemont, *Love in the Western World*, p. 50.

7. Śrīdhara also speaks of these chapters in terms of "*kandarpahā*," the arrogance of Kāmadeva killed in *rāsa-maṇḍala*. *Kāma* as "the enemy" is from the *Gītā* III.31.

8. BhP. X.29.12,13. In Rūpa Gosvāmī's *Lalita-Mādhava;* the *gopīs* Rādhā and Candrāvalī commit suicide because they are unable to bear Kṛṣṇa's separation. They are reborn as Satyabhāmā and Rukminī, respectively, and resume *līlā* with him in Dvārakā.

9. *kāmaṁ krodhaṁ bhayaṁ sneham aikyaṁ sauhṛdam eva ca / nityaṁ harau vidadhato yānti tan-mayatāṁ hi te* // Bh.P X.29.15.

10. Viṭṭhala's commentary on Vallabha's *Subodhinī* cited in James D. Redington, *Vallabhācārya on the Love Games of Kṛṣṇa* (Delhi: Motilal Banarsidass, 1983), 73, n. 24.

11. This reverses the more common motif of an asexual man and an alluring woman, such as Indra's *apsaras* seeking to break the meditation of ascetic *yogins*.

12. BhP. I.4.5.

13. BhP. X.1.15–16,

samyag-vyavasitā buddhis-tava rājarṣi-sattama
vāsudeva-kathāyāṁ te yaj-jātā naiṣṭhikī ratiḥ
vāsudevakathā-praśnaḥ puruṣāṁs trīn punāti hi
vaktāraṁ pṛcchakaṁ śrotṝṁs tat-pāda-salilaṁ yathā.

14. This issue is explicitly addressed in the "*ātmārāma*" verse cited in the first chapter of this volume: BhP. I.7.10,

ātmārāmāś ca munayo nirgranthā apy urukrame
kurvanty ahaitukīṁ bhaktim ittham-bhūta-guṇo hariḥ.

15. Some commentators see "*api*" as showing the greatness of the *gopīs*. For although Kṛṣṇa is *ātmārāma* or settled in his own pleasure, he is exhilarated by the love of the *gopīs*. See BhP. X.29.42:

iti viklavitaṁ tāsāṁ śrutvā yogeśvareśvaraḥ
prahasya sa-dayaṁ gopīr ātmārāmopyarīramat.

16. See Hardy, *Viraha-Bhakti* (1983). The solution here turns around a mimesis of the seasons.

17. NS VI.31, *vibhāvānubhāva-vyabhicāri-saṁyogād rasaniṣpattiḥ.*

18. See C. Mackenzie Brown, The Triumph of the Goddess: The Canonical Models and Theological Visions of the *Devī-Bhāgavata (*Albany: State University of New York Press, 1990), 72–75.

19. BhP. X.29.2.

20. See BG VII.25, *nāhaṁ prakāśaḥ sarvasya yoga-māyā-samāvṛtaḥ*. In BhP. II.7.43. Brahmā declares he and a few selected others know the *yoga-māyā* of the Supreme Being. In BhP. III.5.22, the sage Maitreya tells Vidura that the *līlā* of Bhagavān unfolds through his *yoga-māyā*; whereas in BhP. VIII.5.43, the entire world of *māyā* is said by Śuka to be brought about by *yoga-māyā*.

21. Jīva Gosvāmī says that *yoga-māyā* is the power under which the impossible can become possible, as in Kṛṣṇa expanding himself to being physically present to each *gopī*. Among the many explanations of *yoga-māyā* by the commentators is one in which this potency is the flute of Kṛṣṇa itself.

22. Throughout the *BhP*, *yoga-māyā* is used to indicate a *śakti*, a power or creative potency of the supreme (see II.7.43, III.5.22, VIII.5.42). See S. Bhat-

tacarya, *The Philosophy of Śrīmad Bhāgavatam* (Santiniketan: Visva Bharati, 1960, 1:51 for a discussion of these verses. Dan P. Sheridan, *The Advaitic Theism of Bhāgavata-Purāṇa* (Delhi: Motilal Banarsidass, 1986), relates *yoga-māyā* to allegory.

23. For Hardy the "sanskritization" effort to follow formal Aesthetic conventions here is an attempt to tame "Tamil libido." Sheridan states, "a god whose love play belongs to the standards of poetic conventions surely is intended to have symbolic meaning." Sheridan, *Advaitic Theism*, p. 113.

24. See S. Bhattacarya, *Philosophy of Śrīmad Bhāgavatam*, I: 127–28.

25. BhP. X.29.2, *priyaḥ priyāyā iva dīrgha-darśanaḥ.*

26. BhP. X.29.4,

niśamya gītaṁ tad anaṅga-vardhanaṁ
vraja-striyaḥ kṛṣṇa-gṛhīta-mānasāḥ.

27. *duḥsaha-preṣṭha-viraha-tīvra-tāpa-dhutāśubhāḥ*
dhyāna-prāptācyutāśleṣa-nirvṛtyā kṣīṇa-maṅgalāḥ
tam eva paramātmānaṁ jāra-buddhyāpi saṅgatāḥ
jahur guṇa-mayaṁ dehaṁ sadhyaḥ prakṣīṇa-bandanāḥ

The commentarial understands "auspicious" and "inauspicious" to refer to *karma.*

28. BhP. IV.4.25–28.

29. BhP. IV.4.22,

naitena dehena hare kṛtāgaso
dehodbhavenālam alaṁ kujanmanā /
vrīḍā mamābhūt kujana-prasaṅgatas
taj janma dhig yo mahatām avadya-kṛt //

30. BhP. X.29.11.

31. De Rougemont, *Love in the Western World.*

32. Viśvanātha Cakravartī has popularized the reading of BhP. X.29.18–27 (Kṛṣṇa to the *gopīs*) and BhP. X.29.31–41 (the *gopīs* reply) where all of Kṛṣṇa's remarks are filled with their opposing innuendos as are the answers of the *gopīs*. Ten verses spoken by Kṛṣṇa are followed by a ten-verse rebuttal by the *gopīs* in which each verse can be construed to signify its opposite. Jīva Gosvāmī speaks of Kṛṣṇa as the "master of confusing speech" when referring to these verses.

33. BhP. X.29.27,

śravaṇād darśanād dhyānān mayi bhāvo'nukīrtanāt
na tathā sannikarṣeṇa pratiyāta tato gṛhān

34. BhP. X.29.35,

virahajāgny-upayukta-dehā /
dhyānena yāma padayoḥ padavīṁ sakhe te //

35. BhP. X.29.43, *vyarocataiṇāṅka ivoḍubhir vṛtaḥ*

36. BhP. X.29.46,

vraja-sundarīṇām uttambhayan rati-patiṁ ramayāñcakāra.

37. Redington, *Vallabhācārya*, p. 134.

38. Brown, *Triumph of the Goddess*, p. 74. In addition to *The Triumph of the Goddess* (1990), C. M. Brown, *God As Mother: A Feminine Theology In India: An Historical and Theological Study of the Brahmavaivarta Purāṇa* (Vermont: Claude Stark and Co, 1974).

39. Clifford G. Hospital, "Bhakti and Liberation in the Bhāgavata-Purāṇa, (*Sciences Religieuses/Studies in Religion*, Ontario (automne/fall 1983): 402–03; Kṛṣṇa and the Theology of Play, *Sciences Religieuses/Studies in Religion* (hiver/winter 1976–77); "Līlā in the Bhāgavata Purāṇa," *Purāṇa* 22 (January 1980): 4–22.

40. *atha viśveśa viśvātman viśvamūrte svakeṣu me*
snehapāśamimaṁ chindhi dṛḍhaṁ pāṇḍuṣu vṛṣṇiṣu
tvayi me'nanyaviṣayā matir madhu-pate'sakṛt
ratimudvahatādaddhā gaṅgevaughamudanvati

Therefore, O Lord of the universe, O soul of the universe, O form of the universe please sever this bond of affection to my kinsmen the Pāṇḍavas and the Vṛṣṇis. O Lord of Madhu, as the Ganges ever flows down to the sea, may my mind find its exclusive and continuous delight in you.

BhP. (I.8.42–43)

41. Bharata states that the intensity of love reaches its peak when it is impeded by constant obstacles and the meeting of lovers takes place in concealment and that also very rarely. (NS I.104).

42. BhP. X.30.2,

ākṣipta-cittāḥ pramadā ramā-pates
tās tā viceṣṭā jagṛhus tad-ātmikāḥ.

The word *ākṣipta* has a number of variant meanings (thrown down, cast, overcome, transported (MW) which all imply a state of "possession." Therefore, Viśvanātha Cakravartī describes this state as the beginning of a very particular type of divine madness (*unmāda*).

43. BhP. X.30.3.

44. *gati-smita-prekṣaṇa-bhāṣaṇādiṣu*
priyāḥ priyasya pratirūḍhamūrtayaḥ /
asāv-aham tv ity abalās tad-ātmikā
nyavediṣuḥ kṛṣṇa-vihāra-vibhramāḥ //

45. BhP. X.30.4.

46. Defined in Rūpa Gosvāmī's *Bhakti-rasāmṛtasindhu* (I.2.291). For a modern analysis, see David Haberman, "*Acting as a Way to Salvation* (New York: Oxford University Press, 1988).

47. BhP. X.30.25–26. The footprints of Kṛṣṇa are clearly discernable due to their divine marks, which include a flag, a lotus, a thunderbolt, and elephant goad, and a barley seed.

48. See Walter Kaufmann and F. J. Hollingdale, trans., *On the Genealogy of Morals/Ecce Homo* (New York: Vintage Books, 1989), essay II.

49. Hardy sees this verse as an interpolated interjection of some "enforcement" priesthood. If one consistently adopted this method, the entire text, in fact *any* text, would have to be seen as nothing but a series of interpolations.

50. See Frédérique Apffel Marglin, "Female Sexuality in the Hindu World," in *Immaculate and Powerful: The Female in Sacred Image and Social Reality* (Boston: Beacon Press, 1985), 39–59.

51. See Vasudha Narayanan, "Brimming with *Bhakti*, Embodiments of *Shakti*: Devotees, Deities, Performers, Reformers, and Other Women of Power in the Hindu Tradition," in *Feminism and World Religions*, eds. A. Sharma and K. Young (Albany: State University of New York Press, 1999).

52. BhP. X.30.37, *naya māṁ yatra te manaḥ*.

53. BhP. X.30.28.

54. BhP. X.30.43–44,

> *tan-manaskās tad-ālāpās tad-viceṣṭās tad-ātmikāḥ*
> *tad-guṇān eva gāyantyo nātmāgārāṇi sasmaruḥ*
> *punaḥ pulinam āgatya kālindyāḥ kṛṣṇa-bhāvanāḥ*
> *samavetā jaguḥ kṛṣṇaṁ tad-āgamana-kāṇkṣitāḥ*

Jīva Gosvāmī, for example, claims that this verse reveals the glory of Rādhā, with her name hidden in the word *ārādhitaḥ*.

55. Hardy has noted and documented the strongest insertion of South Indian Alvār poetry and meter here, where separation takes on the mood of *vipralambha* as opposed to *karuṇā*. Hardy, *Viraha-Bhakti*, p. 531.

56. Ibid., p. 535.

57. BhP. X.31.7.

58. *praṇata-dehināṁ pāpa-karśanam*.

59. BhP. X.31.9, *tava kathāmṛtaṁ tapta-jīvanaṁ*.

60. BhP. I.1.1, X.31.10.

61. BhP. X.31.14,

> *surata-vardhanaṁ śoka-nāśanaṁ*
> *svarita-veṇunā suṣṭhu cumbitam /*

itara-rāga-vismāraṇaṁ nṛṇāṁ
vitara vīra nas te' dharāmṛtam //

62. BhP. X.31.15,

kuṭila-kuntalaṁ śrīmukhaṁ ca te
jaḍa udīkṣatāṁ pakṣma-kṛd dṛśām.

63. In BhP. X.31.16, both *acyuta*, "infallible" or "unfallen," and *kitava,* "rogue," "fraud," or "cheater," are addressed to Kṛṣṇa in the vocative case. The "rising desire" of verse seventeen is contrasted with the "heart breaking desire" of verse 18.

64. The derivation of *manmatha* is uncertain. It may be from *math* or *manth*, to churn or agitate, and later, to destroy. Its earliest Vedic usage is in connection with Agni, producing fire from the friction of churning sticks. This form may be an intensive of *math*, but is also possibly a combination of *man*, a form of *manas* "mind" derived from *man* ("think," "consider") with *matha* a derivative of *math*. Thus, Kāma personified is he who churns or agitates (destroys) the mind.

65. BhP. X.32.3,

taṁ vilokyāgataṁ preṣṭhaṅ prīty-utphulla-dṛśo 'balāḥ
uttasthur yugapat sarvās tanvaḥ prāṇam ivāgatam

66. BhP. X.32.5, *santaptā stanayor adhāt,*

BhP. X.32.9, *jahur viraha-jaṁ tāpam.*

67. BhP. X.32.20,

nāhaṁ tu sakhyo bhajato'pi jantūn
bhajāmy amīṣām anuvṛtti-vṛttaye /
yathādhano labdha-dhane vinaṣṭe
tac-cintayān yannibhṛto na veda //

68. *ye yathā māṁ prapadyante tāṁs tathaiva bhajāmy aham.*

69. BhP. X33.29. The use of *īśvarāṇām* in the plural allows for a number of possible translations. But if Śuka was only referring to "God" here, it would be in the singular.

70. BhP. X.32.20

71. BhP. X.32.22,

na pāraye'haṁ niravadya-saṁyujāṁ
sva-sādhu-kṛtyaṁ vibudhāyuṣāpi vaḥ
yā mābhajan durjara-geha-śṛṅkhalāḥ
saṁvṛścya tad vaḥ pratiyātu sādhunā //

72. BhP. X.33.1, *jahur viraha-jaṁ tāpaṁ tad-aṅgopacitāśiṣaḥ.*

73. BhP. X.33.6,

madhye maṇīnāṁ haimānāṁ mahā-marakato yathā

He appeared like a great emerald in the midst of jeweled-gold.

74. *pāda-nyāsair bhuja-vidhutibhiḥ sa-smitair bhrū-vilāsair*
bhajyan madhyaiś cala-kuca-paṭaiḥ kuṇḍalair gaṇḍa-lolaiḥ /
svidyan-mukhyaḥ kavara-raśanāgranthayaḥ kṛṣṇa-vadhvo
gāyantyas taṁ taḍita iva tā megha-cakre virejuḥ //

75. BhP. X.33.16 *svapratibimba-vibhramaḥ*

76. Some *sampradāya* commentators construe this verse (X.33.8) to mean that all the principal *rāgas* originate with the *gopīs*.

77. BhP. X.33.25,

evaṁ śaśāṇkāṁśu-virājitā niśāḥ
sa satya-kāmo'nuratābalā-gaṇaḥ /
siṣeva ātmany avaruddha-sauratah
sarvāḥ śarat-kāvya-kathā-rasāśrayāḥ //

78. Since theological explanations do not fully do justice to the magical nature of the content, it is tempting to see the *siddhānta* as the text's attempt to rationalize the appropriation of "other sources." This is Hardy's position, as he sees a more conservative, sanskritized North Indian tradition trying to incorporate a more sensual South Indian one.

79. BhP. X.33.39,

vikrīḍitaṁ vraja-vadhūbhir idaṁ ca viṣṇoḥ
śraddhānvito'nuśṛṇuyād atha varṇayed yaḥ /
bhaktiṁ parāṁ bhagavati pratilabhya kāmaṁ
hṛd-rogam āśvapahinoty acireṇa dhīraḥ //

Śrīdhara strongly emphasizes "victory over *kāma*" (*kāmavijayam eva phalam āha*) as the reason why one should hear and describe (*varṇayet*) this text.

Chapter 7: Final Partings

1. Barbara Stoler Miller's translation of *brahmanirvāṇa* in the Bhagavadgītā.

2. De Rougemont, *Love in the Western World*, p. 157.

3. S. Bhattacharya, *The Philosophy of the Śrīmad Bhāgavatam*, cites Bharata here (I.104).

4. De Rougemont, *Love in the Western World*, p. 32.

5. BhP. X.35.1.

6. BhP. X.39.14,

kāścit tat-kṛta-hṛt-tāpaśvāsa-mlāna-mukha-śriyaḥ
sraṁsad-dukūla-valaya-keśa-granthyaś ca kāścana

Some, with their hearts burning,
had the luster of their faces dimmed by sighing,
and others had the knots of their hair,
bracelets, and garments loosened.

7. I follow Śrīdhara in his commentary in which he takes *nivṛttāśeṣa-vṛttayaḥ* to be the sensory functions:

tasya śrīkṛṣṇasyānudhyānena nivṛttā aśeṣāś cakṣurādivṛttayo yāsāṁ tā imaṁ lokaṁ deham api na jānanti sma muktā iveti

The suggested terminology of the *Yoga-Sūtra*s is fairly evident, however. For the sensory (*indriyavṛtti*) and mental (*cittavṛtti*) fluctuations can easily imply each other.

8. Sir Monier Monier-Williams, *A Sanskrit-English Dictionary* (reprint, 1981; Delhi: Motilal Banarsidass), 306. Monier-Williams cites the Ṛg Veda, *Śatapatha Brāhmaṇa*, and the *Mahābhārata* for this etymology. Jīva Goswāmī gives the following etymology in his commentary on the *Brahma-saṁhitā:*

kṛṣir bhū-vācakaḥ śabdo ṇaśca nirvṛtti-vācakaḥ
tayor aikyaṁ paraṁ brahma Kṛṣṇa ity abhidhīyate

The work "*kṛṣ*" indicates "existence" (*bhū*) and "*ṇa*" indicates "bliss" (*nirvṛti*). The Supreme Brahma, the "oneness" (*aikya)* of these two, is known as "Kṛṣṇa."

9. BhP. XI.17.53.

10. *aho vidhātas tava na kvacid dayā saṁyojya*
maitryā praṇayena dehinaḥ / tāṁś cākṛtārthān
viyunaṅkṣy apārthakaṁ vikrīḍitaṁ
te 'rbhaka-ceṣṭitaṁ yathā //

11. BhP. X.39.29, *gopyaḥ kathaṁ nvatitarema tamo durantam.*

12. The verse, X.39.35, as Hardy notes, is quite strange:

tās tathā tapyatīr vīkṣya sva-prasthāne yadūttamaḥ
sāntvayāmāsa sa-premair āyāsya iti dautyakaiḥ

Thus, seeing them burning with agony upon his departure, the Best of the Yadus consoled them with loving words, "I will return," sent through a messenger. The use of the *dūta* does not make sense here, *dautyakaiḥ* can be construed as "a message," but that does not help much. For Kṛṣṇa is supposedly talking directly to the *gopīs*. Once again, the commentarial tradition does not always take the Purāṇa's descriptions at face value. Jīva Gosvāmī, for example, in his *Krama-sandarbha*, insists that Kṛṣṇa secretly lamented his separation from the cowherd women (*tāsām iva līlārasāviṣṭasya śrikṛṣṇasyāpi duḥkhām jātameva kintu gopī-tam).*

13. BhP. X.7.35–37.

14. Kenneth E. Bryant, *Poems to the Child-God.*

15. BhP. X.40.15,

tvayyavyayātman puruṣe prakalpitā
lokāḥ sa-pālā bahu-jīva-saṅkulāḥ /
yathā jale sañjihate jalaukaso 'py
udumbare vā maśakā mano-maye //

16. See *Krama-sandarbha* X.39.38, *śrikṛṣṇasyāpi duḥkhaṁ jātam eva*, and *kintu gopitam, gamanāvaśyaka-kāryaviśeṣārtham eva.* In Jīva's *Gopāla-campū*, he even describes Kṛṣṇa's return to Vṛndavana, and has Kṛṣṇa fulfill the *gopīs'* desires by marrying them.

17. One may note, in this regard, that the "happy ending" to courtly romance was not introduced in the West until the allegorical novel of the seventeenth century. The prototype of the courtly romance culminates in death and dissolution into an elevated condition outside the boundaries of the mundane world.

18. Abhinavagupta, we may remember, compares the experience of *rasa* with the experience of the absolute. Viśvanātha, in the *Sāhityadarpaṇa*, equates *rasa* to the other worldly taste of *brahman* that is filled with wonder:

KSS Ed. III.2,3,

sattvodrekād akhaṇḍasvaprakāśānandacinmayaḥ
vedyāntarasparśaśūnyo brahmāsvādasahodaraḥ
lokottaracamatkāraprāṇaḥ kaiścit pramātṛbhiḥ
svakāravad abhinnatvenāyam āsvādyate rasaḥ.

See K. K. Raja, *Indian Theories of Meaning* (Madras, Vasant Press, 1963) for a discussion of the distancing mechanism in *rasa*.

19. BhP. X.46.5,6.

20. BhP. X.46.36,37,

antarhṛdi sa bhūtānām āste jyotir ivaidhasi //
na mātā na pitā tasya na bhāryā na sutādayaḥ.

21. BhP. X.46.43.

22. BhP. X.47.6,

anyeṣvarthakṛtā maitrī
yāvad-arthaviḍambanam
pumbhiḥ strīṣu kṛtā yadvat
sumanasviva ṣaṭpadaiḥ.

23. BhP. X.47.6–8.

24. As a Vaiṣṇava text, the BhP. is referring to Kṛṣṇa in his aspect of Rāma as an *avatāra* of Viṣṇu.

25. BhP. X.47.27, *sarvātmabhāvo'dhikṛto bhavatīnām adhokṣaje.*

26. BhP. X.47.29, *bhavatīnāṁ viyogo me na hi sarvātmanā kvacit.*

27. A similar sensibility is seen in the Christian mystic by De Rougemont. "The saint does not refer to bodily or moral pains arising from the mortification of the senses and the will, but to the soul suffering separation and rejection while its love is most ardent. A hundred pages could be quoted in which there recurs the same lament of the soul about feeling deserted by the divine and being overwhelmingly anguished . . . about the feeling of rejection which counts among the sternest ordeals of purification." de Rougemont, *Love in the Western World*, p. 147.

28. BhP. X.47.44.

29. BhP. X.47.55.

30. Susan Wadley, "Woman and the Hindu Tradition," Introduction, *Signs: Journal of Women in Culture and Society*, 3, No. 1 (Chicago: University of Chicago Press, 1977).

31. BhP. X.47.62.

32. Kenneth Burke, *Philosophy of Literary Form: Studies in Symbolic Action* (Baton Rouge: Louisiana State University Press, 1967), 63.

33. *Gītā* I.1,

> *dharma-kṣetre kuru-kṣetre samavetā yuyutsavaḥ*
> *māmakā̤ pāṇḍavāś caiva kim akurvata sañjaya*

34. Aside from the gruesome epic battles fought at Kurukṣetra, the Bhāgavata notes that it was here that Paraśurāma filled huge pools with the blood of the *kṣatriya* kings in his effort to exterminate the warrior race. The other mythological act that consecrates the field is King Kuru ploughing and thus consecrating the ground. Kurukṣetra is also, of course, the "field of instruction" where Arjuna received the *Bhagavadgītā* from Kṛṣṇa.

35. BhP. X.82.40,

> *dṛgbhir-hṛdīkṛtamalaṁ parirabhya*
> *sarvāstadbhāvamāpurapi nityayujāṁ durāpam*

36. BhP. X.82.48,

> *adhyātmaśikṣayā gopya evaṁ kṛṣṇena śikṣitāḥ /*
> *tadanusmaraṇadhvastajīvakośāstamadhyagan.*

37. Viśvanātha Cakravartī cites BhP. verse I.11.9

> *yarhy ambujākṣāpasasāra bho bhavān*
> *kurūn madhūn vātha suhṛd-didṛkṣayā /*
> *tatrābda-koṭi-pratimaḥ kṣaṇo bhaved*
> *raviṁ vinākṣṇor iva nas tavācyuta //*

insinuating that Kṛṣṇa returned to Braj from time to time: The verse translates as "O Lotus Eyed One, whenever you, desiring to see your friends, departed for the land of the Kurus or the Yadus, O Acyuta, a moment became like millions of years, as if our eyes were deprived of the sun." This verse is spoken to Kṛṣṇa by the inhabitants of Dvārakā, the city that Kṛṣṇa ruled after leaving Vṛndāvana. In his commentary on this verse, Viśvanātha Cakravartī refers to versions in the *Padma-Purāṇa* and other Purāṇas in which Kṛṣṇa returns to Vṛndāvana:

> *tena āyāsye iti dautyakair iti jñātīn vo draṣṭum eṣyāma ityādi yad bhagavatā uktaṁ vrajaṁ pratyāgamanaṁ tat pādmādiṣu purāṇeṣu spaṣṭaṁ sad api, śrībhāgavate tvasminn atraiva jñāpitam.*

The text of the *Padma-Purāṇa,* however, is not clear. There are two divergent recensions, one of which is Bengali and could conceivably have come under strong Vaiṣṇava influence. See Rocher, *The Purāṇas*, pp. 206–208.

38. BhP. XI.7.7,8,

> *yadidaṁ manasā vācā cakṣurbhyāṁ śravaṇādibhiḥ*
> *naśvaraṁ gṛhyamāṇaṁ ca viddhi māyāmanomayam*
> *puṁso'yuktasya nānārtho bhramaḥ sa guṇadoṣabhāk*

Kṛṣṇa will tell Uddhava later on that "it is merely an illusion which shows as difference, which is reflected in the self due to ignorance of its true nature" (BhP. XI.22.56, *ātmāgrahaṇanirbhātaṁ paśya vaikalpikaṁ bhramam* //).

39. See BhP. XI.8.34, for example.

40. BhP. XI.30.39.

41. Many Vaiṣṇavas prefer not to discuss the disappearance of Kṛṣṇa since the sense of separation it engenders is too painful to bear.

42. BhP. XII.5.1.

43. The Purāṇa does not end with the king's death but continues with its *upadeśa*. Parīkṣit's son is angry, as Vālmīki was angry. He curses the entire race of serpents and is finally brought to his senses by Bṛhaspati, preceptor of the gods, who explains that curses, snakes, thieves, fire, lightning, hunger, and disease are results of past *karma* and must be accepted.

44. "The further history of Kṛṣṇaism is intrinsically linked with this vastly influential work. In fact, most of the further developments may be regarded as solutions to, or struggles with, certain problems raised by that Purāṇa." Hardy, *Viraha-Bhakti*, p. 558.

45. See the *Śrī Bṛhat Bhāgavatāmṛtam* (1.7.154–56) of Sanātana Gosvāmī, in which separation is given as the paradigmatic model for the highest devotion. Similarly, the *gopīs*' attainment is reminiscent of the ideal of the Indian wife as depicted by Vaudeville. Her *sādhana* is not meeting but remaining faithful to her *vrata* (vow), not personal love but adherence to a higher principle.

46. A. Gail, in this regard sees the Bhāgavata Purāṇa as steering between "bloodless asceticism and limitless tantricism." A. Gail, *Bhakti in Bhāgavata Purāṇa* (Wiesbaden: Otto Harrassowitz, 1969), 6:96–102.

BIBLIOGRAPHY

Texts of the *Bhāgavata-Purāṇa*

Bhāgavata-Purāṇa. Gorakhpur: Gita Press, 1962.

———, With Śrīdhara Commentary. Edited by Pandey Ramtej Sastri. Banaras: 1956.

———, Translated and Annotated by G. V. Tagare. Delhi: Motilal Banarsidass, 1976. Vols. 7–11. *Ancient Indian Tradition and Mythology*. Edited by J. L. Shastri.

———, Translated and published by E. Burnouf. Vols 1–3. Paris: E. Burnouf, 1840–47.

Śrīmadbhāgavatamahāpurāṇa. With Commentaries of Śrīdhara, Rādhāramaṇadāsa Gosvāmin, Vijayadhvaja, Jīva Gosvāmin, Vallabha, and Viśvanātha Cakravartī, and so forth. Edited by Kṛṣṇaśaṅkaraḥ Śāstri et. al. 12 Vols. Vārāṇasi: Saṁsāra Press, Vim. Sam 2022.

Sanskrit and Indian Language Texts and Translations

Abhinavagupta. *Abhinavabharatī*, commentary on Bharata's *Nāṭyaśāstra*. Edited by M. R. Kavi. Gaekwad's Oriental Series, vols. 1–4, nos. 36, 68, 124, 145. Baroda, 1934–64. Text with Hindi and Sanskrit Commentaries. Edited by A. Madhusudan Shastri. 2 Vols. Banaras: Banaras Hindu University, 1971, 1975. *Dhvanyālocana*. Varanasi: Haridas Sanskrit Series, 1940.

Amaruśatakam. critical ed., C. R. Devadhar. Delhi: Motilal Banarsidass, 1984.

Ānandavardhana. *Dhvanyāloka*. Edited and translated by K. Krishnamoorthy. Dharwar: Karnatak University, 1974. Edited with *Locanā* of Abhinavagupta and *Bālapriya* of Ramaśaraka by Pattabhirama Sastri. Banaras: n.p., 1940.

Bhagavadgītā, Bombay: Gujarati Printing Press, 1975. With Eleven Commentaries. Edited by Shastri Gajanana Shambu Sadhale

Bhaktirasāmṛtasindhu of Rūpa Gosvāmin. Edited and translated by T. S. B. Hridaya Bon Maharaj. Vol. 1. Vrindaban: n.p., 1965.

Bharata, *Nāṭyaśāstra*. Edited and translated by M. Gosh. 2 Vols. Trans. Vol 1. Calcutta: Manisha Granthalaya, 1956, 1967; Trans. Vol. 2. Calcutta: Asiatic Society, 1961.

Bṛhadāraṇyaka Upaniṣad with the commentary of Śaṅkara. Calcutta: Advaita Ashrama, 1941.

Chāndogya Upaniṣad. Madras: Sri Ramakrishna Math, 1984. With Commentary of Ānandagiri and Śaṅkara, Poona: Anandasrama Press, 1890.

Garuḍa Purāṇa (*Sāroddhāra*) with English Translation by E. Wood and S. V. Subrahmanyam. Allabahad: Sudhindra Natha Vasu, 1911.

Gosvāmin, Rūpa. *Laghubhāgavatāmṛtam*. Sridham Mayapur: Sri Caitanya Math, 488 Gaurabda.

Harivaṁśa. Critical ed., P. L. Vaidya, et.al. Poona: Bhandarkar Oriental Research Institute, 1969, 1971.

Kālidāsa, *Meghadūta*. Critical ed. Edited by S. K. De. Delhi: Sahitya Akademi, 1957.

———, *Śakuntalā*. Bombay: Nirnaya Sagar Press, 1958.

Kāma-sūtra of Vātsyāyana. Edited by D. L. Gosvami, with a commentary called "*Jayamaṅgalā*," Translated by R. Burton. 1883. Reprint. Banaras: Chowkhambha, 1929. New York: E. P. Dutton, 1962.

Kṛṣṇadāsa, Kavirāja. *Caitanya-Caritāmṛta*. Calcutta: Gaudiya Math, 1958.

Mahābhārata. Critical ed. V. S. Sukthankar, et. al. Poona: Translated by J. A. B. van Buitenen. Vols. 1–3. Bhandarkar Oriental Research Institute, 1933–66. Chicago: University of Chicago Press, 1973–78.

Manu Smṛti. Edited by J. H. Dave. 5 vols. Bombay: Bhāratīya Vidyā Bhavan Series, 1972–82.

Nath, Radhagobinda. *Gauḍīya Vaiṣṇava Darśana*. Vol. 1. Calcutta: Pracyavani Mandir, 1957.

Padma-Purāṇa. V. N. Mandalika. 4 Vols. Poona: Anandasrama, Sanskrit Series, 1893–94.

Ṛg Veda. *The Rig Veda: An Anthology*. Edited and translated by Wendy Doniger O'Flaherty. Harmondsworth, Middlesex, England: Penguin Books, 1981.

Śiśupālavadha of Māgha. Edited by P. Durgaprasada. Bombay: 12 ed., 1957.

Śrī Bṛhat Bhāgavatāmṛtam by Śrī Śrila Sanātana Gosvāmin. 2d ed. Madras: Sree Gaudiya Math, 1975.

*Taittirīyopaniṣad.*with commentary of Śaṅkarācārya, Sureśvarācārya, and Sāyana. Translated by A. Mahadeva Sastri. Mysore: GIA Printing Works, 1903.

Vālmīki Rāmāyaṇa. Critical ed. 7 Vols. Baroda: Oriental Institute, 1960–1975. General Editors: G.H. Bhatt and U.P. Shah.

Viṣṇu-Purāṇa with the Commentary of Śrīdhara. Ed. Sitaramadason Karanatha. Calcutta: n.p., 1972.

Secondary Sources

Aberbach, David. *Surviving Trauma: Loss, Literature, and Psychoanalysis.* New Haven: Yale University Press, 1989.

Apte, V. S. *The Practical Sanskrit-English Dictionary*, reprinted from the Revised and Enlarged Edition, Poona, 1957, Ed. in Chief, P. K. Gode and C. G. Kurve, Kyoto, Rinsen Book Co., 1986.

Aries, Philip. *Western Attitudes Toward Death.* Translated by Patricia Ranum. Baltimore: The Johns Hopkins University Press, 1979.

Batchelor, Stephen. *Buddhism Without Beliefs.* London: n.p., 1998.

Bhattacharya, S. *The Philosophy of the Śrīmad Bhāgavatam.* 2 Vols. Santiniketan: Visva Bharati, 1960, 1962.

Biardeau, Madeleine. "Some More Considerations About Textual Criticism." *Purāṇa* 10 (1968).

Biswas, A. S. *Bhāgavata-Purāṇa: A Linguistic Study.* Dibrugarh: Vishveshvaranand Book Agency, 1968.

Brown, C. Mackenzie. *God As Mother: A Feminine Theology In India: An Historical and Theological Study of the Brahmavaivarta Purāṇa.* Vermont: Claude Stark and Co., 1974.

———. "The Theology of Rādhā in the Purāṇas." In *The Divine Consort: Rādhā and the Goddesses of India.* Edited by John Stratton Hawley and Donna M. Wulff. Berkeley: Berkeley Religious Study Series, 1982.

———. *The Triumph of the Goddess: The Canonical Models and Theological Visions of the Devī Bhāgavata-Purāṇa.* Albany: State University of New York Press, 1990.

Bryant, Kenneth E. *Poems to the Child-God: Structure and Strategies in the Poetry of Surdas.* Berkeley: Univeristy of California Press, 1978.

Bühler, Georg, ed. and trans. *The Laws of Manu,* in *Sacred Books of the East* XXV. Oxford: Clarendon Press, 1886.

Burke, Kenneth, *The Philosophy of Literary Form: Studies in Symbolic Action.* Baton Rouge: Louisiana State University Press, 1967.

Burnouf, Eugene. *Le Bhāgavata Purāṇa ou Histoire pôetique de Krichna,* tradvit et publié par E. Burnouf, vols. 1–3, Paris, 1840–1847; publié par M. Havnette-Besnault et P. Roussell, vol. 4, Paris, 1884, 1898.

Campbell, Joseph. *Myths To Live By.* New York: Bantam Books, 1973.

Carstairs, G. Morris. *The Twice Born: A Study of a Community of High-Caste Hindus.* Bloomington: Indiana University Press, 1957.

Charlesworth, James H., ed. *The Old Testament Pseudepigraphia.* Vol I. New York: Doubleday, 1983.

Chatterjee, S. C., and D. M. Datta. *An Introduction to Indian Philosophy.* Calcutta: University of Calcutta, 1950.

Coburn, Thomas C. *Devi Māhātmya: The Crystallization of the Goddess Tradition.* Delhi and Columbia, MO: Motilal Banarsidass and South Asia Books, 1985.

D'Aquili, Eugene G., and Charles D. Laughlin Jr. "The Neurobiology of Myth and Ritual." In *The Spectrum of Ritual: A Biogenetic Structural Analysis.* New York: Columbia University Press, 1979.

Dasgupta, Shashibhusan. *Obscure Religious Cults.* Calcutta: Firma Klm Private Limited, 1976.

Dasgupta, Surendranath. *A History of Indian Philosophy.* 5 Vols. Cambridge: University Press, 1922–50.

de Rougemont, Dennis. *L'Amour en Occident.* Paris: Plon, 1939.

———. *Love in the Western World.* Translated by M. Belgion. New York: Pantheon Books, 1956.

———. *Love Declared: Essays on Myths of Love.* Translated by Richard Howard. New York: Pantheon Books, 1963.

De, S. K. with S. N. Dasgupta. *A History of Sanskrit Literature.* Vols. 1, 2. Calcutta: University of Calcutta, 1947.

———. *Sanskrit Poetics as a Study of Aesthetic.* Berkeley and Los Angeles: University of California Press, 1963.

———. *Some Problems of Sanskrit Poetics.* Calcutta: Firma K. L. Mukhopadhyaya, 1959.

———. *Ancient Indian Erotics and Erotic Literature.* Calcutta: Firma K. L. Mukhopadhyay, 1969.

History of Sanskrit Poetics. Calcutta: Firma KLM LTD, 1976.

De Nicolas, Antonio. *Four Dimensional Man: Meditations Through the Rig Veda.* Stony Brook, New York: N. Hays, 1976.

Desai, Sushila S. *Bhāgavata-Purāṇa: A Critical Study*. Ahmedabad: Parshva Prakashan, 1990.

Dimock, Edward. *Place of the Hidden Moon: Erotic Mysticism in the Vaiṣṇava-sahijiya Cult of Bengal*. Chicago: University of Chicago Press, 1966.

Dollimore, Jonathan. *Death, Desire, and Loss in Western Culture*. New York: Penguin, Books, 1998.

Doniger, Wendy, ed. *Purāṇa Perennis: Reciprocity and Transformation in Hindu and Jaina Texts*. Albany: State University of New York Press, 1993.

———. *The Laws of Manu*. Translated by Brian K. Smith. New York: Penguin Books, 1991.

———. *Other People's Myths*. New York: Macmillan; London: Collier Macmillan, 1988.

———, trans. *The Rig Veda*. Harmondsworth, Middlesex, England: Penguin Books, 1981.

———. *Karma and Rebirth in Classical Indian Traditions*. Berkeley: University of California Press, 1980.

Doniger, Wendy, and Howard Eilberg Schwartz, eds. *Off With Her Head: The Denial of Women's Identity in Myth Religion and Culture*. Berkeley: University of California Press, 1995.

Eco, Umberto. *A Theory of Semiotics*. Bloomington: Indiana University Press, 1979.

Erikson, Erik. *Gandhi's Truth: On the Origins of Militant Non-Violence*. New York: Norton, 1969.

Fowler, Harold North, trans. "Phaedo." In *Plato I*. Cambridge: Harvard University Press, 1914.

Freud, Sigmund. *Totem and Taboo: Resemblances Between the Psychic Lives of Savages and Neurotics*. New York: Knopf, 1918/1946).

———. *The Future of an Illusion*. Garden City: Doubleday, 1927.

———. *Civilization and its Discontents*. New York: Norton, 1930.

———. "Mourning and Melancholia." Translated under supervision of Joan Riviere, 152–17. Collected Papers. Vol.4. New York: Basic Books, 1959.

Fruehling, James A., ed. *Sourcebook on Death and Dying*. 1st ed. Chicago: Marquis Professional Publications, 1982.

Frye, Northrop. *The Critical Path: An Essay on the Social Context of Literary Criticism*. Bloomington: Indiana University Press, 1973.

———. *The Educated Imagination*. Bloomington: Indiana University Press, 1964.

Gail, A. *Bhakti in Bhāgavata Purāṇa*. Vol. 6. Wiesbaden: Otto Harrassowitz, 1969.

Gandhi, Mohandas K. *An Autobiography or The Story of My Experiments with Truth*. Translated from the original in Gujarati by Mahadev Desai. Ahmedabad: Navajivan Publishing House, 1927.

Gerow, Edwin. "Rasa as a Category of Literary Criticism." In *Sanskrit Dramatic Performance*. Edited by Rachel Van M. Baumer and James Brandon. Honolulu: University of Hawaii Press, 1981.

Girard, Renee. *Violence and the Sacred*. Baltimore: Johns Hopkins Univeristy Press, 1977. Translated by Patrick Gregory. *Des Choses Cachees Depus Le Foundation du Monde*. Paris: Grasset, 1978.

Gnoli, Raniero. *The Aesthetic Experience According to Abhinavagupta*. Serie Orientale Roma, no. 9. Rome: Instituto Italiano par i Medio ed Estremo Oriente, 1956.

Goldman, Robert. "Fathers, Sons, and Gurus: Oedipal Conflict in the Sanskrit Epics." *Journal of Indian Philosophy* 6: 325–392.

Gonda, Jan, ed. *A History of Indian Literature*. Wiesbaden: Otto Harrassowitz, 1986.

Gosha, S. N. *Studies in Divine Aesthetics*, 44–45. Santiniketan: Visva Bharati, 1974.

Grimes, Ronald, ed. *Readings in Ritual Studies*. New Jersey: Prentice Hall, 1995.

Haberman, David. *Acting as a Way to Salvation: A Study of Raganuga Bhakti Sādhana*. New York: Oxford University Press, 1988.

———. "On Trial: The Love of the Sixteen Thousand Gopees." *History of Religions* 33, No. 1 (1993).

Hacker, P. "Relations of Early Advaitins to Vaiṣṇavism. Vol. 9: 147–54. Vienna: *WZKSA*, 1965.

Hardy, Friedhelm. *Viraha-Bhakti: The Early History of Kṛṣṇa Devotion in South India*. Delhi: Oxford University Press, 1983.

Hawley, John Stratton. *Krishna: The Butter Thief*. Princeton: Princeton University Press, 1983.

———, and D. M. Wulff, eds. *The Divine Consort: Radha and the Goddesses of India*. Berkeley: Berkeley Series in Comparative Religion, 1982.

———. *At Play with Krishna: Pilgrimage Dramas from Brindaban*. In association with Shrivatsa Goswami. Princeton: Princeton University Press, 1981.

Hazra, R. C. *Studies in the Puranic Records on Hindu Rites and Customs*. Delhi: Motilal Banarsidass, 1974.

Heesterman, J. C. *The Broken World of Sacrifice: An Essay on Indian Ritual.* Chicago: University of Chicago Press, 1993.

Hein, Norvin. *The Miracle Plays of Mathura.* New Haven: Yale University Press, 1972.

———. "Comments: Rādhā and the Erotic Community." In *The Divine Consort: Rādhā and the Goddesses of India.* Edited by John Stratton Hawley, and Donna M. Wulff. Berkeley: Berkeley Religious Study Series, 1982.

Hillman, James. *Suicide and the Soul.* Dallas: Spring Publications, Inc., 1965.

———. *Revisioning Psychology.* New York: Harper and Row, 1975.

———. *Healing Fiction.* Dallas: Spring Publications, Inc., 1978.

Hiltebeitel, Alf. *The Ritual of Battle.* Ithaca: Cornell University Press, 1976.

Hopkins, E. W. *The Great Epic of India: Its Character and Origin.* 1901. Reprint, New York: Charles Scribner's Sons; 1969. Reprint, Calcutta: Pustak, 1969.

Hospital, C., and Clifford G. Hospital. "Bhakti and Liberation in the *Bhāgavata-Purāṇa.*" *Sciences Religieuses/Studies in Religion*: Ontario (automne/fall 1983):402–3.

———. Kṛṣṇa and The theology of Play. *Sciences Religieuses/Studies in Religion* (hiver/winter 1976–77).

———. "Līlā in the *Bhāgavata-Purāṇa.*" *Purāṇa* 22, No. 1. (January, 1980):4–22.

Iyengar, K. R. Śrīnivāsa. "Urvaśī." *Śrī Aurobindo Mandir Annual* (August, 1949):46–84.

Jacobson, Duranne and Susan Wadley. *Women in India: Two Perspectives.* New Delhi: Manohar Publishers and Distributers, 1994, 1992.

Joshi, R. V. "The First Verse of the *Bhāgavata-Mahāpurāṇa.*" *Purāṇa*, No. 6 (1964):378–90.

———. "*Catuḥślokī* or *Saptaślokī Bhāgavata*: A Critical Study." *Purāṇa.* No. 16 (January 1974):378–90.

Kakar, Sudhir. *The Inner World: A Psychoanalytic Study of Childhood and Society in India.* Delhi: Oxford University Press, 1978.

———. *The Analyst and the Mystic.* Chicago: University of Chicago Press, 1991.

———, and John Munder Ross. *Tales of Love Sex and Danger.* New York: Basil Blackwell, 1987.

Kane, P. V. *History of Dharmasastra*, Poona: Bori, Vol. I, *The Purāṇas*, 1930, *Origin and Development of Purana Literature*, Vol. V.2, 1962.

Kaufman, Walter, and F. J. Hollingdale, trans. *On the Genealogy of Morals/Ecce Homo*. New York: Vintage Books, 1989. Essay II.

Keith, A. B. "The Birth of Purūravas." *JRAS* (January 1913):412–17.

Kirfel, W. *Das Purāṇa Pañcalakṣaṇa-Versuch einer Textgeschichte*. Bonn, 1927.

Kosambi, D. D. "Urvaśī and Purūravas." *JBBRS* 27 (1951):1–30.

Kennedy, Vans. *Researches into the Nature and Affinity of Ancient and Hindu Mythology*. London: Longman, 1831.

Kinsley, David. *The Sword and The Flute: Kālī and Kṛṣṇa: Dark Visions of the Terrible and the Sublime in Hindu Mythology*. Berkeley: University of California Press, 1975.

Kurtz, Stanley N. *All the Mothers Are One: Hindu India and the Cultural Reshaping of Psychoanalysis*. New York: Columbia University Press, 1992.

Lincoln, Bruce. *Death, War, and Sacrifice: Studies in Ideology and Practice*. Chicago: University of Chicago Press, 1991.

Long, J. Bruce. "Death as a Necessity and a Gift in Hindu Mythology." In *Religious Encounters With Death*. Edited by F. E. Reynolds and E. H. Waugh. University Park and London: The Pennsylvania State University Press, 1973.

Lutgendorf, Philip. "Rāmāyan: The Video." In *Drama Review* 34, No. 2 (Summer, 1990).

Marglin, Frederique Apffel. "Refining the Body: Transformative Emotion in Ritual Dance." In *Divine Passions: The Social Construction of Emotion in India*. Edited by Owen M. Lynch. Berkeley: Berkeley Religious Studies Series, 1982.

———. "Female Sexuality in the Hindu World." In *Immaculate and Powerful: The Female in Sacred Image and Social Reality*. Boston: Beacon Press, 1985.

———. *Śāntarasa and Abhinavagupta's Philosophy of Aesthetics*, Bhandarkar Oriental Series, no. 9. Poona: Bhandarkar Oriental Research Institute, 1969.

Masson, J. L., and M. Patwardhan. *Aesthetic Rapture: The Rasādhyāya of the Nāṭyaśāstra*, 2 Vols. Poona: Deccan College, 1970.

McDaniel, June. *The Madness of the Saints: Ecstatic Religion in Bengal*. Chicago: University of Chicago Press, 1989.

Mehta, J. L. "Dvaipāyana, Poet of Being and Becoming." Paper presented at International Seminar on the *Mahābhārata*, Sahitya Akademi, New Delhi, February 17–20, 1987.

Miller, Barbara Stoller. *The Love Song of the Dark Lord: Jayadeva's Gitagovinda*. New York: Columbia University Press, 1977.

———, ed. *Theater of Memory: The Plays of Kālidāsa*. Translated by E. Gerow and D. Gitomer. New York: Columbia University Press, 1984.

Monier-Williams, Sir Monier. *A Sanskrit-English Dictionary*. 1981. Reprint, Delhi: Motilal Banarsidass.

Mukurjee, Radhakrishna. *The Lord of the Autumn Moons*. Bombay: Asia Publishing House, 1957.

Narayan, R. K. *Gods, Demons, and Others*. New York: Viking Press, 1964.

Narayanan, Vasudha. "Brimming with *Bhakti*, Embodiments of *Shakti*: Devotees, Deities, Performers, Reformers, and Other Women of Power in the Hindu Tradition." In Feminism and World Religions. Edited by A. Sharma and K. Young. Albany: State University of New York Press, 1999.

Neumann, Erich. "Fear of the Feminine." *Quadrant*. New York: C. J. Journal of the Jung Foundation, Spring 1986.

O'Flaherty, Wendy. *Asceticism and Eroticism in the Mythology of Siva*. London: Oxford University Press, 1973.

Paglia, Camile. *Sexual Personal: Art and Decadence from Nefertiti to Emily Dickenson*. New York, Harmondsworth: Penguin, 1992.

Pargiter, F. E. *Ancient Indian Historical Tradition*. London: Oxford University Press, 1922.

———. *The Purana Text of the Dynasties of the Kali Age*. London: Oxford University Press, 1913.

Parry, Jonathan. *Death in Banaras*. Cambridge, NY: Cambridge University Press, 1994.

Perry, John Weir. *Lord of the Four Quarters: Myths of the Royal Father*. New York: George Braziller, 1966.

Plato. *Phaedrus and the Seventh and Eighth Letters*. Translated by Walter Hamilton. New York: Penguin, 1985.

Potter, Karl. *Presuppositions of India's Philosophies*. Englewood Cliffs: Prentice Hall, 1963.

Raghavan, V. *Sanskrit Drama: Its Aesthetics and Production*. Madras: Paprinpack Printers, 1993.

Raja, K. K. *Indian Theories of Meaning*. Madras: Vasant Press, 1963.

Ramanujan, A. K. "The Indian Oedipus." In *Oedipus: A Folklore Casebook*. Edited by Lowell Edmunds and Alan Dundes, 234–61. New York: Garland Publishing, 1983.

———. "On Woman Saints." In *The Divine Consort: Rādhā and the Goddesses of India*. Edited by John Stratton Hawley and Donna M. Wulff. Boston: Beacon Press, 1986.

Redington, James D. *Vallabhācārya on the Love Games of Kṛṣṇa*. Delhi: Motilal Banarsidass, 1983.

Reynolds, Frank, and E. H. Waugh, eds. *Religious Encounters with Death: Insights from the History and Anthropology of Religions*. University Park: University of Pennsylvania Press, 1977.

Rocher, Ludo. *The Purāṇas*. Weisbaden: Otto Harrassowitz, 1986.

Roland, Alan. *In Search of Self in India and Japan: Toward A Cross-Cultural Psychology*. Princeton: Princeton University Press, 1988.

Rukmini,T. S. *A Critical Study of the Bhāgavata-Purāṇa*. Chowkhamba Sanskrit Studies, Vol. 77. Varanasi: Chowkhamba Sanskrit Series Office, 1970.

Sharma, Arvind, ed. *Feminism and World Religions*. Albany: State University of New York Press, 1999.

Sheridan, Dan P. *The Advaitic Theism of the Bhāgavata-Purāṇa*. Delhi: Motilal Banarsidass, 1986.

Sheth, Noel, S. J. The Divinity Of Krishna. New Delhi: Munshiram Manoharlal Publishers Pvt. Ltd., 1984.

Shulman, David Dean. "Toward a Historical Poetics of the Sanskrit Epics." *Journal of South Asian Literature* 4, No. 2 (1991).

Singer, Milton, ed. *Krishna: Myths, Rites, and Attitudes*. New York, Washington, London: Praeger Publishers, 1972.

———. *When A Great Tradition Modernizes: An Anthropological Approach to Indian Civilization*. New York, Washington, London: Praeger Publishers, 1972.

Sinha, Jadunath. *Jīvagoswāmī's Religion of Devotion and Love*. Varanasi: Chowkhamba Vidyabhawan, 1983.

Stone, Michael E., ed. *Jewish Writings of the Second Temple Period: Apocrypha, Pseudepigrapha, Qumran Sectarian Writings, Philo, Josephus*. Philadelphia: Fortress Press, 1984.

Tedlock, Dennis. *Spoken Word and Work of Interpretation*. Philadelphia: University of Pennsylvania Press, 1983.

Thurman, Robert, trans. *The Holy Teachings of Vimalakirti*. Pennsylvania: Pennsylvania State University Press, 1981.

Todorov, Tzvetan. "Recherches Semantiques." *Languages* 1 (1966).

Trungpa, Chogyam, and Francisco Freemantle. *Tibetan Book of the Dead*. Boston: Shambhala, 1987.

Upadhyaya. *Purana-vimarsa*. Varanasi: Chowkamba Vidyabhawan, 1978.

Van Buitenen, J. A. B., ed., and trans. *The Mahābhārata*. 3 Vols. Chicago: University of Chicago Press.

———. "On the Archaism of the *Bhāgavata-Purāṇa.*" In *Krishna: Myths, Rites, and Attitudes.* Edited by Milton Singer. Chicago: University of Chicago Press, 1968.

Vaudeville, Ch. "Evolution of Love-Symbolism in Bhāgavatism." *Journal of the American Oriental Society* 82, No. 1 (March, 1962):31–40.

Wadley, Susan. "Woman and the Hindu Tradition." In *Introduction,* ???

———. *Signs: Journal of Women in Culture and Society* 3, No. 1. Chicago: University of Chicago Press, 1977.

Warder, A. K. *Indian Kāvya Literature.* Vol. III. (1972–77). Delhi: Motilal Banarsidass, 1989.

Watts, Alan. *Psychotherapy East and West.* New York: Vintage Books, 1975.

Weir, Robert F., ed. *Death in Literature.* New York: Columbia University Press, 1980.

Wilson, H. H. *The Vishnu Purana: A System of Hindu Mythology and Tradition.* London: J. Murray, 1840.

Winnicott, Donald W. *The Child, the Family, and the Outside World,* New York: Penguin Books, 1964.

Winternitz, M. A. *A History of Indian Literature.* Translated by Mrs. S. Ketkar. *Vol. I: Introduction, Veda, National Epics, Purāṇas, and Tantras.* New York: Russell and Russell, 1971. Translated from *Geschichte der Indischeṅ Litteratur.* Liepzig: Amerlangs Verlag, 1907.

INDEX